Michelle Payne entered racing ag[...] in Ballarat on Reigning, a horse trai[...] She won her first Group 1 race, [...] aboard Allez Wonder, trained by Ba[...] to three Group 1 victories over the next two years.

Michelle became the first female jockey to win the Melbourne Cup in 2015 on the local one-hundred-to-one horse, Prince of Penzance, trained by Darren Weir and strapped by her brother Stevie.

In 2016 Michelle was named *The Australian* newspaper's Australian of the Year and she won the prestigious Sport Australia Hall of Fame Don Award. Film rights to her life story have been sold.

In the same year she was granted a dual licence, as a jockey/trainer, and had her first win as jockey/trainer on Duke of Nottingham. Her stables, *Nottingham Farm*, are located outside of Ballarat.

John Harms is a Melbourne-based writer, historian, and broadcaster. His books include *Confessions of a Thirteenth Man, Memoirs of a Mug Punter* and *Loose Men Everywhere,* which now form the omnibus *Play On.* He also wrote *The Pearl: Steve Renouf's Story* and has edited nine editions of *The Footy Almanac* annual and the *Doggies Almanac.* He appears on ABC TV's *Offsiders* and is the contributing editor of the popular sports writing site www.footyalmanac.com.au

'Don't get beat, I've got my money on you.'

Stevie Payne

'I was overseas on 3 November 2015, so it was late at night when my phone literally erupted. I received over sixty text messages in under five minutes—friends and colleagues from across Australia and around the world all saying one thing— "Michelle Payne just won the Melbourne Cup". Australia was on its feet.

Michelle's win has changed not only her chosen sport, but the attitudes towards women's participation in all male-dominated sports. It was a watershed moment for sport—not just Australian sport.

Her story doesn't begin and end in under four minutes. Michelle celebrated her thirtieth birthday just before her historic win. Every single one of those years has gone into shaping Michelle as a champion in every respect.'

Katie Page, CEO, Harvey Norman

Michelle
Payne

WITH JOHN HARMS

Life as I know it

**THE BESTSELLING BOOK NOW A MAJOR FILM
RIDE LIKE A GIRL**

MELBOURNE
UNIVERSITY
PRESS

MELBOURNE UNIVERSITY PRESS
An imprint of Melbourne University Publishing Limited
Level 1, 715 Swanston Street, Carlton, Victoria 3053, Australia
mup-contact@unimelb.edu.au
www.mup.com.au

First published 2016
Reprinted 2016 (twice), 2017
This edition published 2019
Text © Michelle Payne, 2016, 2019
Design and typography © Melbourne University Publishing Limited, 2016, 2019

Text design and typesetting by Cannon Typesetting
This edition typeset by Megan Ellis
Cover design by Philip Campbell Design
Printed in Australia by McPherson's Printing Group

 A catalogue record for this
book is available from the
National Library of Australia

9780522876024 (paperback)
9780522876031 (ebook)

Contents

Going to the barrier   ix

1 Christmas at the Paynes   1
2 Loss and sadness   8
3 Playing the cards dealt   15
4 A second home   26
5 We will do much   32
6 A family business   44
7 The horse's way   56
8 In the saddle   67
9 The fallout   80
10 Coming a cropper   85
11 Recovery   101
12 A jockey's lot   111
13 Always a comeback   135
14 Dancing with the princes   145
15 Gathering the troops   169
16 Keeping the faith   185
17 The day of all days   204
18 What a chance   226

How things change   234
Acknowledgements   251

For Mary Payne

She was mother to eleven children but never lived to see them grow up. Sometimes, to help deal with the sense of loss, I tell myself it is a blessing she didn't face the craziness of bringing up ten children. I miss her every day but I feel she is with me always.

And to Paddy Payne

For being the man he is: light-hearted, jovial, positive—but tough on us, all at the same time. He taught us to be polite and respectful and how to work hard.

To my family, friends and the racing community

For everyone who has supported and believed in me, even those I've disagreed with. Every situation helps me to grow and makes me a better, stronger person.

Thank you.

I'm honoured to have a film made about my life, and for my hard work, dedication and persistence to be recognised. It's been an overwhelming experience to see my family's tale up on the big screen, but to see Stevie play himself is the absolute highlight. He is a blessing to our family and now everyone has the opportunity to appreciate him. I hope *Ride Like a Girl* helps others to be inspired.

Going to the barrier

MELBOURNE CUP, 2015. I am cantering Prince of Penzance up the Flemington straight towards the barriers. Past the clocktower. I have just left the mounting yard and walked Prince down along the roses. Darren Weir had wished me luck as he legged me up. And Maddie Raymond and my brother Stevie, the strappers, also sent us on our way. Stevie is already a hero. At the barrier draw on Saturday evening he picked number one. You champion.

I am as calm as Prince. We have become great mates since his debut in front of a handful of racegoers among the gum trees at Stawell in country Victoria in March 2013. He has grown up so much. He looks magnificent—fit, athletic. I can't believe how relaxed he is but so energetic at the same time. Gee, Darren's a good trainer. This horse is spot on.

He rolls along easily; his action is loose. He's as prepared as he can possibly be, and ready to give his best, and I have every faith he will. I love this horse. I believe in this horse.

It's a cracking field: horses prepared by some of the world's best trainers, ridden by some of the world's finest jockeys. And they're trying, just as hard as we are, but I really believe we'll be right there in the finish.

It's a beautiful day. Big blue sky. A few wispy clouds. The slightest breeze. Perfect racing conditions.

The crowd on the lawn cheer and applaud in the sunshine. They are at the Melbourne Cup! Not a care in mind. Drinking. Eating. Cheering. Hoping.

People yell at us.

'Go, Michelle!'

'Go, Prince.'

Not many have backed the Prince. He is an outsider. One hundred to one. Attention is elsewhere. The money is on the international horses.

The Japanese horse Fame Game, the favourite, is up ahead. I can see Ed Dunlop's Trip to Paris. I look at the much-loved Red Cadeaux, and Frankie Dettori on Max Dynamite. Brett Prebble, my sister Maree's husband, is on Bondi Beach. And to my right is Kerrin McEvoy, my sister Cathy's husband, on Excess Knowledge.

I have a lot of sisters and brothers dotted about the place. Wherever they are, they are watching this race. Australia's race. And I am in it; we are in it.

Stevie was so earnest in the mounting yard, and so funny.

'Don't get beat,' he said, as I headed off. 'I've got my money on you.'

Stevie, strapping a Cup horse that his sister is riding. The two of us, who shared a bed all those years ago before we went to school. Stevie, who Dad always called The Little Boy. And me, His Little Girl.

Dad is at Home in Ballarat, watching on our TV, perched on top of some old encyclopaedias on the cabinet. He's by himself, with a cup of tea, I bet. Wishing me a safe ride and the best ride I can deliver. My mother, his great love, is with him in spirit.

My old school friends, the Loreto girls, are scattered, some in marquees here at the track, some at Cup Day functions elsewhere, some at home. Jockey friends sit in their rooms at racetracks watching on. They would love to be taking one down to the barriers. Their time will come. I am the one feeling blessed today.

I canter past Craig Newitt on Sertorius, the only horse at longer odds than us. Stevie and I sat with his owner at the barrier draw. Such a lovely man and just as excited as us to be in the Cup, even if neither of us is fancied. We've earned our places.

Craig and I catch a glimpse of some people on the track. They've been tackled by security. We're laughing as we approach the barriers, wondering what has gone on there. We explain what we've just seen to the other jockeys and barrier attendants milling around behind the start. We assume they're streakers but we later learn they're protesters who've handcuffed themselves to the inside running rail. They're taken away.

We continue to walk around at the back of the barriers, waiting to be loaded. Corey Mallyon, one of the two official starters, is calling out the jockeys and their barriers in order. I will be the first horse called. Glen Darrington, my attendant, offers me some water and I take it from him thankfully. I'm so thirsty.

We are called to load and Glen leads Prince and me into barrier one. It's going to be a bit of a wait while the others are loaded. Frankie Dettori brings Max Dynamite into barrier two. We have a friendly chat. I must be relaxed.

Bart Cummings pops into my mind for a moment. I have a feeling he would want me to do well.

The outside horses are being loaded.

I am quiet.

Alone now.

Waiting.

I think of my mother.

I just know she is with me, as well as my sister Brig and brother Michael. I can feel they're up there watching over me. Prince has a few of us riding with him today.

Jockeys call out.

Barrier five rears; we wait for it to settle. They call out from his stall he's okay. Paul Didham the starter awaits the all-clear from the other starter, Corey Mallyon.

We wait for the all clear, then ...

Crash!

Prince of Penzance ... dawdles out of the barrier. We've missed the start by three lengths.

In the field of twenty-four, we are last.

1

Christmas at the Paynes

EVEN THOUGH WE are spread around the world for most of the year, at Christmas all my sisters and brothers and their families make an effort to go back Home, as we call our place at Miners Rest just outside Ballarat. Mum and Dad bought it in the early 1980s, when they decided to settle in Australia. To come back Home means so much to all of us, especially Dad. He always says how happy it makes him when he sees us all together, getting on so well.

It's a simple family home with stables and yards that back onto the Ballarat Racecourse. I grew up there—one of eleven kids.

It's quiet these days, with only Dad and Stevie living in the house, and me staying over from time to time. But on Christmas Day it is filled with the laughter and happiness (and mayhem) of our childhood. It is *our* place.

People often say we are a racing family and I know what they mean. Racing has been our lives. It's central to who we are—to who I am. But, before everything, we're a family.

By Christmas Eve one or more of my sisters and their families will most likely be staying in the house, having travelled from overseas or interstate. In 2015 it was Cathy and her family from Sydney. She helped get the place ready.

On Christmas mornings family members come from everywhere to gather at Mass. Ten o'clock at Our Lady Help of Christians, the church whose primary school we went to. There's no way we can all sit together, so we spread out around the congregation as we arrive. Noisy kids up the back.

Some don't quite make it to Mass and, as the preparations for lunch begin, more people arrive at Home. Car doors slam. People greet each other. Kids hug, laughing. Dad chats.

'It's good to see you, how are ya?'

My job is to make the punch—one batch for the adults and another for the kids. I'm not far off perfecting the recipe. For the kids it's orange juice, orange and mango juice, tropical juice, pineapple juice and nectar. Same for the adults but with a bit of a kick in it: vodka, Bacardi and champagne. One of the sisters usually picks up the champagne bottle and says, 'Mmm, nice champers, Little Miss Expensive,' because I like to get the good stuff.

As I cut up bananas, strawberries, mangoes and peaches, Therese's husband Jason Patton—they have four kids, the oldest, Jess, is eighteen—helps me. He always does, as I got a little heavy-handed with the portions one year—a funny day. The adults' brew goes into a giant esky and the kids' into a bowl. With so many people in the house it's a challenge to find enough 'nice' glasses for everyone. I hunt around, conjure some up and hand punch to people as they arrive.

When I can sit down with a glass, I watch everything unfold. Fortified by the punch, Therese, Margaret, Maree and Cathy do the turkey and the stuffing, the pork, the chickens. Cathy makes a great sweet-potato bake. Margie and Bernadette prepare the vegies and the salads. Brett and Kerrin do their bit and Jason gets out the electric carver and starts on the meats. I sit back on the rocking chair, sipping on my punch, making wry observations. Jas doesn't find my comments as funny as I do and threatens to claim the easy punch-making job next year.

Christmas lunch is getting closer to being served.

While all that's happening Patrick cooks up some prawns for starters and brings them around. There's a few beers handed out as well. I don't think Andrew does much really. He gets out of it all pretty easily as the official ice-supplier, but at least he entertains all the nieces and nephews. They love him.

Stevie lends a hand. He loves the responsibility and you can rely on him to do a good job. He's good with the kids, too.

Maree often takes care of the setting. We bring in the table-tennis table to join with the one in the kitchen for the adults, and the kids have a long table. She always makes it all look Christmassy.

Dad wanders around, collecting all the news, finding out about all the members of his family: 'How's it going over there in Hong Kong, B. Prebble?' meaning Brett. By initial and surname is how racing people refer to each other.

Meanwhile, the mayhem goes up a notch as the kids open presents and race around outside. When it's hot there are water guns and water bombs and water everythings happening. Along with kids on bikes. Kids forming little conspiracies of mischief.

'How are you, Little Girl?' Dad finds me.

'I'm good, thank you.' And away the conversation goes.

We've always had a few extras over for lunch. Dear friends like Jacq and Karl Schier, who live just around the corner from Dad's, have been coming to Christmas and other Payne gatherings for as long as I can remember. They are a part of the family. When we were kids they always bought us presents, beautifully wrapped with ribbons and cards. Nowadays we include them in the Kris Kringle—there's so many of us a present each would send them broke.

I gather up all the wrapping and packaging and try to tidy up as we go. I put some in my car to take home as it never fits in Dad's bins.

Therese finishes up with the gravy and the kids are served. Then the adults gather around the table. I walk in, late as always, and as I am looking for a chair, say, 'I'd just like to thank you, Cathy, for getting here a few days early and cleaning up —' But I'm cut off.

'We already said that.'

I try again: 'Okay, well, thanks to all the girls for preparing a beautiful lunch.'

'Done.'

Probably best I sit down and shut up!

Cathy says a prayer.

'God, of all gifts we thank you for the many ways you have blessed us this day. We are grateful, each of those who are gathered around this table. In our gratitude and love we remember your humble birth into our lives and pray for those who are without enough to eat. We remember the stable in which you were born and remember those who have no place to live. We remember your challenging message of caring and giving and we pray for peace in families and nations throughout the world. We bless you and give you thanks in your Spirit who brings our hearts to life this Christmas Day and forever. Amen.'

'Amen,' we repeat in unison.

Everyone eats up—even me. I always ride on Boxing Day, but I don't think about that now, I eat without a worry.

One of the great traditions of lunch is that it's a single conversation. I think this proves that miracles are possible, when you consider how chatty everyone is and how many of us there are. It's not a rule, no one ever suggests it—it just happens. There is rarely any racing talk. Just happy chat. And before long someone will start with the childhood memories. Every year, without fail.

'What about the time Therese got hooked on cooking chicken schnitzel!' You can see J. Patton, K. McEvoy and B. Prebble grimace: 'Here they go, again!' Nick Bompas, Margie's French husband, laughs his big, deep French laugh.

Therese laughs, too, a little bit embarrassed because she knows what's coming is completely true.

'It was chicken *and corn* schnitzel,' she corrects us. And someone takes up the story. I was too young to remember, but I've heard it so often I could tell it perfectly.

'Hey, Therese, what's for tea?'

'Chicken schnitzel.'

'Oh yum!' We thought it was exotic that first time, compared with some of our other meals. And it was served with some vegies—we were rapt.

The next day: 'Hey, Therese, what's for tea?'

'Chicken schnitzel.'

'Great.'

This went on for a fortnight until we couldn't stand the thought of it anymore.

'Hey, Therese, what's for tea?' And before she could say 'chicken' we all had our fingers down our throats, gagging.

Everyone laughs. Even the brothers-in-law.

'I still can't look at chicken schnitzel in the supermarket,' Therese says.

That's how it goes, one story after another.

Dessert is served. Rocky road slice and a bit of Christmas pudding and ice cream.

The kids are long gone, wherever kids go, and we summon the energy to get the dishes out of the way. It's a communal effort and after they're put away Home turns into a gamesfest: table tennis (once the tinsel and the tablecloth are off), cricket, basketball, cards, Scrabble, chasey, bike races. Little groups congregate.

Traditionally, at some stage late in the afternoon, we have a huge game of soccer, where Dad mixes it with the young 'uns, but last year we didn't have one. Perhaps it was because Dad hadn't been the best in the months leading up to Christmas. Or maybe it was just too hot.

And then there's a photo. There are always people popping in, which means we can get someone to take a photo of the entire family. We all love this moment. Everyone smiling big smiles that come from deep within, and my dad is so happy.

Late in the afternoon I have to think about driving back to Melbourne for my ride the next day and I work up the motivation to shed the magnificent Christmas lunch. I work out I have about three kilograms to tackle, and I've got eighteen hours. But I've developed a strategy for this over the years.

I put on my sweat gear—a long-sleeved top under a sweat suit, a jacket over it, and leggings—and have one last game of something. It was basketball last Christmas. Red-faced and sweaty, I say goodbye to everyone. I then put a rubber mat and a towel down on the car seat, and wind up the windows. Away I go, back to Melbourne without the air conditioner.

As I drive I mop my neck and forehead with a little towel. It's not very pleasant but it gets the job done. I usually sip on mineral water to help me to keep sweating. I try not to make eye contact with people along the way. If they see me they must think I'm some kind of weirdo. By the time I pull into the driveway at my home everything is damp and I'm around two kilograms lighter. I have a cold shower.

Last year I had rides at Randwick in Sydney on Boxing Day. I had to catch a very early flight so I made sure all my race gear was ready to go before I climbed into bed around 9.30pm. Every year I just lie there and think about the day. These wonderful people with whom I have spent my life. We might not be the most lovey-dovey family, who tell each other how we feel. We just know. These are the people I love and the people who love me. That makes me smile. And I feel blessed.

I also think about the three who are no longer with us.

2

Loss and sadness

B Y THE TIME my mother Mary brought me home from the Ballarat Hospital, a few days after my birth on 29 September 1985, the rhythm of Payne family life was well and truly established. My father Patrick was training racehorses, something he loved doing. Brigid was sixteen and Therese fifteen. They had left school and both were apprenticed to my dad, riding winners for him. Maree was at Loreto College, the Catholic girls' school in Ballarat in regional Victoria. Bernadette was in her last year at Our Lady Help of Christians Primary School in Wendouree, a suburb of Ballarat, with Patrick, Margie and Andrew. Cathy was off to school the following year.

They'd all been born in New Zealand and had spent their early years on the family's dairy farm at Hawera on the west coast in the Taranaki area of the North Island. Dad had also trained racehorses there. By chance, two things changed the direction of their lives. One was a racehorse called Our Paddy Boy. The other was a local council decision, totally out of their control.

Dad owned and trained Our Paddy Boy and when the colt showed so much promise as a two-year-old in 1980, brought him across the Tasman to take on the big races in Australia. The horse did so well Dad was offered a lot of money for him. After selling Our Paddy Boy they returned to Hawera, near Mount Taranaki on the North Island, and settled back into family life. However, their land was required for a major public works project and they were forced to sell.

Saddened at their loss, but always adventurous in spirit, Mum and Dad decided to move to Australia in 1982 because their taste of life here had been so good. They decided on Ballarat as they liked the area, having stabled Our Paddy Boy and his little mate Gentle Joker there with trainer Robert Smerdon on the previous visit.

Dad wanted to keep training horses. They bought our property on Kennedys Road at Miners Rest, which we call Home. It included the stables and a number of paddocks where the horses were during the day, as well as The 40-Acre Paddock, where horses were worked on a dirt track. The house had been built by Tommy McGinley, a wonderful Australian jumps jockey who'd won the Grand National Steeplechase five times in the late 1960s. It had five bedrooms—which was barely enough with the eight children they had then, with two more to follow.

Life was hectic for the family. Dad was training horses and everyone had to pitch in to help feed them, muck out the stables, move the horses, groom the horses, ride trackwork, as well as other jobs around the yard. It was relentless—the life of racing people.

My mother worked tirelessly to keep the family as organised as it could be. She was the bookkeeper, nominated the horses for races, was Dad's secretary, and all the while was bringing up the kids. Being a woman of great love and compassion, she always found time for others. My sisters recall Mum milking the cow we had at the time and taking the milk to the homeless men's shelter in Ballarat every week.

Mum had a delightful sense of humour, which she no doubt needed to get through each day, and put up with the way Dad loved to tease her. He told me she never swore, but he tested her sometimes. He used to say he found it very hard not to smile when she was telling him off, and if he smiled it made her even angrier with him.

As we grew older we would all help around the stables and the house, getting up in the dark to get the jobs done before school. We said Dad had a lot of kids so he didn't have to pay staff! But not all of them were happy with that approach.

'Another one?' the older ones lamented, when Mum was pregnant with me. 'Why do you keep having more children?'

They were also concerned that, because she was older, there might be complications. Stevie, the youngest at the time, was two and had Down's syndrome. From the outset Mum and Dad lived their belief that all children are precious, and that proved true. What a blessing Stevie has been for our family.

My parents also knew the grief of losing a child. Michael was born between Margie and Andrew and died just three days later. He suffered a hole in his heart, which would be treatable today with the advances in medicine.

By coincidence, I was born on the same date as Michael, 29 September, and so I was named Michelle in his memory. Michelle means 'Gift from God'. My middle name is Jacinta, after Saint Jacinta, who was born near Fátima in Portugal in 1910.

One Tuesday morning, not long after Easter when I was six months old, all the jobs were done and the younger kids were getting ready for school. Brigid and my mother were arguing. While everyone usually spoke their minds in our family, this argument must have become heated. Brig was sixteen and having one of those typical teenage arguments with a parent and she left for work with the issue unresolved. Saddened by what had happened, my mum wrote her a note saying sorry and put it under her pillow. It said, simply, 'I still love you.'

Andrew, who was in Grade 1, was also proving difficult that morning. He was annoyed with Mum.

'You never do reading at school,' he said. 'Everybody else's mum does. I'm not going.'

'I promise I'll come and read today if you go to school,' my mother said.

'No. Not going.'

'I promise.'

'No. I'm not going.'

'Well, you can stay in your room until I get home.'

With time getting away from them, Bernadette, Patrick and Margie climbed into the Ford station wagon. Maree didn't go with them as she'd been able to convince Dad to let her go to the races with him. There was a local Ballarat meeting on that day, which Therese was preparing to ride at.

The plan was for my dad to do the school run, but he got stuck on the phone on an important call and signalled to my mum that she would have to take them. Mum drove off along Kennedys Road. At the same time, a local mum was taking her kids to school, and collided with Mum's car at the Gillies Street corner, crashing into the driver's door.

The car rolled onto its side. The kids, who had minor injuries, were able to scramble out of the car but Mum lay motionless, her body hanging out of the driver's seat window.

Petrol spilled out everywhere. 'Everyone run, it's gonna blow!' Patrick yelled.

◆ ◆ ◆

'Pat, you need to come. There's been an accident.' Kenny Williams, a local trainer, went to fetch Dad. Dad knew by his expression it was bad news.

When Dad left, Therese and Maree were still at Home with Andrew, Cathy, Stevie and me, and they waited, sitting on the couch, not knowing what was going on. He came back about ten minutes later with Bernadette, Patrick and Margie. He walked in and all he did was shake his head. And they knew, straight away, that our Mum had been killed.

Father John Keane, the priest who has been closest to our family for many years and a wonderful friend of Dad's, came over. He still describes the moment with total sadness and devastation.

'It was a terrible scene,' he says, in his Irish accent.

I think about my mother a lot. I feel she is always with me. But when I think about that specific moment, when she was taken, which I do from time to time, I don't think so much about an accident I was too young to remember, or of a mother I didn't know for long. I think of my dad and my brothers and sisters. I try to imagine what Dad was feeling. I can't imagine what it must be like to have someone you had made a life with, your best friend, your everything, gone—just gone. Then having to tell your children. If I feel like I'm doing it tough, I think about that and wonder how he got through it, while always retaining his positive attitude and his faith in life. It gives me so much strength, and perspective.

While I am deeply, deeply saddened by what happened I don't have a sense of loss. I know instead the sadness. And I think it is that feeling that has helped me to empathise with others. I don't have an imagined sense of my mother's personality. But I know she is my mother. And I know what a mother is, and what motherly love is. I know mothers. I watch mothers. My sisters are beautiful mothers. My mother's love is an ever-present spiritual love. And I know fatherly love. My father's love is spiritual, too, but I have lived my life with my dad, I know him, and so that love, as tough as he can be, is immediate and real.

The older kids say that Dad became more openly affectionate after the accident, especially with us younger ones. Perhaps he was being gentler, more tender, because we didn't have a mother. Perhaps he was responding to his own grief, which I realise, as I get older, must have been profound.

At the time, my immediate needs were physical. Thankfully I took the bottle without hesitation. A local Irish woman from the parish looked after me, and then Bernadette, who was eleven at the time, took it upon herself to feed me through the night. As I was growing up, Therese then became the motherly figure for me and us all. She just took up the role, taking over the duties, making sure we had dinner, making sure everything was done. She definitely had plenty of little helpers to order around but it amazes me how she coped with that role at such a young age—and without warning.

When I first started to realise what had happened I was about four. The kids were giving me a terrible time, pulling my hair, and making my life a bit of a misery as brothers and sisters do. I yearned for Mum, for her protection.

My dad tells me the story that one night I was lying in bed with him and I'd decided that Mum would be the solution to my problems. She would make things right.

'Can we go and dig her up?' I asked. 'Then the kids won't pull my hair anymore.'

Some days I think my whingeing and complaining about being picked on became too much for Dad. He used to say he would run away from home if I didn't stop. That really scared me. But the next time someone was teasing me I went to tell Dad.

'I'm sick of this whingeing,' he said. 'I'm running away from home.' And he got in his car and off he went.

I was devastated. Who was going to look after us? I stood on our front verandah calling out for my other parent, 'Mum, come back. Please come back!'

When my dad came home I was very angry with him. After that, whenever I was sad, I used to go to the verandah and call for Mum. I'm not sure if anyone heard me. Eventually I realised she was never coming back. This must have been heart wrenching for Dad. But he never showed it.

His approach wasn't a stoic position. And I cannot remember a single moment of self-pity. It was total acceptance, a deep-seated optimism, and a belief that all would work out for the good. Father Keane says that Dad is 'a man of almighty faith', and throughout my life Dad has given me no reason to doubt that.

When I was younger he would tell me every day how much he loved Mum, what a lovely lady she was. He wished he'd told her that every day. He was very affectionate with me and we used to have a little ritual where he would hold his thumb and his index finger about an inch apart and say, 'Your daddy loves you this much.' I would always say back to him, 'No he doesn't, he loves me thiiiiiis much!' and hold my arms as wide as they would go.

My dad's outlook has had a massive impact on us all. He always thinks things can be fixed, that he can fix them. But then he says, 'If you can't fix something with baling twine, you can't fix it.' He usually made things worse but he did always use baling twine for a belt. It did the trick.

When Mum died he knew we just needed to get on with it, and live life as best we could. I think the depth of that feeling of sadness for my father, and for my sisters and brothers, has contributed to how I understand life. I feel close to life. I try to have a sense of what's important. And I believe that things happen for a reason, even if at the time that reason is not obvious.

3

Playing the cards dealt

MY DAD WAS faced with the prospect of raising ten children on his own. The older ones were hard working and independent—they had to be—but Cathy was four, Stevie was two and had his own difficulties, and I was a baby. Dad's approach was remarkable.

He is the sunniest, most optimistic, fun-loving father you could imagine. He was always very tough on us, though, and he could get pretty angry—his voice would bellow through the house or across the yard. But he also loved to pull your leg, to tease you, and to test you. Despite the immense grief he must have been suffering, and the difficulty of being a single parent, he remained so positive, so confident, that we knew, if we got on with it, life would serve us well. Dad often says that despite the challenges, those years together at Home provided him with his most joyous memories.

I remember when I was really little, Dad used to piggyback us to bed.

'Now, who's first?' he'd say, and he would put one of us on his back and gallop down the passageway to one of the bedrooms.

'Who's next?' Eventually about five of us would be carried to bed in this way.

The older kids were simply amazing. Apart from riding and working in the stables, the girls got stuck into the housework. They took to the responsibilities without any apparent questioning or complaint because that's what needed to be done. It was the right thing to do, yet, they were so young themselves.

I used to give Therese a Mother's Day gift, usually some sort of ornament or something simple I thought she might like. Everyone else was buying their mothers Mother's Day gifts and she felt as close to being my mum as anyone did, so it just seemed normal to me at the time. Love and consideration for others produce resilience and a capacity for hard work. Perhaps the hard work was a way for everyone to deal with the grief. But when it came to the horses, even though it was relentless work, it was a field we all immediately took to.

We grew up with horses. We loved them foremost as animals, beautiful creatures with temperament and personality and character—sometimes easygoing, sometimes uptight, sometimes untalented, sometimes brilliant with so much promise. We learned to respect horses and to treat them with affection and compassion. That was Dad's way and it was our way. He'd loved horses since he was a little kid, and he passed that love on to us.

I can't remember life before horses. Horses were part of us, and being with them was as natural as breathing. I always wanted to ride.

'Daaaad, when can I start riding?'

My older sisters were all riding. Brigid, Therese and Maree had begun their apprenticeships at fourteen and a half, the minimum age then. Therese was riding at Moonee Valley the day I was born. She had a nasty fall and broke her collarbone and the family joked that her fall had brought on my birth. I wanted to ride too. But Dad kept telling me I had to wait. I pestered and pestered.

'Daaaad?'

When I was four, Dad put me on Wilbur, our very naughty black Shetland pony. I loved it—until I fell off. Dad had seen it all before.

'You gotta get straight back on, Little Girl,' he said. 'If you don't get back on now you'll never get back on.'

I had a headache from the fall and was a little bit hesitant because it hurt, but I got back on. From that day on, every time something went right I'd feel fantastic, but Dad would make sure I wasn't getting ahead of myself. And every time something went wrong, Dad was there to pick me up and help me and give me a word of advice.

I wanted to be a jockey. My mind was completely made up. And I didn't need to tell the others, they just knew. Part of my wanting to be a jockey was me wanting to be like the others—but I actually wanted to be better than them. Part of it was me wanting to be like Dad.

Wanting to be with horses wasn't just the vague idea of a young child, either. It wasn't that I *thought* I liked horses and riding and racing. I *knew* I did. I wanted to be with horses. I wanted to ride. And I knew I would eventually race.

Before I started school I was into it. After we'd eaten tea and had a game of cards in the evening, Dad would go to bed and he'd be lying there, about to fall asleep, and I'd go in and pick up his hand.

'Dad, don't forget to wake me up in the morning,' I'd implore. 'Please don't forget, Dad.' When I'd wake up and realise he'd already gone and the sun was coming up, I'd run to the stables to find him, half-crying: 'Daaaad! Why didn't you wake me up? I told you to wake me up!'

If I was down at the stables I hoped Dad would put me on a horse and lead me round. Sometimes he would but often he was so busy that it would be a very quick ride, or no ride at all. Even if it was short, at least I was riding. I think I drove him mad and he didn't wake me because it would have been easier for him if I was up at the house fast asleep.

The early hours never bothered me. Five o'clock in the morning, in the middle of a Ballarat winter, is not comfortable, but I didn't think about it. I wanted to be with the older kids, with the horses. Sometimes, though, they didn't want to be out there and they'd manufacture little tricks to get out of work.

Andrew used to sneak out with no boots on and run around the backyard in the frost, come back in and peel off his wet socks as if he'd been out there working hard. He'd say to the others still sleeping, 'Wake up, don't be so lazy. Get up and do some work. I've been out working.' No one argued with him as his socks were wet. But when we were sitting around the table having breakfast, it didn't take long for everybody to work out that no one had sighted him at the stables and he was put back on the roster for cleaning the house.

Stevie and I were The Little Kids, and we were usually left to look after ourselves while the others were working in the mornings. We were like a single entity: 'Where are The Little Kids?' 'Anyone seen The Little Kids?' We'd get up and watch one of our favourite videos. Initially we had four: *Phar Lap*, a documentary about the champion horse Tulloch, *Robin Hood: Prince of Thieves* and *The Sound of Music*. Later came *The Wedding Singer*, *The Lion King* and *Dumb and Dumber*. I think we could act out all those movies we knew them so well. I'm not joking when I say that Stevie and I watched *Phar Lap* five hundred times, often at about 5.30 in the morning. The more I saw it, the more it fed my desire to be a jockey. I used to tell people, 'I just want to win the Melbourne Cup.'

We got up early even if we were tired. A good night's sleep was never guaranteed at Home anyway. Squeezing so many bodies into a few rooms was a bit tricky and there were many combinations of kids in the rooms over the years. Dad often just slept on a mattress on the floor. I would sleep with my dad when I was little, but as I got older I kind of felt it wasn't very cool so I tried to find somewhere else to sleep.

For a while Stevie and I shared a bed but Stevie used to make this noise when he was falling asleep that would always keep me up. I remember waking him up and asking, 'Hey, Stevie, can you wait for me to go to sleep before you do.'

'Yeah, no worries,' he said. Stevie always tried to be accommodating, but then he'd go straight back to sleep, so I'd have to put the pillow over my head to try to block out the noise. That would be when I started looking for someone else to sleep with.

'Can I sleep here, Therese?'

'No, you wriggle too much. Go ask Maree.'

'Can I sleep here, Maree?'

'All right, as long as you don't wriggle.'

'Okay, I won't.'

'Stop wriggling!'

'Okay.' But the more I tried the harder it was to keep still.

'That's it! If you wriggle one more time you're not sleeping in here.'

It was so hard not to move an inch—my nose was itchy, but I figured if I did it real quick she might not notice.

'Right, that's it, you're not sleeping in here.'

'I promise I won't move again.'

'Okay, but this is the last time.'

I almost always found somewhere. If not, it was back in with Dad.

Apart from Michelle, my brothers and sisters called me 'Stinky'. It was one of those names that evolved. They started calling me 'Smelly Shelley', and then that became Stinky. Patrick still writes 'S' in his trackwork logbook when I've ridden a horse for him.

Even in front of horse owners he'll still greet me with 'Hi Stinky'! So nice of him—I always give him a withering thank-you-for-that look.

Patrick and Andrew slept in bunks in The Boys' Bedroom. I remember for a while they used to make me sing to them. I'd sit amid a huge pile of dirty clothes on the floor and they'd say, 'Sing us a song.'

'No, you'll laugh at me, you always do.'

'Come on. Sing us a song. Sing us "Mary had a little lamb".'

'No, you'll laugh at me, I know you will.'

'We promise not to laugh. We promise.'

I'd give up and sing: 'Mary had a little lamb, little lamb, little lamb,' and they'd laugh their heads off.

When I was five I started at Our Lady Help of Christians Primary School at Wendouree, on the Miners Rest side of Ballarat. It was a small, friendly school run by the Sisters of Mercy. We did all the usual subjects, as well as read Bible stories, and learned some of the Bible verses off by heart. I really liked Sister Chris. She was very kind. After school, when we were waiting to be picked up, we would visit her in the presbytery and she always gave us some Maori biscuits or something else nice. Sometimes we'd send Stevie in first because we knew how much they adored him and they would always offer him afternoon tea.

On the day of your birthday the nuns would bake a cake. When I noticed that my birthday was going to fall during the September holidays I went to Sister Chris and announced, 'It's my birthday today!' A cake was baked and brought in to my Grade 1 classroom. Later that day Cathy heard the story and piped up, 'But it's not even Michelle's birthday.'

I learned a lot at Our Lady Help of Christians. I learned that the Melbourne Cup was very special because on that first Tuesday in November the nuns would wheel out the old TV and we'd get to watch. When I was in prep in 1991, my brother Patrick had his first ride in the Cup. He was on Sunshine Sally. I was so proud but I was also so nervous for him. I prayed that everything would go well and he would run a great race.

Patrick led all the way down the straight the first time and was in front past the winning post. But they had to go around again and Sunshine Sally led into the straight but then ran last. I was excited he lasted in front for as long as he did. Sunshine Sally started at three hundred to one and I got $1 from the sweep off my teacher for him coming last. I could tell then how important the day was, how important the race was, and I suspect all that added to my dream of one day winning the Cup.

That year the Cup was won by Let's Elope. She was a mare trained by Bart Cummings and ridden by Steven King, who wore green and gold diagonal stripes with a white cap. We used to have our own races at home—often the Cox Plate but other famous races as well. Andrew and Patrick played the jockeys, usually Mick Dittman and Shane Dye. Stevie and I were the horses—I was always Let's Elope; Stevie was Durbridge or Canny Lad. Sometimes Cathy would play too and she was Empire Rose, because she was so much bigger than us, and Empire Rose was a big mare. We had to crawl around on all fours as the older kids held onto our shirts.

Stevie always used to take off at a full gallop and would conk out in the longer distance races. We would do two or three laps of the rockery, or four or five times up and down the lounge room. I'd sit just in behind Stevie and sprint past him at the end. We tried to coach Stevie but he never changed his strategy. He couldn't help himself. He was like a fiery horse that wanted to go flat out from the start. It did work for him in the shorter races because quite often I couldn't catch him.

We all treated Stevie exactly the same way as everyone else. If we were playing Monopoly or a card game we all played to win. If anyone treated him differently he would notice and get annoyed. You could see it in his face. The smile he usually had would disappear and he'd look both angry and sad.

Dad was always teasing and playing jokes on us. For a long time Stevie had a stutter. Often I was the only one who could understand him and so I had to interpret for him. But Dad wouldn't have it.

'What are you trying to say, Little Boy? Come on, spit it out.' Dad would even make a joke of Stevie's stutter.

'Little Boy,' he'd say, 'tell us one of those d-d-d-d-doggy stories.'

'Ahh, Daaaad!' we all used to cry. Yet we didn't doubt Dad for a minute. We lived in a crazy home of unstated affection, where there was love in the dust.

I made many friends at Our Lady Help of Christians and one of my best friends was Emily Hall. Emily thought she had a big family and she was the youngest of four. Apart from school we'd sometimes see each other at Mass, although the Paynes went to Our Lady Help of Christians on a Sunday and the Halls would go on Saturday night.

Emily came out to our house occasionally for a sleepover. She was very much a town kid and she used to say that coming to our place was better than going to an amusement park. She'd stand there bewildered as Payne life unfolded around her. There'd be horses in our backyard having a pick on the grass, horses in the next yard, horses in the paddock, and the older kids going in all directions doing jobs—riding horses, moving horses, Dad yelling, kids giving it to each other.

Whenever Emily came over I would look after her. Find her a bed, make her bed, and make her meals. I reckon there was only ever one thing on the menu: boiled egg with salt and pepper and toast. We didn't invite too many friends over. I guess we were a bit embarrassed about our crazy life and there wasn't a lot of room to fit in another body.

One day I decided it would be good if Emily knew how to ride. We could ride together.

'Come on, Em, I'll put you on him,' I said as I fetched a horse from the little yard.

'Do you need to ask your dad?' Em asked.

'Nah,' I said. 'It'll be right.'

When Dad spotted me leading the horse he went off: 'What are you doing, Little Girl? Get that horse back in the paddock.'

I think Em got a huge fright. Eventually she just got used to the arguing, and the way we would just not hold back on each other. It was the Payne way. You couldn't be too precious about it.

Feeding the household was quite a task. Maree usually looked after the shopping and Therese cooked in those early days. She learned how hard it was to feed a hungry tribe within budget. While other kids their age were reading *Dolly* and *Cosmo* and watching *Melrose Place*, my sisters would be at the supermarket, wracking their brains, trying to find something that everyone would like. That was the time when Therese brought home a dozen schnitzels, back when not a lot of meats were pre-prepared—I think they had some cheese in them. We loved them at first, but as has become family folklore, we had them every night for a fortnight so we soon turned off them.

Margie tried to impose some order on the chaos. She had that sort of a mind and she would do rosters of jobs. But more time was spent negotiating the roster than actually doing the work.

'But I always have to do that,' I'd complain.

Keeping things clean and tidy was nearly impossible, but eventually we'd just have to make the effort—usually triggered by everyone going nuts because we couldn't find anything, especially shoes, which we would fling at each other when we were fighting.

Margie would have us cleaning up the different rooms: the kitchen, the bathroom, The Next Room, and The Little Passage.

The Next Room, which was the living, rumpus and dining all in one, was called this because it was the next room on from the kitchen. It was a hub of activity and it would get into a real state. It wasn't too hard to tidy up—you just shoved shoes back where they belonged, clothes in the laundry, and the rest of the stuff under the couches and out of the way.

The killer cleaning job was The Little Passage, which got its name because it was the little entry hall at the front door. It was always a mess because everyone would take their shoes and boots off as soon as we got in the door from being at school, sport or working. Ballarat is drizzly wet all winter and so The Little Passage was always a repository for mud and grass and whatever horses left around the place. It was the dud draw in the cleaning lottery.

I always thought the carpet in The Next Room was brown but Therese told me it was actually cream. One day she thought we needed to have it cleaned. A man came out and steam-cleaned it. Dad paid him out the front and they got chatting. That was very much my dad. When he and Therese came back inside there was a perfect trail of hoof prints on the beautiful cream carpet. One of the horses had come in the back door, completed a lap, and walked back out.

We had a lot of laughs but in a household of so many people, tension and upset are inevitable. But as willing as it got during the day, we were a family who went to sleep after having sorted stuff out. Yes, we all stood up for ourselves, spoke our minds and had no trouble defending our positions. And we all seemed to think volume was the key factor in settling arguments, so it could get loud. Sometimes a barney would break out. Sometimes the politics and alliances of the day would put the house at war.

Stevie and I were always allied, even though we had no power whatsoever. The oldest girls formed a group. Patrick would be off riding somewhere, so he was out of it, but the middle kids—

Andrew, Margie, Cathy—were a force to be reckoned with. They were off building cubby houses or exploring, and we always wanted to join them, but they rarely let us. I didn't think anyone should be excluded from anything. I thought so many things were unfair, and I didn't like it. Margie always says she knew when I thought something was unfair because I'd tell everyone to 'get stuffed'.

I would spend a lot of time with Stevie and we were always finding a way to have fun. We used to play cards a lot—Patience or Spit, which was a really fast game. We also loved playing a game we called offices. It wasn't really a game but we just pretended we worked in an office, taking phone calls and writing stuff down quickly.

As unlikely as it might seem, I also spent a lot of time on my own. I used to lie on a bed and think. Or go out into the yard and think. I'd lie in the paddock with one of our horses, laying my head on it, patting it and playing with it. Just me and a horse and the universe.

4

A second home

AFTER HIS LUCK with Our Paddy Boy, the horse Dad had trained before I was born, Mum and Dad had the good sense to invest the money they'd won from racing. This is when they bought two small properties: our house on a one-acre block at Ballarat and what we called The 40-Acre Paddock, about a kilometre down the road next to the members' drive of the Ballarat Racecourse. It was where we did our horse training.

But Dad also needed to make enough money to put the rest of us through school. He was a horseman, a trainer, but he was also a farmer. When I was nearly seven Dad bought a 250-acre dairy farm at Rochester. He thought it looked ideal as another way to make an income. While the older kids remained at Home to look after the horses, Dad took us younger ones, Margie, Andrew, Cathy, Stevie and me, up to live and work on this property, which we came to call The Farm.

It felt so different to have the family divided between Home and The Farm. It was much quieter up there. I really missed Therese's motherly affection and care. Not that Therese has ever been known for being openly affectionate. She's still an awkward hugger now, which we laugh about. But to me she was like a mum and I missed having her around.

Not long after we moved there, and feeling really terrible about everything and rather lost, I decided to run away. Off I went, down the dirt road we lived on and away from everyone. I didn't get far before I stopped and had a rest under a gum tree and thought about things. A few hours went by. No one noticed. No one came looking for me. So I had to go back home.

During those years we were back and forwards between The Farm and Home. One day when I was about seven Stevie and Dad and I were on yet another adventure. We were in the old truck taking horses up to The Farm. Not far out of Miners Rest Dad went to use the brakes but we didn't pull up.

'Oh, geez, the air brakes aren't working,' he said.

We didn't know whether he was teasing us or not, but the further we went the more we believed him. He was using the gears to slow us down. Stevie and I were a little bit frightened because we could hear the worry in Dad's voice but we trusted him to get us home.

'We have to get back to milk the cows,' he kept saying. There was no stopping him.

We made our way along the country roads but not long after we'd passed through Clunes we got to the top of a hill. We could see from there the T-intersection at the bottom. As we hurtled down, the truck built up momentum. Dad gripped the steering wheel, his eyes looking directly ahead.

'Well, kids,' he said. 'We're going to need a bit of luck here.'

We looked at Dad, and we looked at each other, and we grabbed hold of the seat and hoped for the best.

I could see the concentration on Dad's face. He was doing his absolute best as we lurched down the bitumen road. As we approached the intersection he swung the steering wheel and the truck turned on an arc too wide for the road. He knocked out a couple of side reflector posts, which wasn't the worst result. We then bumped and trundled on along the gravelled edge until Dad righted the truck and we were back on the road. Dad looked at us like the result was never in doubt.

After negotiating the traffic lights through Bendigo we made it to The Farm. And the horses were fine.

◆ ◆ ◆

At The Farm, I was riding more and more. I loved riding, especially when Dad would get me to ride one of the racehorses in the morning. But mainly we all had to look after the cows. We always had to get the milking done and then get ready for school. Dad would then drive us to St Joseph's Primary School at Rochester.

At Our Lady Help of Christians in Ballarat we had to wear a uniform—handed down from the older kids, of course. Stevie had colourful tastes. He particularly enjoyed putting on tights and the *Flashdance* leggings our sisters had worn with their big hair in the 1980s.

'No, Stevie, you just can't wear those,' we'd say. 'They'll go nuts at school.'

Stevie was always one step ahead of us, though. He'd wear his tights and leggings *under* his school tracky dacks. He had a favourite iridescent green pair.

Some things never changed. We were always late to school, and Dad was always late to pick us up. Sometimes he'd forget completely. He was often under a lot of pressure. He'd be on the phone organising something for The Farm, out irrigating the paddocks, or talking to Home about the horses. He always worried about the weather. If it didn't rain we would be short of feed.

'Geez, we need rain, kids,' he'd say. 'Don't know what we're gunna do if we don't get rain.' Then the clouds would gather and we'd say, 'It's raining everywhere around us but not here!'

Dad must have wondered why he'd left the lush coastal farming land of New Zealand for this arid place, where farming is a punt. He often reminisced about his homeland, but we'd tune out. We'd heard it all before.

Farming might have been a tough game, but with us kids his spirits remained high. He was forever having fun with us, making our lives happy, even if we were all busy. After tea we'd play Monopoly or Scrabble or Yahtzee or work on a 1000-piece jigsaw. Dad loved quizzes. Driving to the races he'd ask us maths questions or how to spell words. Geography was his favourite. Or at night-time, once he'd finished what he had to do, he'd call out from his desk, 'Who's up for a geography competition?'

'I am.'

'I am.'

'I am.'

'What's the capital of Norway?' he'd ask.

'Ahh, Oslo.'

'What is the biggest city in England?'

'London.'

'Longest river in Africa?'

'The Nile.'

'Prime Minister of Australia?'

'Mr Keating.'

We knew the geography of Victoria pretty well. The older kids were riding all around the countryside, to places like Stawell, Horsham, Donald, Murtoa and Ararat in the Wimmera and Manangatang in the Mallee. We knew about Hamilton and Warrnambool and the towns along the Murray, like Echuca and Swan Hill and Mildura. Racing was popular throughout country

Victoria and when the locals had a good horse they'd send it off to Melbourne to have a go.

Often we'd ask Dad, 'Can we come to the races today?' It wasn't because we wanted to have a day off school. We just wanted to go to the races. I was strapping our horses, giving them a good grooming, from when I was about seven, which must have looked very funny as I led them around the mounting yard. I could still walk under them yet I knew exactly what to do and I had no sense that this might be unusual. I was a Payne and that's what we did. We loved horses and we loved the races.

If we weren't actually at the races we'd listen on the radio—in the car, in the shed, in the kitchen—and once pay TV came along we watched on Sky Channel. Ballarat was our home track, though, and no racecourse in all the world is as special as it was—still is.

Brendan and Christine Atley, whose son Shaun now plays football for North Melbourne, eventually took over The Farm at Rochy as share-farmers and we went back Home to live. After that, I would often go up to the back entrance of the Ballarat Racecourse on our property boundary and walk up a rise to walk the track. We also used to love going yabbying occasionally in the dam that is in the middle of the track. For us, the Ballarat Racecourse was an extension of our backyard, and we felt we could do anything there.

Race day at Ballarat was extra special. We'd stay for the full card of events and then we'd always finish with fish 'n' chips from our local. We'd do a count of how many pieces of fish we'd need and we'd ask for a massive order of chips. We had a rule, though: you had to eat your fish first. Otherwise there was a mad rush to get all the chips as soon as the pack was on the table.

When we moved Home permanently I was given more and more responsibilities. We had to work really hard for a couple of hours in the freezing cold Ballarat morning. Then we'd all race inside and lie on the floor, where the floor heating vents were, to get warm. Some mornings the older kids would take too long in the shower, trying to get some warmth back into their bones. By the time it was our turn there was no hot water left.

If you could survive a cold shower in the middle of a Ballarat winter you were prepared for anything.

5

We will do much

WHEN WE CAME back Home, Stevie went into a special school, which he really enjoyed. He made many friends and was doing really well. He also learned to ride, which could be quite funny. Because we'd watched *Phar Lap* so often, one day when he was on a horse he said, 'That's it, round you go, Bobby boy,' which was Phar Lap's nickname and a line from the movie when Phar Lap is in the middle of his winning streak.

Dad never pampered Stevie and always expected him to pull his weight. As a result he developed the same independence we all had to have to get everything done. He was clever, and he and I were always up to some mischief. Occasionally, to get out of a situation that had landed us in hot water, we would say to the other kids or the teachers that Stevie had Down's Syndrome, as if that was enough to explain away the problem. When that saved us a few times, Stevie picked up on it. Then when he was in strife he'd say, 'I didn't know. I'm Down's Syndrome.'

What we all knew was that he was a joy to have around, and what a lift he gave us. Stevie just has this way about him. He helped bring honesty and openness and perspective to everything because that's just the way he is. He is such a blessing.

When Stevie was about ten, Jack Dalton asked if he'd help him at the races. Jack was a local trainer, a great mate of Dad's and one of those characters who was always popping in. He helped our family out so often. If Cathy or Andrew hadn't been able to organise a lift to the races, and time was getting away, they'd call Jack at the last minute.

'Hey, Jack, we're stuck,' and Jack would come and give them a lift. Or Andrew would ask, 'Could you give me a lift to Warrnambool today, Jack?'

'Yeah, no worries,' and off they'd go, a drive of more than two hours.

Jack would be in our fierce card games of Five Hundred and even now, whenever I see him, he tells me I owe him $20 from a disputed result. My memory is that he owes me! One of us cheated—we just can't remember who.

Jack was famous for his massages. He claimed he was a qualified chiropractic expert who could fix anything. He thought he was a guru. His massages were so hard they were torture. After he gave a rub, if someone was feeling tight after a race, they'd wake up sore and proppy.

'That bloody Jack,' Bernadette would say. 'Makes me feel worse than I was before.'

Jack always had a couple of horses but he couldn't find a world-beater. Like a lot of trainers who just love the game he had to travel a fair way to be competitive. That never stopped him. One day he had a runner at a little Mallee town called Wycheproof, which is not far from the even smaller town of Berriwillock, the hometown of trainer Darren Weir. It's nearly a three-hour drive from Ballarat. After months preparing his horse Jack was very confident he'd win. So the hard-earned went on.

The horse went terribly. Jack was devastated—and broke.

As Jack and Stevie were making their way back, Jack was deep in thought, contemplating what had gone wrong, and then the car overheated in the middle of nowhere. There were no mobile phones then. Nothing. Jack was at wit's end. He got out of the car and started walking down the road, hands above his head, not knowing what he should do. He stopped, stood there, feeling at rock bottom. Lost in his own world, Jack hadn't noticed that Stevie was behind him.

Stevie had wandered up to Jack and then came out with, 'Tough game, isn't it?'

Jack looked at Stevie and gave him a huge hug. He started laughing and laughing. It was the perspective he needed.

He eventually flagged someone down and they got the car going again. Of course it worked out in the end but Stevie always helps you see things for what they are.

While Stevie went to his new school, I went back to Our Lady Help of Christians, where I had Mr Spark as my teacher and my old friendships were rekindled like I'd never been away. Emily started coming over again. I loved that we had the run of the neighbourhood and the racetrack. We had a quad bike, which we used to get around the property and up the rise to the racecourse. Occasionally we'd ride it on the road, but usually I wouldn't be allowed outside the property on my own.

'Come on, Em,' I said, when we were about nine. 'Let's go for a ride.'

I loved going fast—flat out even. This one time we went on the road Em hung on for dear life as we sped along Kennedys Road. When I noticed we were low on fuel I popped into The Shop. It had a bowser outside and Peter who worked there came out.

'Fill 'er up, thanks,' I said. Em didn't know what to think. As Peter was putting the cap back on the tank I said, 'In The Book, thanks.' That's what we said for everything. Lollies, chocolates, chips, drinks: 'Just put them down as bread and milk, thanks.'

Dad would get the account at the end of the month and he'd be amazed that we'd spent $1000 on bread and milk.

'This bill is far too dear,' he'd say. 'How can it be this expensive?'

'Don't know.'

'Don't know.'

'Who did this?' he'd ask.

'Not me.'

'Not me.'

'Not me.'

'That Not Me,' Dad would say. 'He's the worst kid I've got.'

◆ ◆ ◆

I loved sport but Dad was so busy that he couldn't ferry us around.

'Dad, can I play netball?' I'd ask.

'Do you want to be a netballer or a jockey?' he'd say. It was a standard approach of his. If we were stuck in front of the television, he'd come in and say, 'Do you want to be a jockey or a TV watcher?'

Dad did many things for us. One of the most important was to teach us to have a real crack at things, to be the best we could at whatever we were doing. He even gave us handshake practice.

'When you meet someone, give them a good firm handshake and look them in the eye,' he'd say. 'And if they ask "How are you going?" don't say "Good", say "Good, thank you".' He drilled this into us.

Halfway through Grade 6 a couple of teachers from Loreto College came to our school and said, 'If you're going to Loreto next year, come over here.' I joined the group as that's where I knew I would be going. Mr Morris, the Year 7 co-ordinator, talked about Loreto, and its history, and how high school was different and what we needed to do to be ready. He looked up and said, 'Hang on, girls, I've only got four names on my list and there's five of you?'

He knew I was a Payne and he said, 'Michelle, isn't it? I think it's your name that's missing.' Later he phoned Dad.

'Paddy,' he said, 'you've forgotten to enrol Michelle.'

'Well, yes, she'll just be going along to Loreto like the others,' Dad said. The last of my sisters to go there had been Margie, and that was quite a few years before. There'd been an interlude because Cathy had gone to Rochy High when we lived on The Farm.

'No, Paddy, it doesn't work like that,' he explained. 'Getting a place at Loreto is highly competitive these days. You have to fill out all the forms. There's interviews.'

Dad told me he'd work something out, the Payne way.

When I showed up on my first day at Loreto—I'd missed orientation day because I'd been to the races—I went straight to the Mornane lockers. My sisters had told me I'd be in Mornane house because they had been. I went through the list there and my name wasn't on it and so I headed to the office.

'Umm, my name wasn't on the list in the locker room,' I said.

'That's okay, we'll find out what's happened. What's your name?'

'Michelle Payne, P A Y N E.'

'Mmmm,' said the friendly receptionist. 'It appears you haven't been enrolled.'

With a little quivery lip and sad eyes, I said, 'Okay.'

'Don't worry. We'll give your dad a call and sort something out.' She rang Dad.

'Hello, Mr Payne, we've got your daughter here and it appears you haven't enrolled her.'

'Oh, geez, haven't I? Oh, geez, sorry about that. I don't know what happened there. Must have forgotten all about it.' I was eventually enrolled. Dad always had too much on his plate.

Our family was well known at Loreto, and to Mr Morris. Apart from attending school, the girls were often in the news. There weren't a lot of women jockeys around and they were riding really well. The Payne Family had been made (jointly) Racing Personality of the Year in 1994, which was a tremendous honour. Patrick had also become a star. He'd made a name for himself as a naturally talented apprentice. Although he weighed only 33 kilograms then, from the moment he rode in races he was at one with his horse. He'd won the Doncaster Handicap on Soho Square as an apprentice and a string of top-class races on horses like Pontormo, Alcove and Our Pompeii.

A couple of months after Andrew had begun his apprenticeship in 1994, five Paynes rode in a race at Ballarat. Patrick won, leading throughout on the favourite, Titian Moon. Therese finished second on Carajah and Maree made it a Payne trifecta with Caven in third place. Andrew finished fifth on Blatanto, and Bernadette rode Crown of Seaton. That was a big story in Ballarat.

Andrew may not have had as much media as Patrick, but he and Jason Paton, Therese's husband, were famous around the world for a couple of days for an incident known as The Great Jockey Switch. At Caulfield on Boxing Day in 1996 Andrew was riding Hon Kwok Star and Jason was on Cogitate. Jas first came to grief when his mount clipped heels. He fell, safely as it turned out, interfering with Andrew's mount Hon Kwok Star. Andrew also fell but as he toppled he landed across Cogitate's saddle. With lightning reflexes he grabbed hold of the dangling reins of Jason's horse and pulled himself over onto Cogitate's back and finished the race, bringing the horse back to its own trainer unscathed. So he went out on Hon Kwok Star and returned on Cogitate, to the amusement of everyone. It was a remarkable piece of horsemanship.

Racing people had a lot of interest in our family, and I suppose our story was unique and quite interesting to people generally.

Father Joe Giacobbe, a friend of Dad's, wanted to publish a book about us.

A great character, Father Joe was known as 'The Racing Priest', because, trying to turn a dollar for the Church, he had set up *The Winning Post*, a popular racing newspaper with a comprehensive form guide for the weekend races all around Australia. He knew a lot of Catholics loved a punt and that he had to get the cash out of the punters on Friday before the favourite was beaten in the last at The Valley on Saturday afternoon and parishioners were left with nothing for the collection plate. The proceeds of the paper went to Doxa, a fantastic organisation that supports disadvantaged youth.

Father Joe asked racing journalist Tony Kneebone (another Kiwi) to write a book telling our family story: *The Paynes: The struggle, the pain, the glory*. It came out when I was in Grade 5 and all the money made from the sale of the book went to Doxa. The very last line of the book quotes my dad: 'This book on the family is probably premature because the little one is likely to end up better than the lot of them.'

Had he noticed something? What did he mean? I wondered.

◆ ◆ ◆

Being mentioned in a book hadn't made me feel any more confident on my first day at my new school. Landing at Loreto's Dawson Street campus I looked around and wondered how I would survive. I was tiny. I was shy. I was nervous. I was worried. Other people rushed about. They seemed to know what was going on. I didn't.

Our family was also well known at Loreto because we were always late and never organised. Permission slips? Lunch? Parent–teacher interviews? There was more chance of Dad winning the Cox Plate than making an appointment to see a teacher. The school didn't seem too concerned. It was the way we did things, and we somehow managed to make it to the end of each week. Sometimes the girls would write their own notes. Bernadette's homeroom teacher in Year 7, Mrs Fithall, remembers getting a note in Bernadette's handwriting saying, 'Sorry Bernadette is late but we lost Patrick down the paddock.'

One of Bernadette's classmates, fed up after being chastised over being late, blurted out, 'Why don't you ever growl at Bernadette Payne when she's late?'

'Well,' Mrs Fithall said, 'the whole family's done half a day's work before your alarm's gone off.'

When I landed in the grounds of Loreto College, I did so with the family's reputation. I only knew a couple of girls, from Our Lady Help of Christians, and they had been placed in a different class. Most of the girls in my class were from a parish school on the other side of Ballarat, St Francis Xavier's, better known as Villa Maria. Thankfully my sister Margie was great friends with the Duggan girls. Steph was the youngest of the six Duggans and she was in my year. The older ones had teed up Steph to look after me when I got to Loreto.

After sorting out the enrolment problems, I was put into Steph's class, 7 Gold, that morning and I'll never forget walking in the door late. Steph spotted me from the back of the room.

'Michelle, come and sit with us,' she yelled. We have been best friends ever since. She and her friends invited me into their group in a second and I can't be more grateful to have the best friends I could ask for: Bec Ludbrook, Jacinta Bongiorno, Elsie Lardner, Stacey and Jackie Mahar (the twins), Justine Locandro and Liz Francis. That was their nature—they are real characters, lively, bright girls. And so friendly. I felt that being in this school with these girls was where I was meant to be.

We weren't always perfectly behaved but I don't think we caused our teachers too much grief, either. Our hearts were in the right place. Coming from good Catholic homes that valued education and hard work, we had a go, whether it was schoolwork or sport or whatever was happening at school. I loved maths. I really liked the problem-solving part of it. I also liked debating—I'd had plenty of practice, as you had to know how to argue your case if you were to survive in the Payne family.

Apart from being co-ordinator, Mr Morris was my English teacher. He'd grown up on a grain farm at Sheep Hills in the Wimmera in western Victoria. My sister had once won the Sheep Hills Cup raced at the nearby Warracknabeal track, which was one of the girls' favourites. Mr Morris became a little concerned that I had to go to the toilet so often, especially after lunch. One day, I'd ducked out of a different class and just as he was walking by the Mornane lockers he spotted me: I had my little pocket tranny in my blazer, earplug in, helping Andrew get one home at Murtoa.

'Michelle Payne!' he called. 'Michelle. What's going on?'

He knew exactly what I was doing. He knew that racing was in my blood and I just *had* to listen to hear how our horses were going. So we came to an arrangement that suited both of us. At the start of each English class Mr Morris would lay out the form guide on his desk out the front, and I would mark the best bets for him. What he did with that information was entirely up to him. In return for what he called 'good information', I got to go to the toilet whenever I liked.

You can tell when a school is going well. Teachers really get to know the kids. Kids respond to teachers who are understanding. There is mutual respect. Something as simple as a 'good morning' as people walk past each other makes for a friendly school. And moments of upset get sorted out. Loreto for me was a good school.

Even in these early days of school I spent a lot of time thinking about things. And, while we had the usual thirteen-year-olds' conversations, our group of girls would talk about stuff that mattered to us. Rebecca's father had died when she was eight years old and that sense of loss was enormous for her. The youngest of four—the older ones knew my sisters and brothers—she had become very close to her mother. And like Dad and my family, she had faith that things happened for a reason and that everything would be okay.

We played a lot of sport and I loved PE. Although Miss Baird, our physical education teacher and hockey coach, might tell you differently, I have never been a naturally talented athlete. I've simply always been determined and had the will to win. I was fit from all the riding, and the running sessions I did with Patrick and Andrew in Creswick Forest a few kilometres from Home. They were terrific role models, and believed that you just had to be in top condition to be a successful jockey. Patrick was a great believer that you needed to open your lungs up to get fit and he pushed us hard. He usually ran in his sweat gear, not wasting any opportunity to shed a kilo. Then, after dinner—which for Andrew, battling his weight, was a small bowl of pasta with a tiny amount of tomato sauce—we would go for a walk.

We understood it was hard for any of us to play club sport or even participate in school sport as we had so much to do at Home and Dad just couldn't take us here and there. If we could organise a lift that was fine, otherwise it was no go. I would make it into the cross-country team and Miss Baird always laughed at me because she said I was the only kid who could run four kilometres and talk the whole way. When I played netball I was usually centre because I could run around all day.

I also managed a couple of seasons of hockey, which were memorable because I played with that same group of girls who were my friends. One Saturday morning we were up against another school and I got a whack across the nose. I knew it was pretty nasty when, while walking towards me, Miss Baird peeled off her shirt. My nose was gushing; she put her shirt over my face. She rang Home and

Stevie answered, so she had a chat to him and then Stevie put Dad on.

'I think Michelle's broken her nose playing hockey,' Miss Baird said. 'I'm taking her up to casualty. Could you come in and pick her up?'

'She'll be all right,' Dad said. 'Once she's had the X-ray just put her in a taxi and I'll fix the driver up when he gets here.' I can't remember how much the fare to Miners Rest was.

Miss Baird was a fantastic teacher. She also came from a farm, near Learmonth, and I think she really understood me, and my family. She knew we felt a strong connection to the land, and to horses, and we loved the country life.

They were happy days and important days. Looking back I can now see that the philosophy of the school had an impact on me. My family and the school had the same values, so one reinforced the other. The school really believed in the dignity of all people— that everyone matters—and in the importance of working hard to develop the talents you were blessed with.

It was a great school for the group of strong, articulate young women I went through the grades with, and I reckon Sister Mary Ward, the English Catholic nun who established the Loreto order, would have been smiling on us. As our teachers would remind us occasionally, Mary Ward famously once said, 'Women in time to come will do much.' The group of girls I was with were certainly going to give it a good shot!

I really liked school but because we were so busy and so tired some things just didn't get done. I always spent time on the big projects but the day-to-day stuff would be left behind. I was always rushing and doing things at the last minute. Sometimes I couldn't help it as my mind was elsewhere.

'Shit, I forgot to do my Maths Mate homework,' I'd say, waiting for class to start. 'Liz, can I copy yours?' She never hesitated.

'We didn't do too good this week, Liz,' I'd say jokingly when we got our marks back.

By Year 9 our group had grown very close. We'd done so much together in such a short time. But they all knew my passion, that I had racing in my heart and that my time at Loreto would be short-lived. Halfway through that year, 2000, I told them I would be leaving at the end of the year. I was also off to apprentice school.

6

A family business

THROUGHOUT YEAR 9 I led a split life. Already apprenticed to Dad, I was also enrolled in the Apprentice Jockey Training Program run by Racing Victoria near Flemington Racecourse in Melbourne, the track where the Melbourne Cup is run. Then I'd go back to Loreto in Ballarat to write essays and solve quadratic equations.

The apprentice school course commenced with a full week of classes mid year, then we attended one or two days a week. It was a comprehensive introduction to the elements of racing, from riding technique and dealing with stewards to exercise and diet. We learned the basics of balance and general riding skills, and then we'd practise on retired racehorses, ponies and a mechanical horse. We were taught how to conduct ourselves at stewards' enquiries, and the protocols for protests and interference. We also did yoga and spoke with dieticians. Looking back I wish I'd paid more attention to the dietician, it's my one big regret. I got into some bad eating habits early on and I found it difficult to shake them. Relying on energy drinks is no way to live.

The course went for six months then. The only other jockey from my intake of ten young jockeys to make a go of it was Reece Wheeler. The school was very helpful but, really, my dad had been teaching me since I was born. When I signed the papers to become indentured to him in February of that year I was merely formalising my lifelong apprenticeship. I could not have had a better teacher.

◆ ◆ ◆

Dad is the son of Wilfred and Ellen Payne. My grandparents were both born in 1905, in Inglewood in the Taranaki district of New Zealand's North Island. It is a fertile region, very suitable for farming and for horses. My grandfather was from a family of ten children. A scallywag as a boy, he became known as 'Buster'. My grandmother Ellen was also one of ten children, of the Breen family. They migrated to New Zealand from Ireland in the 1890s. Both my grandparents grew up on farms and were devout Catholics who never missed Mass.

Buster worked many jobs on the land. He was a horseman, loved horse racing, especially jumps racing, and could ride anything. One year he won the New Zealand steer-riding championship. Buster and Ellen had two children, Margaret and then four years later, in 1936, Dad, called Patrick Gerard. As a child his week involved school, sport, riding and Mass on Sundays. Dad was an excellent rugby player but not such a good cricketer. He tells the story of his school, Opunake Convent, being bowled out for eight by the Opunake State School. He did contribute one to that score.

Buster and Ellen worked and saved hard to buy their farm and send their two children to high school. Dad later became a boarder at St Patrick's in Wellington, a secondary college run by the Marist Fathers. He was captain of the rugby team, playing as a loose forward. Dad would often duck off to see the races just round the corner at Trentham Racecourse, and then deal with the consequences later. Not an overly dedicated scholar, he missed home, the farm life, and the riding. He left St Pat's when he was fifteen.

Like his father, Dad from a young age just wanted to be around horses, to work with horses, to ride horses and to race horses. He and Buster had a pretty good eye and they started spotting at the sales. They concentrated on jumpers. When my Aunty Margaret wanted a showjumper they found her a beauty at the Waikato sales in Hamilton. That horse, Ronay, turned out to be too good for showjumping so Buster and Dad thought they'd prepare him for jumps racing. They trained him, Dad rode him, and he won eight steeplechase races. They backed him a few times as well.

Dad was an amateur jumps rider. In the early 1950s in New Zealand a professional jumps racing program attracted good fields and plenty of punters. Amateurs were able to ride their own horses. However, when other trainers started to engage the amateurs, the pros weren't impressed. Trying to cobble together a living from riding, the pros didn't like missing out on the prize money—if an amateur won, that prize money went to no one.

One day, when Dad was seventeen, a couple of the professionals threatened him before a race—maybe to scare him off, maybe with the intention of putting him into the running rail—but Dad outrode them and it was one older professional who found himself forced by Dad to ease his horse out of the race.

It seemed the best thing to do was for Dad to turn professional. Concerned that, at 63 kilograms as a seventeen-year-old, he was already heavy, he suspected he didn't have many years left in the saddle. He had to make the most of his time.

Apart from any money Dad made from riding, he and Buster thought they could make a go of the racing game. They continued to trade and train horses. They bought another jumper, Count D'Azure—despite inadvertently bidding against each other at the sale—and it went on to win a number of races and good prize money. No doubt they backed him too.

Keen to further his riding prospects Dad made two trips to England, wanting to break into jumps riding there, but he didn't get the rides he'd hoped for and, on return to Hawera from his second trip, he took up training. Apparently he was a pretty astute punter before he settled down, willing to wait for the right moment to back one of their horses, when it was set to run a big race.

Dad's friends say he was always full of fun, always enjoying himself, always full of possibility. He loved people, and still does. He's so interested in others—who they are and what they do and what they're like. He'll talk to anyone. His Kiwi friends—he is still close to many of them—say he was always warm and friendly and had a bit of the ratbag in him as well. I think he might have been grateful for the Catholic Sacrament of Confession.

After retiring from riding he became friendly with a beautiful young woman with a European accent, Rosa Maria Buhler, my mother. She was never called Rosa. When they went off to the local school, the nuns insisted on calling her Mary and that was how she was known in her new country, just as her sister Berto became known as Bertha.

Mum was one of ten children. Her parents, Robert and Maria Buhler, had emigrated with their children from Switzerland, attracted to New Zealand by the hope of a life better than the hand-to-mouth existence they'd known in Europe. Other Swiss immigrants had settled in the Taranaki district after the Second World War and the Buhlers followed in the mid 1950s. They had a modest dairy farm where they milked their herd. My mum and her sisters and brothers worked other jobs as well. The Buhlers pooled their resources and were able to purchase other land. Their smart investments were soon paying off. Mum was very capable and eventually she ran one of the family's small farms herself.

Pat and Mary met at a local dance and fell in love. Dad was a good-looking young chap in that 1950s way, and Mary was a striking woman. Quite the couple! They were married at St Joseph's in Hawera in 1968. Sadly, Buster had died of a heart attack just months before the wedding. He was only sixty-three. At that time, Dad was offered his father's job as a cattle buyer for Imlay Freezing Works, which would have given him a reliable income. Just after they were married, though, Mum and Dad bought a dairy farm with a hundred milkers on it.

Life was good. They worked, went to the races and to Mass every Sunday. They had many friends in the Taranaki region—in the parish, in the community and in racing. And children came quickly. Brigid was born in 1969, and over the next ten years they had seven more children—Therese, Maree, Bernadette, Patrick, Margie, Michael and Andrew. As devout Catholics they didn't believe in contraception so they used the rhythm method, but Dad used to say they were out of rhythm.

Dad loved the land and farming life and continued to buy and train horses. He was particularly fond of the Waikato sales. In 1978 he purchased a yearling by Blarney Kiss out of Grecian Jade, a Hermes mare. Dad liked the Hermes breed. He thought they were tough and made good jumpers. Blarney Kiss had won derbies in the United States and was to go on to sire two Melbourne Cup winners—Kiwi, who won in 1983 for Snowy Lupton with a young J.A. Cassidy on board; and Kensei, ridden by Larry Olsen and trained by Les Bridge, winning in 1987.

Dad paid $1300 for the young colt in 1978 and then sold a half share to his mate Peter Moran. He'd taken Patrick, still a toddler, with him to the sales that day and when they got home Patrick kept asking everyone to come and look at his horse. So, given the Irish connection in the sire's name, Dad suggested his new purchase be named Paddy Boy.

Their new horse didn't do much in his first couple of race starts as a two-year-old but then, when favourite in a 1600-metre maiden at Waverley, he won by three and a half lengths. Dad then put him in the Group 3 Champagne Stakes at Ellerslie. In the small field, Dad figured he was a chance to nab the prize money for fifth place. A young Greg Childs, who went on to ride the great New Zealand mare Sunline, settled him at the back of the field but he stormed home to win by three-and-a-half lengths. They thought they had a good one. When he dead-heated in first place with the classy Yir Tiz in the Sires Produce they knew they did.

It was exciting times. Paddy Boy was a champion in the making. Dad had his eye on the rich prize money in Australia. It was Winter Carnival time in Brisbane so Dad nominated him for the 1600-metre two-year-old race then called the Marlboro at Eagle Farm in June 1980. The whole family, Paddy Boy, and a second horse, Paddy Boy's companion Gentle Joker, travelled across the Tasman.

Peter Moran was to organise everything but when they got to Sydney there was no car, no float and no booked accommodation. Dad was not impressed. He sorted it out as quickly as he could and the Paynes became the proud owners of a second-hand Kingswood station wagon and a float carrying their talented young horse, which had been renamed as Our Paddy Boy.

I can imagine that adventure, with Dad and Mum and seven kids crammed in the car, driving up the Pacific Highway. There were times when the car and its cargo of people pulling two thoroughbred racehorses, one worth a considerable amount of money, would not make it up a hill. Some of the kids had to bail out and get back in at the top of the rise.

The delay in Sydney meant Our Paddy Boy missed a gallop in his training program and that was to cost him. He ran a brave second in the Marlboro. The family then decided to stay and have a holiday at Surfers Paradise, which the kids loved, before driving south to Melbourne where Dad could prepare Our Paddy Boy for the three-year-old races over the Spring Carnival.

On the way south they'd stop every now and then to let their two horses pick on the grass on the side of the road. At Berrigan in southern New South Wales, Our Paddy Boy got away and disappeared into the scrub. Mum and Dad searched for two hours while trying not to lose any of the kids in the process. Just when they were giving up hope, Our Paddy Boy wandered out of the bush of his own accord.

Dad stabled the horses with Ballarat trainer Robert Smerdon, who they'd met in Brisbane. He became a really good friend of Mum and Dad's. He had suggested that the country feel of Ballarat would suit New Zealanders and offered his facilities. The kids had a ball.

Our Paddy Boy was becoming something of a people's horse. He was a bay and had a great name. People loved the down-on-the-farm tale of Mum and Dad and the kids. Our Paddy Boy was also very, very good.

Dad took Our Paddy Boy to Victoria Park where he won the Adelaide Guineas, Dad's first Group 1 winner, and then to Melbourne for the Moonee Valley Stakes. By that time, Our Paddy Boy was a valuable horse. He had class, he was a competitor, he was tough, and he was bred to stay. He looked like being one of the top three-year-olds of the season, a genuine derby horse. Then, if he stayed sound, he'd be a Melbourne Cup contender the following Spring.

All owners dream of winning a Melbourne Cup, whether they're battlers who spread the cost across large syndicates, or sirs and ladies with plenty to splash around. Some will buy a yearling bred to run two miles and patiently nurture it over the years until it's ready for a crack as a mature horse at the Melbourne Cup. Given the Cup is contested once a year by a field of twenty-four horses, and given the delicate nature of a horse and all of the things that can go wrong, and given the horse has to have ability, the chances of getting into the race are miniscule. To win is nearly impossible. But that doesn't stop people from trying. If anything, those odds are its appeal. That's why the Cup has been so sought after by those who love horseracing. To win it is to defy the odds, and to feel for once, just once, the gods have chosen you.

An alternative way—and this is the much easier way—is to buy a proven young horse with potential. That at least eliminates the first few steps in the four-legged lottery, as Australians have called it. Our Paddy Boy was a very attractive Melbourne Cup proposition and, even before making it to the Cup, if he remained fit and well, he was almost assured of winning good prize money for his owner along the way. He was also an ungelded colt and, with his potential as a stayer, was likely to be an attractive sire once he'd finished his racing career.

The offers to buy him started coming in. Trainer Ian Saunders in Sydney had an interested owner, and the very successful West Australian businessman Robert Holmes à Court, put in a bid. Although tempted by the $200,000 on offer, Dad and Peter Moran held on.

Dad was a battler from New Zealand and his share, $100,000, would have gone a long way to setting the family up. At the time a decent home could be bought for around $25,000. Mum and Dad could have added a few bedrooms and still had change. It was a risk not to take the money. Our Paddy Boy could have been bitten by a snake the next day, or struck by lightning, or damaged a tendon at trackwork, or had bone chips in his fetlock joint. He could have developed colic, or heart arrhythmia. He could have got caught in a fence, or a float could have jack-knifed on an icy Ballarat road. But what racing people know best is risk. So Dad hung on.

At his next start, Our Paddy Boy, ridden by Mick Mallyon, finished sixth in the Moonee Valley Stakes, a run that appeared somewhat disappointing. Dad was concerned he'd blown his opportunity. Colin Hayes, one of Australia's most successful trainers, however, had been keeping an eye on Our Paddy Boy and asked Mick what he thought. Mick gave our horse a good rap. Hayes offered $300,000 for Our Paddy Boy on behalf of the British Pools magnate Robert Sangster, probably the best-known horse owner and breeder in the world at that time.

Dad didn't draw breath this time. The sale was organised immediately and the adventure was over. It was time to head back to the farm in New Zealand.

Our Paddy Boy had made a huge impact on our family. He gave Mum and Dad and the seven kids a magnificent time in Australia, and they made many friends along the way. He introduced them to the beautiful country around Ballarat and he won $50,000 in prize money. As sad as it was to lose him, their $150,000 share from his sale gave our family financial security. Andrew was still a baby and Mum was pregnant with Cathy. They were going home to the farm in New Zealand, returning to the people they loved. They felt blessed.

Our Paddy Boy proved to be a handful for Colin Hayes, who wanted to run him in the Cox Plate a few weeks later. The horse didn't take well to his new surrounds. Stable jockey Brent Thomson couldn't control him and Mick Mallyon was having trouble as well. Hayes rang Dad.

'You've sold me a wild horse, Pat. What's wrong with him?'

'Nothing wrong with him when he left here,' Dad said.

'Well, he's giving us grief. We can't get near him,' Colin explained.

'He must be missing his mate,' Dad said.

'Who's that?'

'Gentle Joker,' Dad said. 'I don't think you've got an option. You're going to have to take him as well.'

'How much?' Colin asked.

'$12,000.'

Gentle Joker was not much of a horse, although he did win a race for the Hayes' stable, but he did ensure that Our Paddy Boy was at his best. Our Paddy Boy became more and more popular. He ran third in that Cox Plate and then third in the VRC Derby the following Saturday. He had a big future ahead of him. When he returned in the Autumn he won the prestigious AJC Derby at Randwick, and then took out the Sydney Cup as a light-weight three-year-old at his next start. Although he experienced injuries over the following twelve months he ran a brave fourth in the Melbourne Cup of 1981 to Just a Dash, having hit the front briefly at the 300-metre mark. Soon after he was retired to stud in Queensland.

Back in New Zealand, Dad began the search for another Our Paddy Boy, or at least another bargain. During 1981, while continuing to farm, he began purchasing stayers with a view to preparing them for Australian and Asian buyers. He had developed a good reputation and some big owners and trainers trusted his judgement. Lloyd Williams, who owned Just a Dash, went on to become a major owner—he has since won the Melbourne Cup three more times with What A Nuisance, Efficient and Green Moon—and purchased a number of horses from Dad. These days, when I ride for Lloyd, I am conscious that he has known our family since before I was born.

Connected as they felt to their homeland, Mum and Dad, now with eight kids, decided to head off on a second Australian adventure in 1982, after their farm was taken over by the local council. Dad was going to have a bit each way as a horse trainer and a farmer.

Dad continued life as an owner–trainer, a role far more common in New Zealand than in Australia. He was also trying to encourage owners to place their horses with him. He didn't ever have a big team of horses but he had consistent success. And, as his kids grew older, one by one they became his apprentices. Until it was my turn.

◆ ◆ ◆

Dad had mixed feelings about my decision to leave Loreto to become a jockey at the end of 2000. He had been pretty tough on me when I rode trackwork for him during those high school years.

'You're keen, but you've got a lot to learn,' he would say. He wasn't convinced I had the talent, although I sometimes wondered whether the sharpness of that criticism was his way of pushing me, and whether he'd used the same tactic with the others. He'd also become increasingly concerned about the dangers in horse racing as time went on.

He thought I needed to get a good education. Dad had read my reports from Loreto, which suggested that, if I applied myself, I would get reasonable results. I think he liked that I was good at geography! Dad believes in education, which is why he worked so hard to put us through St Pat's and Loreto. It's just that we were all so desperate to become jockeys—except for Margie, who went off to study and became an accountant, and Brigid who dabbled in journalism for a while in her early twenties. Therese talked about midwifery and perhaps I could have chosen a profession that involved problem solving—I like the idea of being a detective. My Loreto friends think I would have gone into one of the caring professions. But despite his reservations Dad knew that I was never going to do anything else except ride.

I was already a jockey. It was in me. It *was* me. I'd known since I was five, if not before. Everyone knew. My family, my Loreto friends, my teachers. They all knew that I'd had the passion all my life. Dad had heard me talk about it for years.

'I just want to win the Melbourne Cup,' I would say, and I meant it.

That wasn't just a way of expressing my intention to get as far as I could in horse racing; it was actually what I wanted to do. I wanted to *ride the winner of the Melbourne Cup*. I wanted to stand on the podium with the Melbourne Cup in my hands. That was my aim. I think Dad knew how determined I was, and that I was willing to give it my all.

7

The horse's way

AFTER BECOMING THE eighth Payne to ride, the local television news came out to do a story on me. I was fifteen. 'She's your baby, Paddy!' the journalist says in the story. And he asks Dad if he'd tried to talk me out of it.

'How could I stop her?' Dad asked. It was the right response. I was doing exactly what I wanted, what I believed I was meant to do. When asked what my ambition was I said, 'I just want to be the best jockey I can be.'

When I said that, I could hear my father's voice, I could feel the reassurance of his rock-solid belief. He encouraged us to be thankful for our blessings, to respect others, and to give our best. He had taught us by example in the way he lived, and also by instruction and explanation. He could be incredibly harsh and honest but I always felt he had the very best intentions, and hoped we would find a depth of happiness, if not an inner peace in our lives. If I was to find that depth of happiness, and meaning, in being a jockey then that's what I needed to do. He would support, encourage and nurture me, even though I was going into a profession that he knew only too well was dangerous.

Those best intentions weren't so obvious when he was tearing strips off us in the yard. He was quick to show his frustration, a trait he has passed on to Therese and Patrick, and a little to me. And he can be stubborn, especially when he's convinced he's right.

As he had been to my sisters and brothers when they were apprenticed to him, Dad was my father–mentor, and master–mentor. There was no separation of the roles. The papers to make that official were a mere formality required by the conventions of racing and the law. Life as I knew it went on. Being a jockey wasn't a job, or a profession for me. I felt it was even beyond a vocation. I felt the deepest sense of personal connection with being a jockey. And I trusted that my father understood that—because he was *my father.*

He taught me to be kind to horses, to work with them, to understand them, to love them. I watched him love them and I watched them love him. He also made it very clear, though, that you had to be in control and they had to know you were boss. I learned that from a very young age, when Dad would get us to break in the young horses with him. They have to learn you are in charge from the start and so did I. Horses are very smart and intuitive animals, they know if someone is nervous around them; they know when they can get away with anything they want. And it can be a fine line.

When I was quite young we had a couple of older horses— Moving Away and Colorado Ring—which had over a hundred starts each. Both won more than fifteen races. When Dad walked towards their paddock they'd see him and acknowledge him. They'd start neighing. Dad would look straight at them.

'How's my old mate,' he would call out as he got nearer to them. I could feel the affection between them.

Dad also taught me how to live with horses, in the same place as horses, and to look after them. To treat them with respect, but to also win their respect. To be part of their day. And to ride them. He taught me to believe in the relationship between horse and jockey.

'Some horses go good for some jockeys,' he used to say.

Dad also taught me how to break in a horse. I reckon I was as young as seven when he did. When he brought a yearling back from the sales, he'd put it in a box and put me on it, bareback, as he'd done with most of the kids before me. He'd get me moving its head left and right. He had a consistent message: 'You're the boss. Don't ever let the horse think otherwise. You *show him* you're the boss.'

I heard that over and over again.

Soon after, we'd put a saddle on the horse and go through the same process. Left and right. I progressed from that to being led around on the back of the horses. Dad then started me on a lunging lead, trotting in a circle on the racehorses. I learned to rise to the trot. Once I could trot I was ready to take the next step, to break into a canter. I'll never forget that first day.

The horse I used to ride was a lovely old chestnut called Campaigner. He'd won a few races so he had definitely earned his keep, and he was the perfect horse for me to learn on—placid and obedient. We were in the little circle of one of the small day yards near the stables. I broke into a canter and all I can remember is trying to get into the jockey position. I was all over the place, bobbing along, so tiny, trying to stay balanced like all my brothers and sisters did, like the really good jockeys who were riding at the time did. Cathy and Andrew were watching the lesson and were killing themselves laughing. I was so angry.

I was concentrating so hard and when we stopped, I said, 'Dad, tell them to stop laughing at me.' But nothing could make them stop. Dad was probably trying hard not to laugh himself.

He continued to put me on the lead in the mornings, whether it would be at Home or in the centre of the training track at Ballarat in front of all the other trainers, while the other kids would be working the horses around the track. My practice was used as a warm-up for the more vigorous work the horses would do with the others to build up the horses' fitness.

I was riding more and more but I couldn't get enough of it. Any chance I could get I'd take. But in the afternoons Dad used to take the horses for a stroll and a pick of grass down the road to get them out of the paddocks before feed time. We didn't really like doing this job. I always wanted to ride down the road but he said we had to lead them, which was pretty tiring for a nine-year-old who'd been up since before dawn and had had a day at school. And we were also keen by this time to get home and play on the Nintendo I'd won at the school fete in Prep. We loved Super Mario Kart and Super Mario Bros. Dad was not impressed. He hated us playing electronic games and being inside. He couldn't get us to work. He threatened to cut the cords and we'd keep saying, 'One more game, Dad. I've just got to finish this level.' But then we just did what we were told and tended to the horses.

Our lives revolved around horses. It was a life in two parts: the joy of riding them, and the hard work of looking after them. Even when we lived at The Farm in Rochy, Dad always kept a few horses around. When I first started riding trackwork there, it was on old Rudimentale. He was Therese's horse and he was the horse that in my quiet times I used to go and lie in the paddock in the sunshine with. I'd feel his warmth. Feel his breath. Smell him. And pat him. And then give him something special to eat. He was a lovely horse. He was always placid, so Dad and Andrew decided he would be a good horse for me to learn to canter, without a lead. Being around seven-and-a-half, I was a bit nervous, and despite Rudimentale being super lazy, he sensed this nervousness and the second time I cantered on my own he took off flat out on me.

My first job was to muck out the boxes. I would get up with everyone very early in the morning and go down to the stables to work with Stevie. The older kids would saddle the horses and take them out to work. Stevie and I had to clean out the boxes before they got back. We'd fork and sweep out the soiled straw. Stevie would put it in the wheelbarrow and push it to the heap. He'd take ages to come back for the next load. Time would be getting away and I'd be wondering what he was doing out there. If they got back and we hadn't done the four or five empty boxes the older kids would get so angry with me.

'What have you kids been doing? How come these boxes aren't finished?' I would be trying to do my best but I wouldn't say anything against Stevie.

One day I got jack of it and went looking for Stevie. I found him sitting between the handles of the wheelbarrow on the way out to the manure heap having a spell, talking to himself, laughing away.

'So this is what you do,' I yelled at him. 'No wonder we're always late. No wonder I'm always in trouble.' I was angry. It was always my fault and that wasn't fair.

When he got back to the box we were still arguing. He was making me so frustrated, I punched him in the belly. I have never felt so bad as I did then, because I winded him and he was crying. Although we'd argue and fight, and Stevie had hit me before in a boxing match arranged by the older kids—mainly Patrick—Stevie could never bring himself to hit me in the run of everyday life. Our little touch-up seemed to work, though. He never took as long from then on.

Clocking someone was part of family life. The boys were always fighting—and it was not uncommon for one of the girls to be sporting a shiner as well. Dad bought a pair of boxing gloves and that's how Patrick and Andrew would sort out their differences. I used to put them on as well. So we all learned to handle ourselves.

Feed-up time was a real team effort. Someone had to make up the feeds, and crushing the oats was the worst because it was such an itchy job. Everyone tried to get out of that job and do something else. Someone would bring in fresh straw from the hay shed in a wheelbarrow for the boxes, and someone else would be laying it down in the boxes. Another kid would put fresh water in each box. Anything but crushing the oats ...

When the horses were brought in at night, the chaff also had to be made up, which meant putting lucerne into the hay cutter—just as bad as the oat crusher as all the dust would get down your shirt and make you unbearably itchy. Thankfully Dad used to do this job most of the time if he wasn't at the races. He used to put a towel around his neck to stop it from getting down there. The horses that didn't come in at night also needed their water troughs filled up and feeds taken out to them.

As it was getting dark, Dad would make up the bran mash—fine bran mixed with molasses and hot water. I would do the final round with him, giving the horses a couple of handfuls each of the mash. We'd go to each box inside, where the better horses were stabled, and he'd put his big hands in the white buckets and feed them. The horses loved it and there was no doubt they were Dad's mates. They'd rub against him affectionately as he'd give them a pat with his clean hand and some of the older ones would give Dad a little neigh as he opened the box door.

As we turned off the lights I would take hold of Dad's hand and we'd walk home under the moonlit sky back to the house to have dinner. I used to hold Dad's hand wherever we walked and usually I'd have to break into a little jog to keep up with him.

◆ ◆ ◆

After we had returned to Home from Rochy, some of the older kids moved away. Their blossoming riding careers took them to Melbourne and around the Victorian countryside. Bernadette was based in Adelaide for a while, where she had a lot of success. Patrick was riding in Hong Kong. I remember the day Patrick won the Doncaster Handicap when he was sixteen. Seeing him ride and win, I was just thinking about what he was doing—how he rode, his patience, his hands. He has the best hands to get a horse to settle, and patience in the finish. You'd be thinking he was waiting too long but then he'd pull it off. He just knows his horse; knows how to read them. And he was never much of a whip rider. He always got the horse going more through encouragement rather than the whip. He's like that now with his training. He's very kind to the horse. It's all about the kindness, unless they obviously need some standing over. But when I did a lot of trackwork for him, when I was about fifteen and onwards, he was very hard on me, a real arsehole at times. Looking back now it toughened me up and made me a lot more capable.

Once the older kids moved on it meant I was given more of the responsibility of working the horses in the mornings. Maybe two or three horses would need a gallop. From when I was about eleven Dad would let me gallop up the paddock in a straight line with Cathy and Andrew. The horses knew to stop at the top. As I got older I progressed to riding beside the car. He'd get me to rate the horse. We'd do evens, which is 15 seconds for 200 metres, and then we'd work a little faster. Dad taught me the importance of knowing precisely how fast your mount was going, to develop a way of understanding time and speed. It took a lot of practice, a lot of hours in the saddle.

Because I was little and not very strong, I knew I had to develop a technique to get the horse to do what I wanted it to do. And when you're a little kid from Our Lady Help of Christians hurtling along at 45 kilometres per hour on a frosty Ballarat morning, you have to concentrate. Technique was everything. I had to learn to find the rhythm, learn to soften my hands and the horse's mouth to have it come back underneath me. Dad would get me to practise riding on the bomby old pushbike, as if it was a horse, for balance. When I was going as fast as I could along the members' drive of the Ballarat Racecourse, I'd pull out the whip and get that pushbike first over the line. It helped me develop the rhythm of the action while staying balanced.

At the end of each gallop in the mornings, Dad would make a few observations and suggestions. Then I'd go in for a shower and something to eat and we'd head in to school, arriving four hours or so after I'd first woken up.

By the time I was thirteen I was riding on the training tracks at Ballarat. I felt very much at home there, and I was looking forward to the day when I got a start in an actual race.

Dad taught us to walk the track. He reckons it's one of the most important things, to find out where the better going would be. One time there was a meeting coming up at Ballarat and Therese was riding one of our horses. She was in The Next Room, lying on the couch watching *Days of Our Lives*.

'Like sands through the hourglass,' came the voiceover, 'so are the *Days of Our Lives*.' Dad was in the kitchen.

'Come on, Therese,' he called. 'We're going up to walk the track, for the races tomorrow.' Dad thought his horse could win and the track was heavy, so he was after any advantage. The horse had drawn wide, and would start from an outside barrier, and he thought that if Therese plotted a course out wide, down the back straight, the ground might have been firmer and faster and would save the horse's energy for the finish. But he had to check it out and show Therese where to cut across before the corner so she didn't waste too much ground on being wide by the time she turned.

Therese didn't move. This was her favourite show.

'Therese! Come on!'

Grudgingly she trudged out with him, into the mist of the Ballarat winter. She knew she had to go but she was back pretty soon.

Dad always brings this story up because Therese hadn't really paid attention and when the time came for the race she just got beat. Dad was so angry. He was certain she had misjudged it. After much debate he dragged her back out again into the cold to look at where the footmarks of the horse were to make his point. She was the only jockey who took that path so it was clear where she had ridden. Dad was right and still to this day he says she would have won if she'd listened and not been annoyed about missing *Days of Our Lives*. It was a valuable lesson about how racing is a game of tiny margins.

As I got older I could see the benefit of walking the track, to see where the muddy patches were, to see where the divots were messy, and to see where the better going was. It was a sensible and practical thing to do, so I have always done it. It leaves one less thing to chance—to decide whether going the extra distance of sitting away from the running rail or going through the muddy patch can be a real equation. Sometimes it can be a real advantage to put in the extra thought and effort.

Dad was definitely not infallible, though. Sunny Glow was a grey horse we got from Kevin 'Dummy' Myers. Dad always used to say Dummy by name but not by nature. The Myers were really close family friends from New Zealand. Sunny Glow was taking off in his trackwork with Cathy and me—Dad's main trackwork riders at the time—so he had nothing left for his races.

Dad thought he'd try working Sunny Glow behind the four-wheel drive in The 40-Acre Paddock, telling both Cathy and me to take turns in riding him just behind the car. Cathy or I would start him off, cantering behind the car, but neither of us would get far; he'd just go flying past the car. He'd gallop flat out for a lap, about 1800 metres around. By the time we stopped, Dad would be going mad.

'What happened? I told you to stay behind the car.'

'Dad,' we'd say each time, 'he's going to run into the back of the car if we do.'

'He won't run into the back of the car.'

'He will, Dad.' He would send us back out next time and once again we'd fly past the car. Dad got so angry. After a few goes at this he came up with a plan.

I'd drive, even though I didn't have a licence, Cathy would ride and he'd sit on the back of the car with its tray down. He was going to shoo him away from the back of the car if he got too close. As we got to cruising speed I looked back in disbelief—Sunny Glow was galloping all over the tray at the back of the car, right near Dad's legs, which were hanging over it, and Dad was unable to do anything to stop him.

Cathy was completely out of control. I was in shock, and I didn't think to drive faster. They were yelling, 'Speed up! Speed up!' So off I went.

Thankfully both the horse and rider were okay when we came to a stop. Cathy and I just looked at each other. Dad was shaking his head.

'Well, I didn't think he would do that.'

'We told you he would, Dad.' It was one of the only times I've seen Dad beaten.

'Who'd have thought?' he kept saying, 'that a horse would run into the back of a car.' We didn't try it again.

After I left Loreto I felt I was ready to ride in a race and in February 2001 Dad agreed to let me. He put me on Reigning in a very average 2200-metre race at Ballarat.

The days leading up to the race passed slowly. I would be on a gentle giant, seventeen-hands high, trained by my dad; I was nervous and excited. I didn't sleep well maybe for a week before—running the race over and over in my head, thinking of how I wanted to ride a horse I knew so well. I ran the course every day the week before, planning my race, imagining what I would do at what point.

Sitting in the barriers before the race I must have looked really anxious. My barrier attendant was Darren Browell.

'Just take a deep breath,' he said to me. 'It'll be okay.'

I've never forgotten that, it's something that's stuck in my head my whole career. Even to this day, whenever I feel a bit nervous, I say to myself, 'It'll be okay.'

The gates opened and away we went. Reigning went to the lead and travelled beautifully in front. I took him easy up the hill and let him slide down it as I strode along the back straight. Approaching the 1000-metre mark I allowed him to quicken slightly. He was a big striding horse and a bit of a lazy bugger, so I felt if he had a bit of a break it might encourage him to try a bit harder. When I turned for home and balanced him up I increased to full speed. He lengthened beautifully and went on to win by three lengths.

My school friends from Loreto College were cheering me over the line. I was so thrilled the girls were there. It really was a fairy-tale start to my career in the saddle. Dad looked really pleased, and maybe a little surprised.

Suddenly I was getting offers from all over the place.

8
In the saddle

WHEN YOU FIRST become an apprentice you can claim 3 kilograms, which makes you attractive to some trainers. It means if a horse is handicapped to carry 59 kilograms, you can ride that horse if you are 56 kilograms. The less weight a horse has to carry the easier it is for it to run. It's a trade off. You are less experienced but the horse carries less weight. So, after my debut at Ballarat, my 3-kilogram claim looked good to owners and trainers. The phone kept ringing.

My second day of racing was at Warracknabeal, about two-and-a-half hours northwest of Ballarat, and I was booked for six rides. My sisters loved Warracknabeal, a classic country track, but I had a shocker of a day. I was thrown in the deep end. One horse took off on me and led by eight lengths and basically carried me around. Generally the racing there was rough, which I just wasn't prepared for. I was getting bumped around all over the place. Nothing like that had happened in trials. I just didn't have the awareness; no race smarts whatsoever. I was devastated. It did my reputation no good, and no doubt it fed the prejudices of some trainers and punters who thought female jockeys were a risk.

Dad was concerned too.

'All the other kids showed a bit of promise, but I don't think you've got it. Maybe you should go back to school. You're good at school.' That made me all the more determined. I was going to show him. He probably knew it would get a rise out of me. He'd used that tactic on the older ones. He once said that all Maree could do was put a leg on either side of a horse and move her little fingers.

Dad told me I had to practise on the chaff bag. I would practise my style with the whip but I had to find the rhythm of the horse. I stuck at it. Dad believed in technique and he helped me a lot with this. And I'd spend a lot of my time talking to Andrew. He gave me good advice. He liked talking about racing craft and he wanted to see me improve. Andrew was a typical older brother when we were growing up because he picked on me so much and loved making me cry, but when the time came for me to be a jockey he really couldn't have been more helpful. I can't thank him enough for that support. He bought an equiciser (a mechanical horse) more for himself but he would make me get on it for practice all the time. He later gave it to me. I called it Our Paddy Boy and still have it to this day.

There was no substitute for race riding, though. Like all young jockeys I had to get a feel for how to ride in a field where every jockey was doing their best to win the race. While the rules of racing are very strict, the experienced jockeys have all the tricks. They have a personal interest in beating you. The ride you get from a trainer is the ride that jockey had missed out on.

Some jockeys offered suggestions, or an encouraging word, and my sisters and brothers were fantastic. Cathy was very supportive, even though she was living in Melbourne and we were often bidding for the same rides in the country. She was still a good advocate for me. After riding one for the Maldon trainer Brian McKnight, Cathy suggested he should engage me as I could claim the 3 kilograms. I rode two winners for Brian that day, and seven more soon after. I was in his good books and became his rider. We had many wins, thanks to Cathy. She didn't ride for him much after that but she laughs about it now.

Not long after I started riding in races and I was getting more rides, Dad thought it was a good idea to get me a manager. He asked his friend Joan Sadler if she would take the job on. Joan was apprehensive initially, as she had never been a manager before, but she said she'd give it a go. She took all of the requests from trainers and helped me find rides, mainly on the phone. She is such a generous and warm-hearted woman, and she really looked after me. We grew very close. She was so supportive, and a great listener—and talker! Joan also started managing Cathy and became like a mother to us. We used to joke that all we needed to do was sign the adoption papers.

Therese, Maree and Cathy lived in Melbourne and were riding for city and country trainers with good success. When I started going to Melbourne to do some trackwork in the second year of my apprenticeship, I'd stay with either Maree or Therese. Initially I worked a lot for trainer Brian Mayfield-Smith through a connection of a friend of ours, Stuart McLay. I was also riding trackwork at Caulfield when I could. It was a matter of getting to the track before dawn and standing around waiting to be asked to ride a horse, or being a bit more assertive and approaching trainers to see if they needed anyone to work one of their horses. Once you ride a horse at trackwork there is a chance you'll be asked to ride that horse in a race. I was gradually building relationships with trainers but it was going to take a long time.

Joan was finding me rides in the city and the bush. My 3-kilogram claim was always a big plus and I was working hard on improving my fitness and strength, and on the technical elements of riding in races. Apart from doing a lot of Brian's trackwork, I was riding for him in races and had numerous city winners: Gussy Godiva, Ella Fire, Dual Spark and Penny Opera. I was riding for other trainers as well.

No matter what aspect of my technique I was working on, I felt I was at my best when I was building a relationship with a horse. I really clicked with Sir Chuckle, one of Mike Moroney's horses. He had a wind, or breathing, problem and he needed to get into a rhythm. I also worked out he was better away from the pack, he just relaxed better. We won four races in a row, three of them down the straight at Flemington. Michael let me ride him in a listed race—a top-quality event where trainers usually use senior riders because apprentices cannot use their weight claim—just because we got on so well. He ran a gallant second. I also rode a few winners for Therese, who was training by then.

I was developing my understanding of the tactical side of racing, studying the form guide to learn the pattern of racing of the horses, where they settled in the running, and what they were capable of, to anticipate how races might play out. At seventeen I was still so young, so inexperienced, but keen and ready to learn.

I used to speak with Andrew after just about every ride. His opinion mattered to me. He has always been a thinker, open and honest. Over the years it's been nice to put our heads together to see what we can come up with. We'd talk about relationships, beliefs, just life in general. He had his own concerns, as he was dealing with the issue of becoming too heavy to be a jockey.

My relationship with Patrick has been quite different, especially when I was young. Being older he was more likely to tell me what to do rather than discuss things with me. I didn't mind; I respected him so much. He always has a lot of theories—I think that runs in the family. Patrick gave me other advice as well. He told me about boys and how they think and to be wary of their intentions. He made Cathy have that boy–girl chat with me when I was sixteen—which was very awkward for both of us.

Patrick's style was to throw me in the deep end, getting me to ride horses that were difficult. It was a test. He wanted to see how I'd cope. He taught me that the easy way isn't always the best way and that struggle is sometimes valuable. I agree and I think that understanding has helped my riding because I have never wanted to fail. I've valued the struggle. It's amazing how when you really give something everything you've got, a situation that might seem impossible can actually become achievable. Patrick always used to say '"can't" is not a word'.

With all of this experience around me I was soaking it all in. From the time I began riding I realised how competitive it was. It was hard to get a ride, and it was hard to keep the ride. I was trying to make an impression, trying to do what I thought was the right thing, which, as an apprentice, was to show trainers I could ride at very light weights—around 50 kilograms and occasionally less. I thought I had a short period of opportunity to make a name for myself and that I would be tossed onto the heap of failed jockeys if I didn't. I was constantly in a battle with my weight and because I was trying to please everyone, I didn't know how to just stop and say, this is totally unreasonable.

I had started riding when I was a 47-kilogram girl but, as I matured and grew, it was harder to remain in that lightweight category. By the time I was eighteen, even with the sort of discipline jockeys impose on themselves to maintain their weight, I settled in at about 53 kilograms. As an apprentice, I still had to make the lighter weights, with the claim, to keep the rides, so I had to go a step further. I had to starve myself before the races. Literally starve myself. No food for a day. Often I would be physically weak and have no energy. And there was the psychological element, of stressing about gaining weight. You are constantly delving into your deepest physical and emotional resources at times like that. There is no doubt being caught in that cycle means your well-being suffers.

To compensate, during a race I'd try to look strong and vigorous on my mounts. It was wrong—all I did was compromise my technique. I would lose the shape and balance I'd be trying to maintain, particularly over the concluding stages of a race. After I ran third in a 2500-metre race one Saturday at Flemington, the stewards called me in because I looked so weak on my horse.

'What is going on here?' Chief Steward Des Gleeson asked.

'I'm just exhausted,' I said, fighting back the tears. 'At Cranbourne yesterday I rode nineteen horses in trials and that was after riding seven horses at trackwork at Caulfield.' What I didn't say was that, because I had to get down to 50 kilograms for the Saturday meeting, all I'd had during the day was two cans of V drink.

'Maybe you need to look at managing yourself a bit better,' they suggested. 'Maybe you should say no to some of those trials. You need to pace yourself.' I tried to explain to them my dilemma as a young jockey.

'It's hard because if people ask you to trial their horse you can't say no, because they know you're not on another one, and they'll think you're lazy. You don't want to let them down. If you don't do the work, they won't put you on the horses in races.'

Des was kind and he said, 'I understand. But it's something you have to address. You have to be as strong as you can be, for lots of reasons. Maybe you could raise your weight a little, so you can eat more.'

'Yes, Mr Gleeson,' I said. 'I understand.' But I knew it would cost me rides.

Des was being helpful. He was a wonderful chief steward, a warm-hearted man who wanted what was best for you. From Yangery, just outside of Warrnambool, he loved racing and he wanted racing to be fair and just. He had a good sense of where young jockeys were in their development. I was just starting out. But I was determined. I was trying to be honest with myself. I found positive people—people like Des Gleeson who treated others kindly—so encouraging.

It wasn't the only time the stewards wanted to talk to me. One of their more mundane jobs is to sign off on an apprentice's phone bills and organise for the money to be paid from their apprentice's account, where prize money and riding fees are deposited, for transparency. When I was first going out with Rhys McLeod— jockeys tend to go out with jockeys or people from the racing industry because no one from the real world would ever put up with the lifestyle—text messaging was introduced. Being madly in young love, Rhys and I spent all day sending each other text messages. Des Gleeson called me in.

'Michelle,' he said, 'I need to talk to you about your phone bills. We are concerned you are spending too much and would like to advise you it would be in your best interest to cut them down.'

'Yes, sir,' I said. 'I completely understand.' I couldn't get out of there quickly enough.

Rhys and I were both apprenticed at the same time. A bit older and ahead of me, he was apprenticed to Pat Carey at Huntly Lodge in Sunbury. We were living similar lives under strict apprenticeships, and found comfort in texting each other. He was my first true love! We were so young. Unfortunately we didn't last the distance and went our separate ways after four years. He is still one of my closer friends, someone I can count on through anything.

When you are a young jockey it's not easy to measure your progress. Where you finish in the field is not the only indicator. The best ride in the race does not guarantee victory. You can win because you ride a good horse adequately. You can win because you're on the very best horse, and all you have to do is sit and steer. And sometimes you can give a horse the very best ride but it still finishes back in the field. Occasionally there's a moment when you know you've made progress.

Quite early in my career, I led all the way to win a 1400-metre race at Sandown. Many people would have said the horse jumped, led and won well, and that the jockey played little part. It was actually a difficult ride that required soft hands and intense concentration. On one of the racing programs on television, racing commentator Richard Freedman noticed that it had been a delicate operation and I had really nursed the horse home.

'This girl can ride,' he said. It gave me a real lift. I had put a lot of thought and preparation into how I was going to get that horse to travel sweetly on the day and it was reassuring that someone noticed.

Riding is such a complex skill. There are endless debates over what jockeys should and shouldn't have done, often ending in arguments between owners, trainers and jockeys. Owners are quick to sack jockeys and put another one on their horse. They often respond emotionally rather than rationally. The jockey is the first one to cop the blame when a horse does not perform to expectations, because the owners are often thinking about the prize money they've missed out on—only the first five horses get the reward—and often their losing bets as well. They don't necessarily understand that races are made up of a whole series of related and intersecting events that don't always turn out as you expect. One thing leads to another and suddenly a new set of circumstances exist and a new path has to be forged. There are so many variables.

Racing is not random, though. People have the capacity to influence the outcome. Owners, trainers and jockeys are always planning, theorising, strategising. Stables employ specialist analysts whose job it is to anticipate the positions horses will take up in the field, based on their record and their barrier. These are called speed maps, and increasingly they were appearing in form guides when I started as an apprentice. These analysts also anticipate what jockeys will do at what stage in a race: a horse that has no sprint might have to start its slow grinding run from the 1000-metre mark; a horse that is not good enough to win a race might be ridden for luck on the off chance it gets an inside split and bursts to the front at the right instant, because that's the only way it can win against better horses. And sometimes races do go to plan and everyone looks like a genius.

But, as Dad always says, 'There's always luck. You could go inside and get a clear run or you could go inside and not get the run. Who's to know?'

Races don't unfold the way you think they will every time. A horse can pull you forward to the front of the field when you were instructed to sit back at the tail of the field. A horse can miss the start and won't go forward when you've been instructed to lead. A horse can get caught three and four wide without cover and will be out of fuel as the field turns for home. A horse can get buried away on the rails and get shuffled back by tiring horses. A horse can be in the ruck with no opening and never get a run.

Even as a young jockey all this seemed obvious to me: you can read a race only when you're in the middle of it and then you can act. That's when you can anticipate what's about to unfold, and you make a rational decision in the split second you have to process the information. You can respond to your intuition and instinct, and the combination of both, which is best called 'experience'. But one thing is certain: a jockey *cannot* control what other horses are doing. I've also learned that not everyone realises this. I see how jockeys are sometimes blamed for things that happened *to* them. When you are a young female jockey you really get blamed. It is unfair and frustrating. I want people to know that things don't go wrong because you are a woman. They just go wrong.

When I was starting out, male jockeys—the senior riders and the apprentices—did not cop the same degree of criticism as women. They were more likely to be forgiven. Poor rides were not blamed on their maleness. While some owners and trainers were very fair the tendency was that women were less likely to be forgiven. Then, if a horse won only because of the tactically and technically outstanding ride from someone like Clare Lindop or Holly McKechnie, there would be this sense of surprise: 'Who would have thought? A brilliant ride from a woman!'

I was always aware of this attitude. I'd seen it with my sisters. I'd see it at trackwork. I'd see it on race day. It is a culture, a set of assumptions that affects the lives of female jockeys. It is unjust. But it is the way it is and we have no choice but to exist within this culture, while working to change that culture.

I would speak up and argue my case when it happened to me. I think the Loreto girls were not surprised when I defended myself to racing people if they were with me when I got a phone call from an owner. I would stand my ground, try to give rational explanations to people who had not experienced the hurly-burly of what a race is like. I would get so disheartened by the attitudes. I spent a lot of time talking with Joan about it. She knew how hard I tried, how hard I worked.

'Women jockeys have to be twice as good to be considered half as good,' Joan would say.

There were some moments when I felt I made progress. Not long after my eighteenth birthday, Heath Conners, for whom I was riding trackwork at Caulfield, nominated Gaju Chief, a wet-tracker, for a Randwick 2400-metre race. It had been raining up in Sydney and Heath gave me the ride. After coming across from barrier four, Gaju Chief settled well, handled the wet ground comfortably, and

I got a nice split in the straight and went on to win the race—my first winner in Sydney. The crowd was very welcoming, cheering me back to the winners' circle.

However, two very experienced jockeys, Larry Cassidy and Corey Brown, protested, claiming I had interfered with their horses as I came across from my barrier. Larry Cassidy argued that my action caused his horse to over-race. In the hearing I suggested that Larry Cassidy had slapped his horse out of the barriers and that his actions caused his horse to fire up, definitely not mine. The stewards agreed, and the protest was dismissed. I didn't think much of it—I was just arguing what was reasonable. Joan said it showed I was willing to stick up for what I thought was right, something some in racing weren't expecting from a young female apprentice.

I stuck at it. A number of trainers were continuing to give me opportunities, taking advantage of my claim: Brian Mayfield-Smith, Brian McKnight, Mike Moroney, Heath Conners, David Hall, Andrew Noblet and others. When John O'Connor came across from South Australia he'd often get me to ride for him. He'd ring Joan: 'That you, Joan?'

'Yes.'

'Michelle Payne's Number One fan here.'

A young jockey needs a bit of that.

◆ ◆ ◆

It got to the point where I was spending most of my time in Melbourne, which was easily the best thing I could be doing to make my way in racing. Dad didn't agree. I think he was getting a bit lonely as it was just him and Stevie left at home. It was very quiet and Dad wasn't handling it well. He was used to a house full of activity, laughter, good fun, hard work, and all those things he loved so much when we were all young. Not that I thought about it at the time, but he probably realised that he was getting older. He had some health concerns. He'd had a minor heart attack when he was the age his father was at the time of his death. It was generally a time of change for him.

Towards the end of 2003, when I was in Ballarat, Dad offered me a deal to come back home and take a half share of the prize money on the horses he trained. But he only had two horses, and that meant opportunities for me were going to be limited. It was impossible for me to get to early morning trackwork in Melbourne from Ballarat—I didn't have my driver's licence. I didn't have to think too long about his offer.

'No, I think it's better for me to stay in Melbourne, where I work, because I'm getting plenty of rides,' I said to let him down as gently as I could.

'Go then. You can find another trainer to look after you,' he shouted.

I didn't say anything; he had never been so angry with me before. Cathy was with me, and she could see how upset I was and how furious Dad was.

'Come on, let's go,' she said, and drove us back to Melbourne.

Dad and I had had heated arguments before and they had always blown over. This felt very different. The next morning, when I was on my way to the races at Kilmore, he rang.

'Now, if you don't find yourself another trainer by tomorrow, I'm going to stand you down. That was a good deal I offered you and I can't believe you don't want to take it,' he lectured. I knew he was hurt. I didn't argue, as unfair as it seemed. Although I was disappointed by his reaction I understood it.

It was a pretty drastic threat, though, and he certainly had the power to make it happen. Perhaps he thought he could force me to change my mind. But I wasn't going to cave in. I thought he was being unreasonable and I was determined to stick to my guns.

I was riding for Brian Mayfield-Smith that day and explained the situation to him. He didn't hesitate. He was happy to take me on as an apprentice. I rang Dad on the way home.

'Brian's going to take me on.' That's when Dad and I stopped talking. For the first time in my life I was estranged from my father.

9

The fallout

BEFORE OUR DISAGREEMENT, I was speaking to Dad once or twice a day, sometimes more. No matter how busy I was in Melbourne, through 2002 and 2003 I'd ring for a chat or a word of advice. That was part of daily life. After our falling out towards the end of 2003, Dad was extremely unhappy. And so was I. I saw it as a matter of principle. I thought Dad was being unreasonable, or even unfair, and when I feel something is not fair I'll hold my ground. I thought he was being selfish, putting himself ahead of what was best for me—something I'd never seen in him before.

There's a point at which my dad's determination can become stubbornness—I know that because I can be the same. He wasn't budging and neither was I. It wasn't that I was ignoring Dad, far from it. It was more about my focus—I was on my way, concentrating on the path I'd chosen and determined to do my best. In this case I don't think I had a blinkered view at all.

My sisters were concerned, especially Cathy, but no one was going to get involved. They thought we needed to sort it out ourselves. They were busy with their own lives and responsibilities, anyway. Therese's tribe was expanding. I felt I was taking good steps as a young apprentice and I knew I was with one of the very best trainers in Brian Mayfield-Smith.

Of all the people in Australian racing, Brian was one of the most respected. He was a horseman's horseman, who still rode his stock pony during trackwork. He was a purist like Dad. He loved horses, and his primary concern was the welfare of his, and of all, animals. He hated anyone being cruel or even rough to horses. He loved his horses.

Brian had grown up in far north Queensland, where he'd been a bush stockman. His work with horses there directed him towards racing. After moving to Sydney he became the first trainer to knock T.J. Smith, Gai Waterhouse's father, off the Trainers Premiership Table. T.J. had won it for thirty-three years in a row. Brian went on to win it a couple more times, so it was no fluke.

Not long after his Sydney successes Brian and his wife Maree began travelling to Africa. The more they went, the more they wanted to be there, working in animal conservation. They moved to Africa for a period, concentrating their efforts on saving the white rhino, which proved to be somewhat frustrating. On their return to Australia Brian established stables at Flemington and built a strong team. Again, he became one of the country's best trainers.

Although I was signed over to Brian for three months, Dad was ultimately still the master of my apprenticeship and he retained the final say in what I could do. But day to day, I worked with Brian. His home was just around the corner from where I was living with Maree and Brett. Still without a driver's licence, I relied on Brian. He would pick me up at 4 a.m., six days a week, and I'd ride trackwork for him. He'd drop me home when we finished at 9.30 a.m. I had to work until then, even though we had finished riding around by 7.30, to earn my wage of $215 a week with the afternoons off. By this time in my apprenticeship I was riding almost every day. I remember once riding twenty-six days straight. Nowadays apprentices are only allowed to ride nine days straight. It was incredibly tiring and I would become so sleep-deprived an afternoon nap would sometimes carry me through until the alarm went off at 3.30 a.m. the next morning. I'd also sleep for six hours during my days off to catch up.

When it came to my technique Brian was a helpful critic, encouraging me, but letting me know when I'd made a mistake. He was a natural teacher. He taught me patience and that, while strength was valuable, there are other ways to get the best out of a horse. His way was all about getting horses into a rhythm and having them travelling well on a nice rein, getting their breathing right, and keeping them balanced. That's what I'd learned at Home, so we basically had the same philosophy. It was reassuring.

Most trainers watch trackwork from the tower, a tall structure with an enclosed platform from where they can keep an eye on the horses being worked. It's a place of binoculars and stopwatches and horse talk. Brian was different. He liked being out in the middle. He sat on his pony at the end of the straight so he got a closer look at the horse's action and was able to listen to the horse's breathing as it pulled up.

Once I signed on with Brian, though, I did not get nearly as many city rides and Dad did not think Brian was doing the right thing by me. He wanted to change the nature of the apprenticeship again. He delivered a second ultimatum: 'If you can't find another trainer by tomorrow night I'm standing you down from riding.' He had the power to do that.

By then Therese had her trainer's licence and was based at Rockbank on the western outskirts of Melbourne. I rang her.

'Therese, Dad won't let me stay with Brian. I need to find a new master. Can I sign with you?'

'No worries,' she said. 'Of course you can.'

Sorted in a minute.

Dad and I still weren't talking and there was no end in sight to the trouble between us. Neither of us was giving an inch. I'd wonder, was I really gambling my relationship with my father against my riding career? This was constantly on my mind, but I continued to think he was trying to make life harder for me in Melbourne in the hope I would return to Ballarat. That still didn't seem fair to me.

One afternoon in late winter I went Home. The house was a mess. The Next Room hadn't been touched in ages. I spent the afternoon tidying, sorting and cleaning, just getting the place respectable, if not organised. Then I cooked Dad dinner. Hardly a thing was said between us all afternoon. I felt tense until I left to return to Melbourne.

Dad later rang Cathy and said, 'It's Little Girl's birthday coming up. Could you buy her a present for me, please? She came and cleaned the house and cooked me dinner and I didn't say thank you. So could you do that for me, please?'

When Cathy mentioned it I was a bit shocked. I thought he was going to remain angry with me forever. It was the first sign he was coming round.

'Did he really say to buy me a present?' I asked.

'Yep. He said he felt bad,' Cathy assured me. I think she was relieved, too, that finally he was trying to make amends.

Dad and I started to rebuild our relationship. Dad was being very supportive. He offered me a ride on Shelley's Trick, a horse he'd named, in part, after me. He was one of my favourite horses. Dad had let me break him in when I was still at school so I had helped bring him right the way through. I won on Shelley's Trick in a moderate race at Ararat. I'd never felt so happy. To win on Shelley's Trick was one of my great thrills in racing. Shared victory in racing is a powerful thing. Shelley's win meant a mighty lot to both of us.

By Christmas things were back to normal and I was Dad's Little Girl again. Although it had been painful at the time I always knew that ultimately our relationship was never under threat.

10
Coming a cropper

THINGS WERE TICKING along and I was riding my share of
winners. Just after Christmas 2002, I had my one hundredth
win on The Mighty Lions. It was a blessing to have come
that far. Although life was hectic and the hours were tough and I
battled with my weight, I felt it was all worth it. I loved what I was
doing. I felt I had so much to give to so many horses.

Riding in a race is a feeling like no other. Riding is of the mind,
of the body and of the soul. Physically, it fills you with adrenaline
and puts you in a heightened state—a zone. It also elevates your
spirit, takes you to places that ordinary life is less likely to. When
a trainer has prepared a lovely horse for you and you have ridden
her as well as you technically and tactically can, and misfortune has
not intervened, and you cross the line first, you punch the air with
a delight and a satisfaction that comes from deep within. I'd seen
that depth of gratification expressed by Patrick when he'd ridden
Northerly to win the Champion's second Cox Plate in 2002.
I wasn't riding that day—I was elevating my spirit with a picnic on
the lawns at Moonee Valley with the Loreto girls.

I also knew that the wonderful feeling I got from racing could come at a price. The evidence was all around me. There were always jockeys on the sidelines nursing serious injuries, waiting to come back, forced to retire through injury, and worse. Some sad, some disappointed, some shattered. Some no longer with us.

The Melbourne Cup of 2002 was a classic example of the bittersweet nature of racing. Just two days after Patrick had won the Cox Plate, Jason Oliver was involved in a fall when riding in a trial at Belmont Racecourse in Perth. He died the next day. His renowned jockey brother Damien was distraught. The family was no stranger to tragedy. Their father, Ray Oliver, had been killed in a terrible race fall during the Boulder Cup in 1975, when Damien was three and Jason was five. Damien was down to ride Media Puzzle for Dermot Weld in the Melbourne Cup. Having just won the Geelong Cup, Media Puzzle was one of the favourites. Damien chose to take the ride and, in one of the most heartfelt scenes in Cup history, Damien raised his hand heavenward as Media Puzzle crossed the line first.

Sadly racing exists at the point where triumph and tragedy too often intersect. Racing is dangerous. There is no point dressing it up, or trying to suggest otherwise. Horses are beautiful animals but they are much bigger than you think they would be. Racehorses look so sleek and fine, yet they weigh over 500 kilograms. They have delicate legs that are surprisingly skinny with hard hooves. They run very fast—at about 60 to 70 kilometres per hour. That's 100 metres in six seconds. Black Caviar could run sectionals of 31.5 seconds for the last 600 metres. So, whether horses are bowling along comfortably in the middle of a race, or giving everything in the final charge to the line, that weight and speed combine to generate enormous momentum and energy. If a horse falls that energy has to go somewhere. If a galloping horse falls on you, you cop the full force of that energy. Jockeys are also injured when they are dislodged, falling a long way down to hit the ground; when their own horse falls on them; or when horses around them fall on them or clip them with sharp, hard hooves and strong, bony legs. That's when you're in the lap of the gods.

In Australia horses run on grass tracks, occasionally on fibre or sand. The state of grass tracks changes according to how much moisture is in the surface. When they become wet, the heavy turf can shift under the weight of the horse. Sometimes races are called off because the track is too heavy and unsafe. When tracks are very dry, horses can skate on the hard surface if there is a small amount of rain. Despite the very best preparation and maintenance on race days, tracks are hard to get perfect. Horses' hooves remove divots and leave marks and the surfaces then become more and more uneven as more races are run on the track.

A jockey's job is to get the best out of their horse, settling it in the early and middle stages of the race to preserve its energy, before urging it forward and releasing it to go as fast as it can in the final stretch of the race. This is a complex skill that requires balance, co-ordination and strength, and awareness of the other horses.

Horses aren't always predictable. They race in a tight bunch and they bump into each other. Sometimes the horse causes the bumping, sometimes the jockey does. Horses are flight animals, which can make them erratic, and a panicked racehorse, however well trained, will be too strong for any rider.

In race conditions jockeys make mistakes that can have dire consequences for themselves, other jockeys and the horses. Those who control racing are dedicated to the safety of jockeys and horses. Hence the rules of racing are very, very strict. If jockeys cause interference to other riders, they will be charged with care-less riding and, if found guilty, will be suspended and fined. Given the significant prize money on offer, jockeys can be tempted to push the limits of those racing rules. Largely, jockeys are respectful of each other, as they share the same plight, and they have the shared understanding, often unspoken, of the courage it takes to ride in races.

As dramatic as it may sound, when jockeys leave the mounting yard they know that they might not come back. My dad has always had a sense of perspective when it comes to riding in races. If I've been upset by a poor day when things haven't gone well, where I've ridden poorly, or I've had no luck, he says, without fail, 'At least you got to pack your bags and come home.'

When Cathy was twenty-two and in good form, and I was eighteen and doing well as an apprentice, we decided it would be a good idea to buy a house together. That had always been the Payne way. Frugal Dad taught us that if you don't spend it wisely it will soon disappear. We were looking for a little while around the Essendon–Moonee Ponds area and one day we found the perfect one. We knew it was ideal as soon as we saw it. By coincidence Margie and Therese, who were helping us househunt, had seen it earlier in the day. Cathy and I weren't the most experienced negotiators but by some miracle we agreed on a pretty fair price. It was a simple little house in Essendon, a perfect spot close to Moonee Valley and Flemington racecourses and handy to get onto the highway to go Home. It also had a bungalow out the back where we could set up a gym and spa.

The sale went through in March 2004 but there were a few more papers to sign. We were feeling very grown up and excited. Around that time Cathy and Margie were out shopping for furniture for the new house while I had some nice rides at Sandown. One was on an old grey, Vladivostok, trained by Colin Alderson. There was nothing special about the race but for some reason my sisters took a break from their shopping to listen, which, given how many races our family has been involved in, was rather unusual by this stage of our lives. They just wanted to see how I went.

Vladivostok didn't run much of a race, finishing eleventh. Around 200 metres after the finishing line, Vladivostok did something that even very experienced racing people had never seen before. Although being eased down, while still galloping at a reasonable pace, he fell over. I went straight over his head.

I don't remember the incident at all, but the newspaper reports used words like 'torpedoed' and 'speared' to describe how I was propelled headfirst into the turf. Footage of it remains horrible to watch. I'm lying on the ground and I don't move. Race-caller Bryan Martin sounds terribly concerned. I just lie there, unconscious, on the track.

Cathy and Margie got straight in the car and rushed to Sandown. They were beside themselves as the paramedics were putting me on the stretcher and placing me in the ambulance, and I was taken to emergency at Dandenong Hospital. I was diagnosed with a serious head injury and transferred immediately to the Epworth Hospital in Richmond.

Cathy and Margie tell me that when they first saw me they were shocked. I had dilated pupils. I was looking at them but not seeing them. Cathy says I had the blankest stare, I had no life in me, I appeared to recognise them but I have no memory of that time. Dad apparently phoned, but I don't remember our conversation.

Joan Sadler had also been watching the race at her home. She arrived at the hospital just after the girls left. She says I seemed like an empty shell. The whole episode really shook her up and soon after she resigned as my manager. She felt so responsible for me.

I had a fractured skull but doctors could not determine the extent of my head injury. Only time would tell, they'd said. They were difficult days for the family, more difficult than they were for me. One of the many symptoms of brain injury I had was the loss of insight. I was assuring everyone I'd be all right to take my ride for Trevor Bailey on the next Saturday.

'I've nearly got my balance back. Couple of days and I'll be fine,' I said. 'When can I go home?'

The initial press reports suggested I'd be out for six weeks, but it seems that was mere speculation. I was actually in a very bad way, but I just didn't realise it. I had injured my right frontal lobe, my right temporal region, and my parietal lobe. The nurses were magnificent while I was in the ward for those first couple of weeks. I was asking them the same questions over and over and over. They were so patient. But they'd seen it all before. Their compassion in dealing with trauma victims is so admirable. We talk about sportspeople being heroic, but it's those who work in medicine and other caring professions who deserve the most praise. I just ride a horse around in circles.

My slow recovery was very sad and confronting and I felt I would be better in a different environment.

'When can I go home?' I kept asking. I was unable to acknowledge in the first few days, and even many weeks later, that I had suffered serious head trauma. Slowly, very slowly, I regained the capacity to understand and began to appreciate the impact of my injury. I was going to need twelve months of intensive rehabilitation and a full recovery was not guaranteed.

In my dark moments, lying in my bed in the ward, I felt totally alone. Would I ever race again? Would I ever ride again? Would I ever drive again? What would happen to my memory? Would I slur my words? Would I need a walking stick? Could I cross the road? But then I would find heart. I would tell myself to be strong, reminding myself that whatever happened I would do everything I could to help the recovery process. I just wondered if I would ever be normal again.

I was a jockey and I was just starting out, and I was determined to ride again. I was determined to find the inner resolve to do everything possible to get back on a horse. I wasn't on my own,

I had the best help: medical specialists, physios, speech therapists, nurses, and so on. I also had many, many supporters. I received hundreds of greetings, cards and floral gifts from my family, friends and even the media. I reckon every punter who'd ever put me in their quaddie was wishing me well. There were so many flowers my sisters put them in other wards around the hospital.

But just as I thought I was getting better, I would crash again.

'Why is this happening to me?' I would ask, not expecting an answer. 'Why am I so unlucky?' Des Gleeson, the chief steward, certainly thought I was unlucky

'I just can't explain it,' he told one of the newspapers. 'Normally, if a horse knuckles or falters, you can see it unfolding in the few strides before they go down.' Accidents like mine, unexplainable ones, just happen.

After I started to improve I joined patient meetings, where we told our stories and offered each other support. Some accident victims had been very unlucky, and some had been fortunate to survive. Some weren't taking it well, others knew they had a fight on their hands and were up for it. One guy had come off his motor-bike and his MRI not only revealed a brain injury but a tumour as well. It was removed and, although he was left with slight brain damage, the accident had saved his life. Try to navigate that path of fortune!

I spent about two weeks in hospital. On the day that I was to leave I was sitting on a chair outside my ward early in the morning and the chair rolled back and I smacked my head on the desk. Everyone, all the nurses, rushed over to me. I tried to make nothing of it because I wanted to go home so badly. The neurologist came to see me and said I had to stay in for another week. I was extremely upset.

After that I was moved to the rehab ward. All I remember is the green walls and the awful tragedy of severely injured patients.

I begged the doctors to let me be an outpatient, I couldn't bear being away from Cathy and my family any longer and I found the ward depressing.

'Please let me go home,' I said over and over. I think they could see I was going to struggle as an inpatient so they drew up a plan. I was permitted to go home if I caught a taxi every day and came into the Epworth rehab unit to spend time with the various therapists involved in my care. I had a lot of ground to cover.

I worked with an amazing rehab specialist, Chris Byrne, an exercise physiologist. By coincidence he and Miss Baird, my old physical education teacher from Loreto, are best mates. They know each other from their university days. While I don't remember a lot of the details from that time, Chris Byrne has since explained to me what happened. I now have a pretty good understanding of my injury and recovery.

The human brain is suspended in fluid and sits within the skull. There is space between the brain and the bone. When there is a severe impact the brain reverberates inside the skull cavity, causing it significant damage. That's then followed by bleeding, swelling and increased pressure. Physical, sensory and cognitive functions are affected according to the part of the brain that is affected.

After my injury, I had post-traumatic amnesia. My speech was slowed and delayed but not impaired. The things I had previously learned, even simple things like the alphabet, had been lost. I was easily confused. I had trouble with concentration, struggled to read a single article in the newspaper. I was easily fatigued. My personality had dulled. I had balance issues. I had reduced postural tone. I had lost some cognitive function. My capacity to process information was slowed. What really intrigued Chris was that I had not lost any understanding associated with horses and riding. I could speak coherently about those things and this, he believes, showed how deeply ingrained they were within me. Maybe that's what 'innate' means.

Talking about riding a horse and riding in a race was my motivator but I was jumping miles ahead. I needed to take small steps on my road to recovery. I needed to regain the function that would allow me to cope with daily life, initially with the support of a carer, and then learn to be independent. The injury was much more serious than I understood at the time.

Chris was superb. He explained the neuroplasticity of the brain to me—where regions of the brain can alter their function to allow for the re-learning of skills. These alterations occur when the brain is set with the task of learning a new or previously learned skill. This is a large part of recovery from a brain injury. My brain had to relearn how to make me stand, and how to hold my body in a position, and how to walk and eventually run. He also understood my state of mind. He could tell when I was down and when I was strong. He knew when to set me a task I could complete successfully and when it was the time to challenge me. He knew that I was relearning how to do things in the right order—how to pay a phone bill, for instance. I was relearning how to process information effectively. Together we made those small advances.

Chris set me challenges in the morning and afterwards I'd wander down Bridge Road with a carer to have some lunch. Slowly I improved my day-to-day functions. My cardiovascular fitness also needed a lift. Being knocked unconscious and the significant periods of time I spent in hospital meant I had a long way to go to build up strength. But I felt that that was just a matter of time.

At home, Cathy and my other sisters were brilliant. Cathy became my principal carer, something I will never forget, helped by the others. They all took their turn. They knew I wasn't the real me, but that wouldn't have made it any easier for them. They looked after all my needs, even showering me. And all I gave them in return was grief.

Because of my injury my nature had changed. It seems I felt free to say what I liked: 'Your pants are too old-fashioned, Therese. You need to update your wardrobe.' I'm embarrassed that I was so rude; I'm glad we can laugh about it now.

Once I had relearned some of the basics we all worked together on the next steps. Foremost for me was getting back to riding a horse. Towards the end of my rehab Dad was pretty vocal. He didn't think I should ride again. But I was determined, even if there were obvious limitations as to what I could do. When Chris and I thought I was ready to at least sit on a horse, we drove to Ballarat. Dad picked the horse for me. Apart from the body's position on a horse—your brain needs to learn how to control all the muscle groups needed to stay there—there's the co-ordination that needs relearning, and there are even changes in vision. A brain injury can affect how you see.

As Chris and I ticked the recovery boxes the last one left was decision making. I could hold my position on a horse and I could gallop. But we wondered what would happen when I got into the barriers and became part of the frenzy of racing. How would I respond? Having spent a lot of time with elite athletes he knew that one of the key factors for them is the pace at which they react to visual cues. It was at that point I understood the degree to which being a jockey requires many skills in concert with each other.

During those months, I spent a lot of time on my own. I went to church at St Therese's in Essendon. I'd ask God for help and to help me be strong. I felt Mum was always with me, comforting me, guiding me, helping me maintain my faith in life.

Seven months after the fall I was cleared to ride trackwork. At Caulfield, trainer Colin Little asked me to ride a horse for him, a young, uneducated horse that still needed a lot of training. Going out onto the track the horse whipped around and tipped me off. I was unimpressed and took him straight back in.

'I can't believe you put me on this one.'

I got on well with Colin and I was probably a bit disrespectful.

I was down the street shopping later that morning when Colin called me and asked if I wanted to ride Krasky at Moonee Valley on the Thursday night. It would be one of my first race meetings since I got my medical clearance. I was thrilled to be given the opportunity. Krasky had a good chance, I thought, and I could hear confidence in Colin's voice.

It was early October, a week after my nineteenth birthday, and the crowds were starting to come out for the Spring racing meetings. Krasky was about $10 in the market, so other horses were more favoured to win. The punters might have been hesitant about backing me so soon after returning from injury but I thought we could do it. Chris had been training me hard. My weight was down to 52 kilograms and I was ready. I settled him back off the leaders over the 1000-metre journey, we were four wide but we were having a nice run off the fast tempo. He then swept around the pack at the 500, took over, and he was just too good. We won, and we went on to win again in his next start.

The support for me at the time was phenomenal. I was given a huge reception as I brought Krasky in after that first race. The fraternity is like that. As competitive as racing is, when someone is seriously injured or struggling with an issue, people rally round them, wish them a speedy recovery and a rosy future. But once you're fit and racing again, it's on for young and old.

Soon after, while still very much in comeback mode, I was in a race where, coming around the corner, the horses got a bit tight and Damien Oliver got a little closer to me than I thought he should have. I was really angry.

'You could have given me a bit more room,' I said, as we pulled up.

'Oh, do you expect us to lay out the red carpet for you,' he scoffed. It was pretty barbed. We had an argument over what had happened and who was in the right. He didn't like it.

'Go back to the bush where you belong,' he said.

'You're just an arsehole,' I said in the heat of the moment. He laughed. I don't think he was expecting me to say anything.

We had to face the stewards over the racing incident but I didn't make a song and dance about what I thought had been a dangerous situation. You can't take another horse's running. They are entitled to continue running in a straight line without interference. In the end, neither of us was penalised, which was a relief.

When we were waiting outside the room I said to him, 'I would have expected a bit more respect.'

'I would have expected more respect from you,' he said. 'We'll shake on it.' While we shook hands and agreed to disagree, I was still angry.

I needed to build some more confidence and re-establish myself. Having won on Krasky, I continued riding trackwork for Colin Little and he put me on a young horse that I could tell immediately had some ability. In March 2005 this horse was having his second start, at Cranbourne. I rode him and he won well.

'I reckon he's outstanding,' I said to Colin.

'I think you're right,' he said.

The horse was El Segundo, who was indeed top class. He'd just broken the track record. This was the sort of horse I'd been waiting for. I really fancied him and I was hoping to make him my horse. I wanted to ride him in all his race starts, and all his races, and to build up the rapport needed to get the best out of a horse. Other jockeys also had their eye on him. When a horse shows exceptional ability word soon gets around. Although he had no reason to, Colin kept me on for El Segundo's next start, which was at Geelong.

At trackwork at Caulfield on the morning of the race, Colin got me to ride Thunderous Applause. She was another immature horse and I fell off, landing on my hand and hurting my wrist. I also hit my head pretty hard, which worried me but I wasn't going to let

on to Colin because I was desperate to ride El Segundo that afternoon. To show I was fine I worked a horse for Mick Price. I didn't
often work for Mick. I was struggling to put my hands on the
horse's neck while working it and felt that I had possibly sprained
it a little. Then Colin asked me to ride another. The pain in my
wrist was tolerable but the young horse bucked 400 metres into
the work and I fell off again. I was holding the horse as I fell. Not
wanting to let him go I'd hung on, and he pulled back and tugged
and twisted my sore wrist even more. I was actually brought to
tears by this stage, but managed to swing back on and worked the
horse. I was in much more pain than I made out.

'You right?' asked Colin.

'Yeah, I'm fine,' I said. 'Bit sore, but nothing to worry about.'

When I got to my car I couldn't turn the key in the ignition.
I went straight to my doctor in Essendon, thinking it was prob-
ably (hopefully) just a sprain and he could wrap it up. But Dr Paul
Mulkearns was thinking broken wrist and an X-ray.

'Can't you just wrap it up?' I pleaded. 'I won't need to touch
this horse. He's just going to win.'

The X-ray showed Dr Mulkearns was spot on. Blake Shinn was
the late replacement rider on El Segundo and he got hemmed
away in a pocket and ran a very unlucky second. I was out for at
least six weeks while El Segundo became a star, winning seven of
his next ten starts and moving up to Group 1 level. Every time
senior jockey Darren Gauci won on him I thought of what might
have been. He won the 2007 Cox Plate for Luke Nolen.

My wrist took a month and a half to heal and then I had to
come back yet again. All I wanted was to get a decent run at being
a jockey, to stay fit and healthy for long enough to build proper
relationships with trainers and with the horses, especially. I wanted
to find a horse and be part of its development. To take it from being
an immature and inexperienced horse with potential to success at

the highest level of which it was capable. It was about the horse and about the jockey, and about the entity that is the horse and jockey.

It wasn't long after that I had another setback—at Bendigo. When the pack was racing tightly, a horse came down right in the middle of the field. Instinctively the horse I was on, Transferral, and I went to jump the fallen horse but it was awkward and I fell down heavily. I was knocked out again and didn't wake up until I was in Bendigo Hospital. That concussion put me on the sidelines for more than three weeks. I had also fractured a vertebra in my neck, which was cause for concern.

These falls, either at trackwork or in races, were happening far too frequently. On my return after this accident I was successful on Dirty Denim for trainer Mick Kent. Mick was a great help and support in getting me back in form.

With all the interruptions due to injury I had to apply for a three-month extension to my apprenticeship, so that I could continue to claim until I had outridden my metropolitan claim. My goal from the outset. My extension was granted. A week before the extension started, though, I had my sixtieth win—on Leroy the Boy on a heavy track at Moonee Valley in the middle of winter. So then I had to apply to cancel the extension. I was now a senior jockey!

I was so proud to have become the first female to ride out this claim. It was something my sisters hadn't done and it had always been a goal of mine. It's hard to set goals in racing, such as winning certain races, but this was something I had thought I could achieve if I worked hard enough. I think it was something that helped me fight my way back from the falls.

I knew I had to work extra hard to make it as a senior jockey. That's what makes or breaks any jockey, the transition from having a claim to being on your own. I was up for the challenge and I knuckled down. Unfortunately, not long after becoming a senior jockey I had yet another fall.

When I rode Greek Adonis in a race at Sandown I was crossing the field to take a position up with the leaders when another horse came around me and across my path. My horse clipped heels with that horse and I fell at the worst possible place: in front of the entire field. This is the only fall I do remember. Of the half dozen or so major falls I've had, this is the only one where I haven't been knocked out and I remember it vividly.

I can still see in my mind the ground coming up to meet me, and then being acutely aware of what was about to happen as the field tried to jump over me. Every horse passing was its own small lottery. It was an all-in moment in my life. Of all the places I could have been—a lecture theatre at Melbourne University, a pub in North Fitzroy, a beach in Bali, a winery in the Barossa Valley, an armchair in front of the TV—there I was, a nineteen-year-old woman, being stampeded by a dozen horses.

I tucked myself up in a tight bunch to try to protect myself, minimise the damage. The first horse missed me. I won that lottery. And the second and the third, even though, by then, I was being rolled along the course like a ball. I survived another, and another. Would I be lucky enough to survive them all? The last horse went past and I felt incredibly relieved—that's it, there's no more behind me!

What I didn't know, though, was that a good friend of mine, Jade Darose, was five lengths behind the field. She tried to dodge, but her horse stepped on me. I sat up on the track and gathered my bearings. I could move my legs. Phew! But I was in all-consuming pain. I could see the medical attendants running towards me.

'I think I've broken my leg,' I called out. 'I can feel the bone coming through the skin.'

They immediately put an air boot on me. It is the worst pain I've ever had; the skin was taut because my ankle was dislocated. For some reason I then had to wait forty minutes in the racecourse's casualty room before an ambulance came to get me, and all I had was the green whistle, a hand-held device allowing me to inhale an emergency analgesic. I told them it was having no effect. I was in agony, shaking, sweating. They suggested I suck on it again, I did, but nothing. I threw it at the wall. When the ambulance came they intravenously injected morphine into me and knocked me out.

I woke up in casualty at the hospital as they were taking the air boot off, and the doctor explained the nature of the dislocation, and that I needed a knee reconstruction immediately. I don't know how long it took them to put me back together. But I was now out of racing for another three months.

When I returned I couldn't get the vision of my Greek Adonis fall—of crashing to the turf and being run over—out of my mind. During a race at Hamilton I felt genuinely frightened and you cannot race frightened. It's not fair to anyone. I was really troubled. For the first time I felt I might have to retire.

My family were supportive, suggesting that my reaction was understandable, and encouraged me to work through it. I went to see renowned sports psychologist, Lisa Stevens, who was also a counsellor at Racing Victoria. She had encountered this problem many times before and assured me it was easily fixed. The strategy she suggested was to repeat a single word over and over in the barriers to block out the fear. I used two, 'win' or 'straight'. To my amazement it worked.

I was very relieved.

11

Recovery

WITH SO MANY falls and so many injuries and my health always a topic of speculation—'Should Michelle keep riding?' everyone kept asking—I was becoming frustrated by the interruptions to my career. I felt I had the motivation and direction but things just weren't going my way. I continued to wonder why I was so unlucky, and kept pestering the people closest to me to find an answer.

'Ah well, when things are bad there's always something good round the corner,' Dad would say. He was in a difficult situation. He wanted to be supportive, but he needed to be protective.

The dangers of racing had been highlighted again in the winter of 2006, when not only had I had my nasty fall from Greek Adonis, but Brigid was involved in a barrier incident while working for trainer David Hayes, the son of Colin Hayes, at Euroa. She was airlifted to the Alfred Hospital and placed in an induced coma for a week. She returned to light duties at the Hayes stables.

Brigid, who was always a big character, had had a somewhat unsettled life, but had been happy in her new role. Not long after our family came to Australia, and Mum had died, she'd left home to work with a different trainer. She rode for a while but then moved to Perth to take up a job as a journalist at a suburban newspaper with the prospect of also completing a university course in media studies. While in Perth, she and her boyfriend had a child, Sam. When things did not go so well she returned to Ballarat as a single parent. After a few endeavours, she worked for a number of trainers before settling on the position with David Hayes.

While working on light duties after the fall, Brigid suffered an aneurysm. She was taken straight to Shepparton Hospital. Dad drove across to visit her. Seeing she was stable, he was on the way Home to feed the horses when she went into cardiac arrest. He had no mobile phone.

The instant I heard the news of the cardiac arrest I raced to the hospital from Melbourne. She died that evening in January 2007. I then drove straight to Ballarat to tell Dad. He was still feeding the horses. It was a terrible time. Sam, who we are all so close to now, was fourteen at the time. It tore me apart to see him lose his mum. Dad took it very hard as well. His wife, newborn son Michael, and now his oldest child were all gone.

The congregation at the funeral service at St Patrick's Cathedral in Ballarat was enormous. Brigid was such a character. Inevitably the discussion turned to the dangers of racing. My brother Patrick spoke to the media afterwards, telling *The Age* newspaper, 'You have to enjoy what you are doing or you'll just be unhappy. I think none of us are content sitting in the safety of a comfortable couch. The bond with horses is the same for all of us. We tried to talk Michelle out of becoming a jockey [after a serious fall] but she wasn't happy on the sidelines at all, and she wasn't [happy] until she started back riding again.'

I felt at times Dad really wanted me to give it away. The doctors' warnings were clear: another concussion injury could have a serious impact on my health in the short and long term. Increasingly reports were coming out in America about sportspeople and the neurological and mental health issues that were plaguing them. Boxers. Footballers. Anyone in collision sports. Medical science was developing its understanding that concussion had serious implications. I had to live with that. I had to weigh up the risks.

But Dad knew how much being the best jockey I could be meant to me. He did not want me to go through life wondering what might have been. So he encouraged me to stick at it. But Patrick probably said it best in that interview when talking about my future: 'If you're not doing what you really want to do, you're not living.'

We weren't scientists. We were horse people—trainers and jockeys—and we knew the best minds at the CSIRO weren't going to be applying for research grants to pursue an understanding of the chemistry of the magic of horse racing. We were better off talking with Father John Keane than them anyway. He was on our wavelength, especially after he'd backed the winner of the last race of the day and celebrated with a couple of whiskies. Father Keane was from Tipperary, horse country, the home of Dermot Weld and his horses Vintage Crop, which had won the Melbourne Cup for Micky Kinnane in 1993, and Media Puzzle, which had won in 2002. Horse racing helped Father Keane understand what went on in the human heart, what mattered to people, and what grace and fortune were.

Me? I just wanted continuity, a run of reasonable luck, even neutral luck if there's such a concept, a run that allowed me to improve to the point where I could at least feel like I was starting to become the jockey I believed I could be. The luck of the Irish would do, as ironic as that concept might have been. I had my doubters, and my detractors, but I just wanted a chance to give my best. If it wasn't good enough—well, that wasn't the worst thing, because at least I would know I'd given it a real crack. It was like being caught in the pack, bolting, but unable to get a clear run.

I was trying to be really disciplined, working incredibly hard on all the physical elements of being a jockey—good diet to keep my weight right, which was always a major challenge; fitness, aerobic and strength; and technique, constantly discussing that with those around me. I slept well. But just as I was building momentum, and just as I was winning the confidence of trainers and owners, and the respect of those who mattered to me, and of fair-minded punters who follow racing closely, I would have a setback. A fall, literally.

I'd then have to have three months or so off, during which time I just wasn't as disciplined. But who would be when the lifestyle of a jockey is so unnatural? You go out more, you eat more. There's no *immediate* reason to resist the temptation of something as simple as a banana smoothie, or even the basic chocolate milkshake that has been a favourite of many a Payne. There was no *immediate* reason to push myself on the bike along the Maribyrnong. I was rarely totally carefree, though, because I knew how hard it would be to return to racing weight and fitness.

Once my injuries were healed and I had been through physios and received the all-clear from the doctors, I'd be in the comeback part of the cycle. That was always intense because I had ground to make up and I had to push myself, trying to catch up. I was impatient. I wanted to accelerate the process, to get to where I wanted to be more quickly than I should have. So I would get tired and rundown, and a little off colour. And when I'm not quite right, that's when something would happen on the track. It's like being a boxer who goes into the ring only three-quarters fit—it's dangerous. Later in my career I have become more conscious of the warning signs and I have learned when it's time to have a break.

As frustrating as it was, during that spate of falls, it did allow me to get away from Australia from time to time. I love to travel. I have always been fascinated to see how people live, what they do, what matters to them. What's different? What's the same? Seeing how cultures have developed in response to life and its challenges and questions. So for a few years I got into a bit of a routine of spending the miserable Melbourne winters overseas.

I had heard about the Lake St Moritz White Turf race meetings, which are held each February, and I thought it would be fun to ride. I contacted the organisers and explained I was a young jockey from Australia, that my mother was Swiss and I was intrigued by their festival. They invited me over. My school friend Liz Francis was living in Amsterdam at the time and she came too. Racing on a frozen lake is quite an experience. So is skijoring, which are races where horses pull people on skis. The event attracts the rich and famous from around Europe and we were treated by the wealthy guests, taken out to dinner, with Liz and I looking like a couple of backpackers among the glitterati. When we pulled out our 20 euros to help pay for the lavish dinner, everyone just waved us away. They were very welcoming and generous.

I also visited my mother's home village of Aufiberg in the Swiss Alps, four hours from St Moritz by train. The trip was spectacular and I was captured by the beauty of the place. Although no relatives live in Aufiberg now, some of my cousins met me at the site where the Buhler home once stood. It was great to be there, with them.

After he won the Melbourne Cup, Cathy and Kerrin McEvoy were married. Kerrin became the stable jockey for Godolphin Racing, the worldwide racing enterprise of the Al Maktoum family, the royal family of Dubai, who are besotted by horses and horse-racing. With the massive financial resources available, Godolphin is at the very top end of the racing game, very different from our down-on-the-farm facilities, albeit, that's what we love about Home. Godolphin has complexes in Dubai, Newmarket in England, and in Sydney and Melbourne. Everything is the very best. From stables for the horses to veterinary services to the private training facilities, the operation is superb, and expensive.

Sheik Mohammed bin Rashid Al Maktoum, who is the head of state in Dubai, part of the United Arab Emirates, has a deep affection for horses and loves racing, and is desperate to have in his palace the most sought-after trophies in world racing. The Melbourne Cup, which has eluded him, is probably number one on his list. The family has come close a number of times, with Crime Scene, for instance. Their approach, apart from running a first-class racing operation, is to remove as many of the chance elements as possible. If only it was that simple!

Why does a horse win the Melbourne Cup? Who knows the minds of the racing gods? In 2000 Kerrin was just twenty when he produced a fantastic ride on Brew to win. Given his talent, and his ongoing success, a few years later Kerrin was invited to ride for Godolphin, initially in Dubai and then at Newmarket—so different from Streaky Bay on South Australia's Eyre Peninsula where he grew up. Occasionally I would visit Cathy and Kerrin, wherever they were. I saw them in Dubai in 2004, and that's when I first met Frankie Dettori, another of Godolphin's jockeys.

In 2008, I visited them again at Newmarket, the famous horse-racing town just north of London, a few kilometres from Cambridge. I love being there. It is just beautiful. The stables are nestled among stately trees, and grounds with gardens. The Godolphin complex is made up of the century-old Stanley stables built by Frederick Stanley, the sixteenth Earl of Derby, and a complex known as Moulton Paddocks.

I love the feel of history, the sense of permanence. That people have and still share the same passion; they speak a common language. I love that the estate attracts people who are into horses and racing, from England and Ireland and around the world. Some stay, totally infatuated by the place. Everything that they've ever hoped for is there. It's not just Newmarket either. There are racing towns all over England, Ireland and France, and their carnivals are legendary, just as they are in Australia. So, when people descend on Warrnambool in south-western Victoria for the annual three-day carnival, you can understand its origins, even if Warrnambool has such an Australian flavour.

Cathy worked for the successful trainer James Fanshawe at Pegasus Stables at Newmarket. She got me a job there, too. James was a character. Everyone called him Gov'ner. He didn't really insist, it was just the way it was. Imagine calling a trainer in Australia 'Gov'ner'. Not one for lords and station, I couldn't bring myself to do it. It was a spectacular place to work and it didn't feel like work. It was more like spending pleasant days with people who've spent a lifetime developing their craft, and trying to understand what it means to live with horses.

Dad had been doing the same thing at Home. We didn't have the resources, but the soul of racing was present in everything he did. I reckon if Paddy Payne and the Sheik sat down together they'd find plenty to talk about.

I loved Newmarket so much that I went back a year later, on my own, and rented a place from David Redvers, a very success-ful bloodstock agent. I lived just behind the High Street. I worked for Luca Cumani, an English trainer who has had starters in the Melbourne Cup and very nearly won with Bauer and Purple Moon, and Jane Chapple-Hyam, an Australian trainer based there. Jane is the daughter of former leader of the Liberal Party Andrew Peacock.

I was getting a few opportunities to race for Luca and Jane and this one day Luca put me down to ride one of his horses at York Racecourse up in north Yorkshire. As it turned out, on the same day I had a ride for Jane Chapple-Hyam at Salisbury, near Stonehenge in the south of England. I like an adventure so I thought I'd see how I would go getting to each track on time. Jane was relaxed and confident I could make it. At least the Salisbury race was the last one of the night so I was in with a chance. While waiting for the York train at Newmarket that day, Frankie Dettori wandered along the platform and saw me. He was riding at York, too. Despite having a first-class ticket he decided to sit in economy with this Aussie traveller, who was not quite a backpacker. We chatted all the way to the races. I ended up running second and beat Frankie home! Then it got interesting.

To get to my next race, I took a train to London, caught two underground trains to get to Waterloo Station and took a British Rail train to Salisbury. Once I arrived, I got a cab to the track. It was a marathon trip, especially dragging my race bag through the crowds in the underground station, but I got there in time—and finished last. A couple of the jockeys drove me back to Newmarket. It was a long day.

During the same trip, thanks to Kerrin, legendary Irish jockey Johnny Murtagh, who is now a trainer, arranged for me to spend ten days with Aidan O'Brien, one of the world's best trainers, at his complex at Ballydoyle in Ireland. It was another one of those epic trips that started at Newmarket. On the flight to Dublin, I sat next to a very friendly Irish guy. When we landed he offered me a lift to the train station in his car. We'd got on so well I would have offended him if I declined. There I was in Dublin in a car with a complete stranger, but that's where life takes you sometimes. I then caught the train to Cashel in County Kilkenny, which is classic horse country two hours out of Dublin.

It is gorgeous country, as green as you would expect in the Emerald Isle, and Ballydoyle was a superb place. A woman called Eileen was so obliging, showing me to the room in the house where I was staying and explaining how to get into Cashel. The Irish being Irish, we went into town together to the pub with the workers. I also went off to the races with Colm O'Donoghue, a jockey who has ridden winners all over the world, and I enjoyed hanging out in the crowd with the punters. Everyone was so friendly. They reminded me of Dad. Even Aidan O'Brien reminded me of my dad. I felt so at home over there. They felt like my people. Aidan's brother Walter was the truck driver on the Ballydoyle farm and we got on really well. He took me to meet their parents, that's how hospitable they were.

After being there for nearly a week Aidan asked if I had a release from the Australian stewards to ride. I jumped at the opportunity and it was quickly arranged. They put me down to ride at Cork—in a 2400-metre race. The distance was going to really test me as I hadn't ridden competitively in a month. I was riding Dylan Thomas's sister but she wasn't as good as her brother, the European Horse of the Year in 2007 who had been retired to stud after winning the Prix de l'Arc de Triomphe. She was one of seven runners for Aidan O'Brien in a twenty-four-horse field. I was supposed to be the pacemaker in the race but she had no early speed and I couldn't get her to go forward. She actually ran on quite well to finish fifth.

Aidan also had a runner in Deauville in France and he asked if I would like a ride. To get there was going to be another travel adventure—train, plane and train. Johnny organised for me to travel with Aidan. Aidan said there was a spare seat in his four-seater private jet, and the airport was just up the road. That made it somewhat easier—a quick flight across the channel and we were there.

I not only loved Ireland because of the people, who were so openhearted, friendly, willing to chat and genuine—and who made me realise that there was still a bit of old Ireland in our family—I also learned a lot about training and riding. Everything is so much more relaxed there. Things happen at a reasonable pace. Horses do a lot more walking. And there's less pressure on the stable riders who work the horses. The system is completely different.

When you are working a horse—whether in Ireland or England—you are responsible for one horse at a time and you do everything. You saddle them, work them, walk them, pick them, hose them and put them back in their box. That will take an hour or so. Then you do another one. Both the horses and the people are more leisurely.

Because horses are trained differently, they race differently. Jockeys get rolling very early on their mounts, urging them forward from a long way out, and riding vigorously to get them all the way to the line. In Australia we tend to wait, and then finish with a burst. Because of my training my timing was always out and my horses were getting to the line too late and, when I adjusted, I was going too early. Of course, just as I began to get it right, I had to come home.

I found the French racing much the same as ours, but with far stricter whip rules. I think the riders in France are the most stylish, polished—the best I have seen in the world. They are beautiful to watch.

While in England, Ireland and France, I was inspired by these old stables and farms. They made me want to create my own place in Australia, in Ballarat, just like them. I loved the idea of living on a beautiful property, with a home and stables, and my own tribe of kids.

12

A jockey's lot

COMING INTO THE Spring Carnival of 2009 I was hoping a few opportunities would come my way. It was always a tussle to get the rides, and then keep them. Competition between riders for the good horses can be fierce. The race calendar is set: Turnbull Stakes Day, Caulfield Guineas Day, Caulfield Cup Day, Cox Plate Day, Derby Day, Melbourne Cup Day, Oaks Day and Stakes Day. It finishes at Sandown. If you add in the major country cups, like Geelong, Bendigo, Ballarat and Kyneton, there is a lot of fun to be had. This time of year has a wonderful rhythm. Everyone's trying to get their horses ready; some are well prepared through targeting early Spring events. The punters are trying to jag a winner. Women are buying hats.

Colin Little asked if I'd like to ride El Segundo in the Group 1 Turnbull Stakes, one of the lead-up races to the Melbourne Cup. The champ didn't fire a shot; his best was behind him. It was four years since I rode him in his maiden at Cranbourne. So much had happened to El Segundo. So much had happened to me.

I was getting a few rides for Bart Cummings. Perhaps it was because I was kind to horses, like he was. Reg Fleming, Bart's

Melbourne foreman, liked how I rode, and maybe he put my name forward because he knew my sisters and Jason Patton. Maybe it was a more practical reason: I could still make the lightweights. Whatever the reason I was grateful when he offered me the ride on Allez Wonder in the Toorak Handicap on Guineas Day. She had been handicapped at 52 kilograms, a weight I worked hard to maintain.

The moment certainly wasn't lost on me. I was honoured to be riding for one of the great characters of Australian sport. At that time Bart had trained twelve Melbourne Cup winners and about 250 Group 1 winners. He was the grand old man of racing, and still had a magnificent head of wavy grey hair and a sparkle in his eyes. I loved his style. He was always looking for a laugh, always keeping everyone guessing.

I don't think he was confident Allez Wonder was going to add to his tally of Group 1 wins, although he'd chosen to put her in the Toorak Handicap ahead of a very suitable mares' race she would have dominated the night before at Moonee Valley. She was a sixty to one shot in the Toorak. But there was some money put on her and she got into the forty to one odds. She'd won her previous start with Damien Oliver in the saddle, but it was me who was offered the Toorak ride. Damien was riding King Mufhasa for Kiwi Steve McKee.

It was a magnificent day at Caulfield and Bart was probably the jauntiest eighty-two year old on the course. As the owners were standing around in the mounting yard, and Bart was cracking jokes, I had to prompt him for my riding instructions.

'Ask the horse,' suggested Mr James Bartholomew Cummings, who'd seen it all, and done it all. I looked at him puzzled. Then, very casually, he said, 'She likes to get back, so let her get back. And bring her to the outside and we'll see what she can do.'

With that I was away and, thanks to Bart's advice, feeling very relaxed.

I trotted down the straight before a really great crowd; I was riding for Australia's greatest trainer in a Group 1 race. I smiled to myself as I let Allez stop, stand and take in the atmosphere. It was okay for me to enjoy the moment too, but getting the horse into a good frame of mind was more important. I gave her a pat and took her around as nicely as I could to the barriers. You need them to work with you and to give their best. Everything counts when it can come down to a matter of inches.

When we jumped at the fall of the barrier Allez Wonder, who could be fierce, went forward of her own accord, immediately. I wasn't doing as instructed: let her settle back at the start! She found a position, fifth or sixth, near the rail, and travelled beautifully. Approaching the 600 I was going well and coming to the corner I felt I was a sneaky possibility. I stayed in—failing to honour the master trainer's advice on that one as well. I needed luck. I waited, realising that timing would make the difference. I wanted to have a clear run before I asked her for an effort. Coming to the 300 I thought, I'm a chance to win this, I just need a split. It came and I shot through and hit the front just before the line. My first Group 1—and for Bart Cummings!

I didn't get a chance to speak to Bart until the presentation.

'Well done,' he said. 'Can you ride at 50 kilograms?' I didn't hesitate.

'Yes!'

J.B. Cummings was offering me a ride in the Caulfield Cup.

Riding at 50 kilograms was a tough ask; it is my absolute rock-bottom weight, but I was determined to do it. I would do it!

The media interest in me that whole week was off the charts. It was mad. I was trying to starve and at the same time train hard whenever I could. At one stage I did a workout at the local gym and when I got back to my car there were sixteen missed calls from media outlets around Australia. When I rang Mark Zahra, another jockey and my boyfriend at the time, I burst into tears. It was difficult to handle the uncertainty. It was all too much! I knew physically that I could get to 50 kilograms—a weight I hadn't been in six years, but mentally I was beginning to struggle.

'I can't do this,' I blubbered. 'It's too hard.' But then I sat in the car and told myself I had dealt with harder times and that I could do this. It was the Caulfield Cup! I soldiered on. Mark was in the same boat, riding 53 kilograms, which is his absolute minimum. Having someone do it with you made it a bit easier to handle.

My diet and exercise regime for the week leading up to the Caulfield was:

Day	Weight	Brekkie	Lunch	Dinner	Exercise
Sun	53	boiled egg	nil	fish and fresh vegies	None
Mon	53	¼ cup muesli	can of tuna	grated raw vegies, brown rice, sweet potato	30 mins on running machine, interval training (walk, run, walk, run), 30 laps in pool, sauna, spa
Tues	53	¼ cup muesli	nil	small can tuna, water, raw vegies, brown rice	Rode eleven horses at Caulfield, then five rides with two winners at Echuca (drove to Echuca), 2 laps of the track at Echuca in between races
Wed	53	¼ cup muesli	nil	tuna and brown rice, special caffeine drink	Two rides at Caulfield, one hour on treadmill
Thurs	52.5	¼ cup muesli	nil	sweet potato and raw vegies	20 mins on gym cross trainer in sweat gear; 40 mins on treadmill, sauna, spa
Fri	51.9	¼ cup muesli	nil	orange	Trackwork (including with Allez Wonder), six trials at Flemington, one-hour walk, nap, another walk, sauna

The night before the Cup I was 50.7, which meant I was on track. I was so thirsty and hungry, though. I felt I just had to have something to eat. I thought an orange would do the trick, with its juice and fibre. What I failed to anticipate was that as my stomach was so empty, citric acid would eat the lining. I ended up in such pain. I slumped to the floor and crawled to bed.

Lying under the covers, in agony, I wondered how this could possibly be worth it. Then I thought, this is what you train your whole life for: to compete at the top level. You've endured the falls, come back from them. Pull yourself together.

◆ ◆ ◆

On the Saturday morning I woke up and weighed in at 50.5. Half a kilogram—I could do this! No breakfast for me. I hit the gym.

At the Windy Hill gym, with the sweat suit on, I did twenty minutes on the cross trainer and an hour and a half in steam. I sipped on a quarter of a bottle of soda water to help me sweat while in the sauna. Normally I'd drink the whole thing but I had to be getting close! I stood on the scales: 50.7.

What!

I had four hours to lose it. I went home to get ready as I had a ride in race one and the Cup was race eight. I also had a radio interview at 9.30 a.m.

'So, Michelle, it's been well documented that you've been working very hard to get to the 50 kilograms, how's that going for you?'

'Oh, yes, on track. I just have a bit more to go while I'm at the races but I'll get there.' I wasn't sure, but I wasn't about to give up.

After the first race, Channel 7 asked again about the weight.

'Yep, on track, just about to go lose the last half a kilo now before weigh-out time.'

I was sweaty from the race and I jumped straight into my bathers and into the steam room at the races. You're allowed fifteen minutes at a time, and then a forty-five-minute break. Next to the steam room at Caulfield is a hot spa, which provides another place to lose weight until the break is up. I made slow progress, but at 50.4 I was getting there. Back in the sauna, running on the spot, doing push-ups, sit-ups, then back in the spa. I can do this. On the scales.

Fifty kilograms! Yes!

I sat in a cold shower, so happy. It was like I'd won the race already.

Going to the weigh out, looking the gauntest I'd ever been, I passed Bart.

'How'd you go, did you make the weight?'

'Sure did.'

'Good girl.'

Afterwards I made myself a shot of coffee with milk—I needed some fluid intake. I stood up with all the best jockeys from around the country being introduced to the crowd and felt immensely proud.

Allez Wonder was in fine order. When I looked at the big screen I saw she was fourth favourite. Wow.

She'd drawn barrier five and she flew out. Before I knew it we'd landed in the box seat. I was supposed to have her further back in the field at the start. Even so, she had a great run but finished eighth. Bart wasn't impressed. He took me aside: 'You rode her too close.'

I didn't hold much hope for getting the Melbourne Cup ride on her. But I was happy to finish in the top eight, which meant prize money for the owners. Despite being annoyed, to my surprise, Bart kept me on Allez Wonder for the Cup. I think Su-Ann Khaw was helpful for me with that.

I was going to ride in the Melbourne Cup! This was what I had dreamed about my whole life. I was so glad I had toughed out that week. I was so excited. I was also lucky that Mark Zahra was going through the same routine as me for the lead-up week, so I had company. Allez Wonder had 50.5 kilograms in the Melbourne Cup and, having got down to that weight, I hoped sustaining it would be easier.

It was still hard work and I felt preoccupied by the worry of it all week. It dominates your mind, and your body. There was still much that was good about the week. For a start, that of all the jockeys in Australia and the world, you are one of the twenty-four is a real thrill. This is the race all jockeys want to win, all jockeys want to be in. For the opportunity I felt blessed, and thankful to Bart and to owner Su-Ann Khaw and the other connections. I'd make the weight and we'd see if their horse could handle the 3200 metres.

On the Saturday morning before the Cup I worked Allez Wonder and she was peaking in absolute tip-top shape. For years people had been talking about how Bart was the master trainer and could get his timing spot on. I was experiencing this firsthand. It was why the term 'a Bart Cummings preparation' had entered the language. It described anything that was perfectly timed, especially in sport. Having a horse in that sort of condition eliminated one element of chance. If she stayed the distance, and was good enough, her fitness was not going to give out.

Bart had three runners in that year's Cup, with one of the favourites being the previous winner Viewed. The others were Roman Emperor and, of course, Allez Wonder. He was short and sharp with my instructions: ride her back in the field. I knew he was concerned that the only hope she had to stay the distance was if she wasn't used up in the first three-quarters of the race. Bart always made you feel confident in your own ability, whether he believed in it or not.

Going to the barriers Bart had her timed exactly right. I cantered up thinking, no wonder he's won twelve cups. Allez Wonder had drawn right in the middle of the field. She was the last horse loaded of the inside bunch, and then we were ready.

The gates opened and I actually heard the almighty roar of the crowd. We were away and it was a tremendous feeling. She began well, but I took her back as instructed. We found the rail just behind midfield and we were in a nice spot for how she was to be ridden. The speed was an absolute dawdle going down the straight the first time and a lot of horses were over racing. I was following Bart's other runner, Viewed, and he was travelling strongly.

As the other horses crossed to gain position, Viewed clipped one of the hind heels of one of the runners up ahead, faltered, and then knuckled over. Thankfully, not enough to fall. I checked my mount away from his heels when this happened. We approached the first bend and I found myself up inside Viewed. As we travelled along the back straight I was following a line of three runners, including Shocking to the outside.

Allez Wonder was travelling well and I was happy. Coming past the 800-metre the tempo was starting to quicken, the runs were coming and she was taking them. Passing the 600 metres I thought, I have a sneaky little chance here—and this is the Melbourne Cup! Alarm bells started to ring pretty soon after that, though. As we approached the straight and neared the 300 I had no carrots—gas in the tank—left to make up the six lengths or so and we plodded away, into sixteenth place. Shocking was the eventual winner.

I'd given it my best. I then understood what it meant when they say, 'You find out at the clocktower if they're a true two-miler.' With just 300 metres to go the horses that have the extra stamina quicken. Unfortunately, Allez wasn't a two-miler.

I explained that to Bart and the owner Su-Ann Khaw and her syndicate members, and all the other connections involved, when we returned to the mounting yard. That's just the way it was and they understood. I was grateful to Bart and the owners for giving me the experience. I enjoyed the satisfaction of making the weight and giving it my best. It was not that I finished in the second half of the field, it was the blur of spending the week worrying about making the weight. It puts you in another world. But that's what jockeys have to do. I had done the best I could—in the circumstances.

◆ ◆ ◆

The life of a jockey sometimes borders on the absurd, and when you stand back and look at it you wonder why anyone would pursue it. A typical day begins at around 3 a.m. after just four, five or six hours of sleep. I sleep very soundly because I am constantly tired. I use any spare moment I have to catch some sleep, even if it's only thirty minutes. Better than nothing.

I drive myself to the city venues for trackwork and race meetings, and often to country meetings. It takes over three hours to get to Warrnambool and Hamilton and four hours to Horsham. But if I am getting a lift with someone I will try to sleep, or catch up on phone calls and text messages. Jockeys are always on the phone communicating with trainers and owners, even when they have managers. Phillip Roost has looked after my rides since Joan retired. He has been a fantastic manager.

Trainers want to talk about recent performances and what's next for a horse. While they know their horses well and generally have in mind the direction of a horse's campaign, and have worked out where the horse will start next; sometimes it's not so clear-cut. They seek the advice of a jockey and discuss the previous start in a race, the nature of the performance, and the qualities of a horse. You become closer to some trainers and, as they respect you and your performances, they might use you for all of their horses. Or you might develop a relationship with a single horse, and the trainer lets you become that horse's rider. That doesn't always work out because jockeys get injured, suspended and have schedule clashes, having to ride at other venues. But a jockey will stick to a good horse and do whatever they can to retain the ride. Hence jockeys also develop relationships with owners.

A horse might have a single owner or be owned by a syndicate, and then owners might have numerous horses, in which case you might ride a few different horses for the owner/syndicate. Brad Rawiller has ridden a lot for trainer Darren Weir. Luke Nolen has ridden a lot for Peter Moody. Luke Nolen also became the jockey of Black Caviar, and when the owners of Black Caviar became involved in another horse they would have it trained by Peter Moody and ridden by Luke Nolen. So owners want to get to know the jockey and they want to know how their horse is going. They're desperate to know the potential of their horse—everyone's trying to win the Melbourne Cup or one of the big races.

You build real friendships with trainers and owners, which means chatting to them on the phone is a very natural thing to do. It just takes time, and the closer you become to them the more likely they are to ring.

At trackwork a jockey might ride half a dozen (often more) horses, and the work might be all over by 7.30 a.m. Then there may be trials at that venue or somewhere else. This is where horses are given a run in a race that has the appearance of race conditions—it starts from a barrier and you race against other horses. It doesn't count for anything other than to give the horse a trial run. There's no prize money. Horses may be asked to give their full effort, but that's not likely. It just depends where the horse is in the lead-up to a start in a proper race. A horse gets fitter during these campaigns but will eventually become a little jaded and is then given a spell.

We were always going to be a horse-loving family. From left: Brigid on horseback, Lucrezia Martelletti, Dad steadying Andrew on the pony, Nicola Gordon and Therese holding the reins, Bernadette on the bike, and Patrick chewing on a table-tennis bat.

The Payne family at Home on the verandah. Dad is holding me, Mum has Stevie. Seated, with other friends, are Maree, Patrick, Andrew, Bernadette, Therese, Cathy and Margie.

In Loving Memory

Rosa Marie Payne
Born 29-1-1941   Died 15-4-1986
May she rest in peace

My mother's funeral card.

Sitting on Therese's lap. I'm about six months old and learning to take the bottle.

Paddy with Stevie and me before bedtime in 1988.

Proud as punch. Therese kneeling with her trophy in 1988 surrounded clockwise from bottom left: me, Cathy, Margie, Patrick, Andrew and Stevie.

A day at the Ballarat races with big sister Therese.

Early ambitions. Dressed as a jockey in 1989.

Getting to know our neighbour's foal. *Gay Harbord*

In prep at Our Lady Help of Christians primary school in Wendouree, Ballarat.

All in the family. Five Payne jockeys in the same race at Ballarat in November 1994. From left: Andrew, Therese, Maree, Patrick and Bernadette. Patrick won. *Fairfax Syndication*

Dinner duty. Stevie and I are working the BBQ like old hands.

My final year at Loreto was busy as I was also at apprentice school for the last six months. I am in the front row, third from left. Lifelong friends Elsie Lardner, Rebecca Ludbrook, Stacey and Jackie Mahar, Liz Francis, Justine Locandro and Jacinta Bongiorno were also in this class. *Williams Studios, Ballarat/Loreto College Ballarat Archive Centre*

LORETO
COLLEGE
YEAR 9 RED
2000

Trackwork on Reigning at Home a week before our first win at Ballarat racecourse in February 2001 and after the win with owner/trainer/master—Dad. *Ken Irwin/Fairfax Syndication; Michael Perini/Newspix*

Leading the way. Patrick, with trainer Fred Kersley behind him, holds up the Cox Plate he won on Northerly, 26 October 2002. *Mark Dadswell/ Getty Images*

Unlucky. My first major fall, from Vladivostok, at Sandown, 24 March 2004. *Nicole Garmston/Newspix*

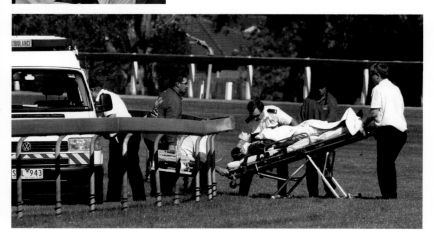

Another world. Racing in St Moritz, Switzerland, in February 2008.

Better than it looks. Fall at Trentham, New Zealand in 2008 involving jockey Corey Brown (left) and me. *Trish Dunell*

Trackwork at Flemington on Allez Wonder the week before our Caulfield win in 2009. *Vince Caligiuri/ Fairfax Syndication*

With the legendary Bart Cummings after my win on Allez Wonder in the Toorak Handicap at Caulfield, 10 October 2009. This was my first Group 1 victory. *Paul Rovere/ Fairfax Syndication*

Stevie and me with Patrick's horse Awakening Dream.

Everyone loves a Melbourne Cup parade. Enjoying the mood with jockey Corey Brown's daughter in 2009, before my first ride in the Melbourne Cup on Allez Wonder. *Fairfax Syndication*

Making weight. On the scales after a win on Sunday Rose at Flemington in 2010 for Bart Cummings. *Bruno Cannatelli/Ultimate Racing Photos*

Hugging orphan Kevin in Rwanda, 2010. *Gabby Engelbrecht*

With trainer brother Andrew after a win on Clanga's Glory at Flemington, 20 July 2013. *Vince Caligiuri/Getty Images*

Victory in the Thousand Guineas on Yosei at Caulfield, 13 October 2010. *Paul Rovere/ Fairfax Syndication*

Swapping identities with world champion surfer Layne Beachley for Beachley's charity Aim for the Stars, on Thirteenth Beach in 2015. *Darren McNamara/Racing Victoria*

Aboard the equiciser, Our Paddy Boy, in my home gym. *Tom Elliott (The Woolshed Company), G1X*

A good feeling. With Prince of Penzance a week before the Cup. *Colleen Petch/Newspix*

On Prince of Penzance with trainer Darren Weir and Irish jockey Johnny Allen on Dandino after a final track gallop at Terang Racecourse, a week before the Cup. *Colleen Petch/Newspix*

The best draw. Stevie, elated, when he drew barrier 1 on the Saturday before the Melbourne Cup. *Robert Prezioso/ Getty Images for the VRC*

Leaving St Francis's church after having my saddle blessed, on Sunday, 1 November 2015, at the racing fraternity mass. *Frank di Silvestro*

History-making. We are first across the finish line of the Melbourne Cup 2015.
Colleen Petch/Newspix

All in the family. Congratulating Stevie, who was Prince of Penzance's strapper, moments after the victory. *Scott Barbour/ Getty Images*

Proud strappers Maddie Raymond and Stevie Payne flanking Prince of Penzance. *Stuart McEvoy/Newspix*

Local heroes. Darren Weir and I holding up the Cup trophies. *Colleen Petch/Newspix*

The family: Andrew, Cathy, me, Stevie, Margie, Bernadette, Patrick and Therese celebrating at the racing pub, the Emerald Hotel, in South Melbourne on Cup night. *Yuri Kouzmin/Newspix*

Front page news. Dad at Home the day after the Cup. *Tim Carrafa/Newspix*

With Patrick after my win on Husson Eagle at the Magic Millions carnival on the Gold Coast in January 2016. *Steve Hart*

Family Christmas 2015. From left in the back row: Jason, Sam (Brigid's son), Emma (Patrick's partner), Therese, Paddy, and Andrew holding Jake (Cathy and Kerrin's son). Fourth row: Jordan (Patrick and his previous partner Sharna's son), Patrick, Nick (Margie's husband) and Margie. Third row: Harry (Therese and Jason's son), me, Lachlan (Patrick and Sharna's son), Kerrin and Bernadette. Second row: Estelle (Margie and Nick's daughter), Jessica (Therese and Jason's daughter), Cathy and Stevie. Front row: William (Therese and Jason's son), Cash (Margie and Nick's son), Henry (Therese and Jason's son), Rhys and Charlie (Cathy and Kerrin's sons). The Prebbles—Maree, Brett, Georgia and Thomas—didn't arrive in time for the photo.

Such an honour. Holding The Don Award at the Sport Australia Annual Hall of Fame on 13 October 2016. *Vicki Jones/ Sport Australia Hall of Fame*

Reunited. My last ride on Prince at Lady Bay Beach near Warrnambool. *David Caird/ Newspix*

Second win. Congratulating my brother-in-law jockey Kerrin McEvoy on his 2016 Melbourne Cup win while talking to Cathy in Sydney. *Ian Currie/Newspix*

Double header. My first win as a jockey/trainer on Duke of Nottingham at Swan Hill Racecourse on 27 November 2016. *Brendan McCarthy/Getty Images*

Nottingham Farm: A place to call home.

During a spell it has a lazy time in a paddock somewhere, doing whatever it likes, eating what it likes (almost), and not being worked. When they come back into work they start with light runs and build up towards resuming.

Trials might be finished by midmorning. If there are no trials and you are riding at a race meeting in the afternoon, you may well have to attend to your weight. I might be 55 kilograms but have to ride at 54 kilos that afternoon. I try to eat something, even if I have to lose a kilogram. Often it might be quarter of a cup of muesli. Because I have gym facilities at home I will have a workout on the treadmill and cross trainer with my sweat gear on, and a hot spa. While I am in the spa I'm either on the phone, or I am doing the form for the afternoon's races. If I'm on top of things, I'll be listening to music or watching the TV.

If I'm riding at Moonee Valley or Flemington it's just ten minutes away from home, but Swan Hill is half a day's drive. As hungry as I might be, and as magnificent as food smells, there will be no grabbing a potato cake from the warmer when you're filling up with petrol along the way. I have survived on a lot of cans of V over the years, but I try to stay away from them if I can.

At the track you complete your book of rides. On an eight-race card you might have seven or eight rides, and each one requires energy, especially the distance races. Then the phone starts ringing and you have a variety of conversations, some celebratory, hope-fully, and in others you find yourself explaining what happened and why the horse finished where it did and what to do next. You are defending your ride and presenting a case for why you should keep the ride next time. Sometimes I'll give Andrew or Patrick a call to get their opinion if I need it, and I'll usually speak to Dad and he'll give his opinion to me, whether I ask or not.

The travelling can become exhausting, but riding in a race if you haven't done any trackwork that day isn't tiring. I find driving to and from the races is a nice time to catch up on news from my sisters, and what is happening in their lives and with their kids. It wouldn't be rare for me to speak to four or five family members in between races.

Riding in races after a busy morning is extremely draining, physically and mentally, and you often feel flat the next day—but you have to find a way to ready yourself for that day's riding. When I get home after the races I'm wrecked and all I can think about is getting to bed because the alarm's going to go off early again for trackwork in the morning. Quite often I go to bed hungry and can't wait to get up in the morning and have a bit of muesli. I usually start with just a coffee and have my muesli midmorning, after trackwork.

This is what we jockeys do, over and over and over and over again. When we finally get a day off, we just plonk on the beanbag, unable to move. But the reality is, if you are a mid-ranking jockey you find it very hard to let any opportunity pass.

Sometimes you might feel your own fitness is not up to scratch, so you'll squeeze in a workout, a few interval sprints up to the local oval. Lately I've been doing that in conjunction with a tabata session, a Japanese workout I picked up working with trainer Wes Clarke from the Melbourne Victory soccer team, who I met through my friend Grant Brebner when I came back from holidays before the 2015 Spring Carnival. He's put me on a regime and a different fitness program. I don't have too many more Spring Carnival years left in me and so I don't want to leave any stone unturned. It has helped me become the fittest and lightest I have ever been.

If you look at how professional sports clubs control their players' diets, you'd have to say jockeys have looked after themselves by comparison. Some have worked with dieticians, but when I was starting life as a jockey I just felt my own way through it, doing what my brothers and sisters did without even thinking about it. That led to a vicious cycle of starving, sweating, eating. Andrew and I joke about it now, as I was a bit of a guts when I was younger. But I blame Andrew for that because he always told me before I started riding to eat as much as I could while I had the chance because that would come to a halt pretty quickly.

At one stage I considered being hypnotised to help me control my eating habits but I decided I had to use the power of the mind to change for the better. I had to want it. I found strength and motivation from Steven Arnold, one of Australia's finest jockeys and best mates with Patrick. Steven has to lead the most disciplined life to maintain his weight, which is still high by a jockey's standards. He can sit at dinner and sip on half a glass of water and watch others eat and not let it affect his mood. Patrick was also incredibly disciplined but always referred to Steven's discipline as extraordinary. My new ability to maintain close to a contestant weight definitely helps, but I still treat myself from time to time and gain weight on holidays. It's always hard coming back.

◆ ◆ ◆

I was twenty-four when I rode Allez Wonder in the Melbourne Cup of 2009 and, having seen what it was about, I really hoped I would get another opportunity. But the reality is, with the international horses and their fly-in riders, there are fewer places for an Australian jockey. I still wanted to find horses that I could follow through on, and ride throughout their careers, even if that did not take them into the Cup. You just never know when one is going to bob up and involve you. Sometimes they come out of nowhere.

For me, it was in the new year of 2010, when young horses make their debuts and try to qualify for some of the rich two-year-old races, like the Blue Diamond at Caulfield and the Golden Slipper at Rosehill. Owners and trainers are eyeing off the big Autumn prize money and jockeys are hoping they land a few good rides in the hope of getting a start themselves.

I'd driven up the Hume Highway to Benalla, east of Shepparton in the north of the state, to ride La Spiel. If he won, his trainer, Henry Dwyer, was going to give me the ride in the big Moonee Valley race that was looming. He ran second.

As luck would have it, Stuey Webb asked me on the day if I'd ride his unraced two-year-old filly, Yosei. I'd never seen her before. She was tiny. As he legged me up, Stuey said she'd run well, and was a pretty good chance of winning. Cantering to the barriers I was surprised at how impressive her actions were for such a small horse. She had a really relaxed, flowing action with quite a big stride.

I had a nice run and was in the box seat, going well, when she got severely checked. But just as I was feeling disappointed, Yosei picked herself up. I spotted a little gap on the fence, aimed her for it and she burst through and won by four lengths.

'Wow! This one's got some motor,' I thought to myself. 'I like her.'

Henry took me off La Spiel, which was disappointing, especially when he went on to win the Moonee Valley race. But at least I'd met little Yosei. It's funny how things can work out.

I also met John Pittard, a farrier and good mate of Stuey. He had bought Yosei for around $15,000 and later sold a half share to Rob and Barbara McClure, who have a stud farm at Red Hill on the Mornington Peninsula. Yosei was a cheapie and, like Dad, I love a cheapie.

Given she had ability, Yosei and I went across to Adelaide for a $100,000 two-year-old race. She ran a gallant second but when I gave her one with the whip she swished her tail. I took note. I reckon she'd have won that day if I hadn't used the whip as much.

By then Stuey and I knew she was a real quality filly. She was accepted for the Sires Produce, a Group 2 race at Flemington. She ran third behind Shamrocker, who went on to run second in The Oaks in the Spring, so she was up to mixing it with the best of them. Every time she went out to race she improved, and she learned a bit more. It was clear she was a trier. She just needed encouragement and then she would give you her best. There was no need to stand over her and create fear. That was the wrong thing to do.

The two-year-old season was underway in Sydney.

'Should we go up there?' Stuey asked.

'Why not?' I said.

She ran fourth in another Group 2 event, the Reisling Stakes in Sydney, racing greenly in what was only her fourth start. But I was learning about her as well and I think we were starting to understand each other. We were aiming at the Champagne Stakes but also to enter her in the Sires Produce the week before against the male horses. Coming down the Randwick straight in the Sires I gave her a couple on the left with the whip, which balanced her up—she had a tendency to want to run to the left under pressure— and she hit top pace so athletically. She didn't have a long sprint but a sharp burst that was very effective, so you had to be patient and not push the button too soon.

I tried to stay as balanced as I could on the little filly, encouraging her by my voice and a wave of the whip. She gave everything she had and we just got home by a nose. She was a sixteen to one shot but she'd held off the favoured runners and had a Group 1 race to her name.

When I spoke to Andrew and Patrick they were all questions.

'What were you doing?' Andrew asked.

'What?' I said.

'Why didn't you hit her, it was such a tight finish.'

'Because I didn't need to,' I explained. 'She was giving me everything. She couldn't go any faster.'

I was going on instinct, having only ridden her a few times, but that's what she'd shown me and so that's how I treated her. I only used the whip to straighten her up. All I wanted to do was keep her balanced because she was so small.

My style might not have been as flash as others but it was effective and at least I was having a go. Some jockeys can't use the whip in both hands and they won't even try. It was something I'd worked on and practised my whole life, as it can be the difference between winning and losing. I was so proud to have been confident enough to do it in a Group 1. To be made fun of by my brothers over that really got to me, and it has been a running joke between trainer Robert Smerdon, an old family friend, and me to this day—that I would choose a Group 1 race to practise using the whip in my left hand.

She ran fifth in the Champagne Stakes and it was discovered she had a virus, so her performance to be beaten by a length was gallant. She was sent out for a well-earned spell but would be back in the Spring. She'd had an excellent campaign. I was so keen on her.

◆ ◆ ◆

On the day Yosei won the Sires Produce in April in Sydney, I was sitting in the jockeys' room with Kathy O'Hara, one of Sydney's top jockeys. She was best friends with Gabby Engelbrecht, a very young trainer—as young as us—from Warwick Farm. We got chatting. We had a lot in common. Her father Steve is also a trainer at Warwick Farm in Sydney, and Gabby grew up with horses and wanted to be with them. All she wanted was to win the Melbourne Cup as a trainer. She also wanted to make a contribution in other areas as well, as she has a strong sense of social responsibility.

She planned to travel to Rwanda to spend time helping in an orphanage. I was really interested in what she was telling me and, as I was looking to go away for the winter, I asked her if I could join her. Most of my friends had volunteered to work with kids in Tanzania and Ethiopia and other African countries. They felt they'd done something worthwhile by doing this, and they'd loved the experience. So I was looking forward to doing the same.

A few weeks later, Gabby and I finalised our arrangements and headed off to Kigali. I was on another one of those long trips: Melbourne, Sydney, Johannesburg, Nairobi, Kigali—it took thirty hours, including the delays. Where we stayed was a ninety-minute walk to the orphanage, which was run by the Faith Victory Association, or FVA. We would walk halfway and either bus or moto the rest. It was fairly hectic, to say the least. It was set up in 2002 by Dr Immaculate Mukatete and some of her colleagues, in response to the shocking suffering of the children whose parents were slaughtered in the Rwandan Genocide in 1995.

The first time I saw the orphanage I was overwhelmed. The children, aged from two to nineteen, had no one. Some were the victims of circumstance—the horrible realities of politics and ethnic hatred. Some were unwanted. One child had been found in the mouth of a dog, having been abandoned in a nearby forest. I contemplated the fate and chance in that. Was that an example of fortune? Or misfortune? To be born into that situation, then found by a dog. And then to be retrieved from the dog.

Many of the older children we helped out were orphaned by the conflict in 1995, while the parents of most of the younger children had died of HIV/Aids. If you don't think chance plays a part in life, if you don't think hope and possibility and opportunity are at the heart of well-being, go and visit an orphanage in Rwanda. I so admire the people who are determined not to give up on the kids. They are giving the children in their care the means to work towards building a life for themselves.

I thought of the hope my little mare Yosei had given me, how she kept me going. But that was inconsequential compared with the hope those who work so hard to keep these orphanages going have created. Apart from caring for the children and looking after their basic needs, of food and shelter, and medical care, FVA provides scholarships to orphans, job training for women, counselling for genocide survivors, domestic violence education and a range of therapies.

It made me realise that my life was not that hard. I had all the love in the world as a child but these kids hadn't, and they then had to find the strength and a reason to believe in life, to have the faith that things would work out. Some were terribly afraid—of everything. Some ran away when they saw our white skin. But together we built genuine trust. Working to attend to their needs helped build that. Showing them that people cared for each other helped build that. I think they could tell we wanted to help them, out of simple human compassion. To see them was to feel for them.

Many newly arrived orphans were malnourished. Others, while grateful for the food they were given, were stuck in a routine of milk porridge in the morning and a rice and bean dish in the evening. We put together a small collection that we called The Fruit and Vegetable Fund. Each day we would walk to the busy market, which was just a series of stalls along the dirt roads, to buy fruit and vegetables to add variety to their diet.

We read the kids stories and played games with them. We'd have dancing competitions with some of the older ones. Those times were fun. All in all, it gave me such a sense of perspective.

On the long walk home along the dirt roads after a lively day I'd feel pretty buggered. And we'd be hoping the running water was on at the place we were staying—quite often it wasn't and we'd have to wash with water from a jerry can. It was the first time I had ever had to pray for running water. Rwanda taught me not to worry about the little things. To focus on the things that really matter.

The oldest boy at the orphanage, Elias, was quite a character. He lived with the memory of atrocities and the ever-present sense of loss. His stories made me grimace and it was hard to imagine the scenes of violent hatred he had witnessed. But I could relate to his sadness. We talked a lot. I admired his spirit. His determination to build a future for himself, and for others around him. He had nothing, and he knew it.

'The only thing I have in my life,' he told me, 'is my brain.'

He wanted to go to university and I decided to fund his education. Initially, he flew to India but found it very difficult to secure and maintain a place at the university he'd chosen. He seemed more suited to an African campus. He enrolled in a Ugandan university but corruption and blatant theft drained the funds I was providing. He did, though, finish his course and came up with a plan. He wanted to start a chicken farm but it was going to take forever to save the money to get started. He asked me to help.

'Everyone likes to eat chicken,' he said. 'And there's a shortage of chickens.' He found a site to build the pens and approached local restaurants. He was so keen to give it a red-hot go.

It was very hard to know how Elias would go investing what was a substantial amount of money. After much discussion with my dad, who always loves to help others but was a bit skeptical, and Mark Zahra, who thought I was odds-on to be taken for a ride, I decided to go with my gut instinct. I sent Elias the money to set up his farm. He stays in contact and he tells me it's set up and going. We've hit a few bumps along the way but you can only live in hope, and trust, and I certainly hope his venture will turn into something substantial one day. And if it doesn't, the money is gone and we carry on. At least we had a go.

We were sad to leave when we did. Gabby and I went on to Nairobi and then to Mauritius before returning home. Sitting in the comfort of my Melbourne home, reflecting on my time away, I concluded that you cannot expect anything. All the great moments of your life, all the joy you experience, have to be thought of as a blessing.

This renewed sense of perspective gave me a feeling of release. It helped me understand the things that mattered most to me— my family, my friends, the people around me. I would be the best jockey I could be, but I'd try not to stress about it. I had to learn to understand things and accept things. Acceptance was the key.

◆ ◆ ◆

I was looking forward to getting back on my little mate Yosei. When she resumed in the Spring she didn't do much in her first two starts. She was racing against the best three-year-olds and she remained one of those horses that, despite her successes, and her form, was never regarded as top class. Punters kept sending her out with double figure odds.

Stuey took us to Sydney again, to run in the Flight Stakes at Randwick. She was caught wide and didn't feature in the finish. Our run was okay, but it looked disappointing. I copped a bit of heat over my ride and there was talk of taking me off her. But Stuey stayed loyal and argued my case. Yosei and I went well together.

She was one of a handful of chances in the Thousand Guineas at Caulfield. I thought she was in good nick and, after spending a long time studying the form, I thought we could run a tactical race that would serve her well. I was confident I'd be four back on the rails in the run, with the on-pace Sydney runners somewhere in front of me. When I walked the track that morning I found that the best ground was hard up against the inside rail. I felt a sense of quiet confidence come over me. If we could hug that rail we were right in this.

Yosei sometimes missed the start and liked to get back and finish over the top of them. Given the Sydney fillies were used to running the other way round—clockwise, yet another thing Melbourne and Sydney didn't agree on all those years ago—I thought they might drift off the rail on the corner and an inside run would present itself. And that's what happened—just.

The Sydney fillies half hung out, leaving only the tiniest gap. Yosei was so game, she'd take any run. Turning into the home straight we had made our way up behind the leaders and all we needed was a run. It came around the 300-metre mark and little Yosei didn't let me down. She shot through and won. Her second Group 1 win. She was a beauty.

Stuey tried her against the country's best fillies and mares in the Myer Classic but she wasn't yet up to that class. Back to her own age, she ran in The Oaks on the Thursday of Cup week, unsuccessfully as it turned out. I didn't ride her very well; she struggled at the distance and she finished well out of it. It was time for another spell. But we had a horse and I loved her. Stuey was doing a terrific job and the owners were having a good time of it. I really felt I knew this little horse.

◆ ◆ ◆

At Christmas time the family all got together, as we always did. We caught up with what had been happening. There were a lot of laughs. Stevie was happy in his job at Darren Weir's stables.

He'd been working there for a couple of years and they loved him. He had a little scooter to take him about the place.

I was looking forward to a big year. Yosei was going to be a highlight for me, and who knew what she could do. She would be contesting the best races all over the country. At last, I thought, I might get a decent run at things. I might even find another Yosei or two. I was certainly working hard at it.

Towards the end of that summer I was riding Suite Success in the Blue Diamond Prelude for two-year-olds. Shortly after the start, as jockeys were jostling for positions, she clipped heels. I fell heavily and was again knocked unconscious. Concerned I'd injured my neck, the paramedics took me straight to Epworth Emergency for X-rays. Lying still in my neck brace waiting for the results of my CT scan, I talked myself into thinking I was fine and that I would be right to ride the next day. I had a good book of seven rides for some great trainers. Surely I could just walk out. Then a doctor came in.

'Now, it's a bit worse than we first thought,' he said. I started to cry. 'You have a fracture in your neck.' This certainly wasn't trivial.

Mark Zahra took me home. When I left the hospital I was sore but comfortable, but at two in the morning I headed to the bathroom for some painkillers and deteriorated very quickly. I started sweating and shaking uncontrollably and was rocking back and forth on the floor. My brain felt swollen, like it was too big for my skull. It just wasn't right. Mark came in to check on me but didn't know what to do either. I vomited my painkiller up and I sat beside the toilet and then had to lie down on the cold floor of the bathroom, I couldn't have a shower, I couldn't stand and I couldn't take off my neck brace.

I took more painkillers and with Mark's help got back into bed. I just held on until the medication eventually kicked in. For two days I couldn't get out of bed. I was vomiting and sleeping. I was so ill, and I was also sad. Yet again I was injured and I was worried. Since the first fall I had lived with the prospect of far-reaching injuries. Was this what that meant? Would I be going back to the Epworth?

Mark made an appointment to see Gary Zimmerman, the jockeys' doctor, the next morning. I was too crook to go, so I cancelled. A second appointment was made, but I couldn't get out of bed. I cancelled again. Finally Mark talked directly with Gary, who said that I couldn't keep sleeping, that it was possibly dangerous for me to be sleeping so much. So we went in to see him and there wasn't much he could do. I had to see it out. The vomiting lasted another couple of days and Mark just sat with me, rubbing my back, unable to do anything else.

By the fourth day I came good. I had to rest and let my neck heal, which was going to take at least three months. And what then? Where would Yosei be by then? Who would be riding her?

I had to get through the recovery time, but I'm not very good at being inactive. I painted the cupboards and did a stack of jobs around the house. I also got to travel overseas again.

While I was out of action the Loreto girls came over for dinner a couple of times. One of the positives about being injured was that I could also eat whatever I liked for a couple of months. When I'm able, I cook roast lamb. The girls would bring bubbles and red wine and we'd talk. They still laugh about the time I played hostess with my neck brace on.

At those dinner parties we'd all end up in the spa, without a care in the world—for once. We'd inevitably talk about the past, and the future, and have those late-night, glass-in-hand conversations that people close to each other have. The Loreto girls were always concerned for my well-being. But they knew me, and what I hoped for—to race again.

I hadn't fully recovered by the time Yosei resumed with a run up the straight at Flemington. Stuey gave Mark the ride. It was a fair run. Then Stuey took her north to Brisbane for the Winter Carnival. I was close to a full recovery but Jason Maskiell rode her in her first start up there. Yosei didn't do much.

I was riding trackwork and working hard in the gym to get back to riding my little mare. I was so lucky to have a horse I wanted to push myself for. Stuey was slightly concerned I'd only be back racing for two weeks before the Group 1 race Yosei was aimed at next, but I assured him I'd be okay. I'd had a few winners; I was ready.

I flew to Brisbane to work her five days before her race. She felt really strong.

'Gee, her work was good,' I said to Stuey. 'She'll go well.'

The exceptional Sydney mare Beaded was the odds-on favourite for the Tatts Tiara that Saturday. She looked the winner so I rode Yosei to run a place, in the hope she might even snatch the win. Dropping to the tail, Yosei travelled well within herself and came to the turn. I just needed an ounce of luck. We'd wasted no energy and I knew she had a really good sprint left in her. I thought she was going to storm home. Beaded shot clear like a good thing but, in a spectacular burst, Yosei came out after her. My little filly really lifted and she got home! It was a brilliant win—her third Group 1.

13

Always a comeback

RACING IS MADE up of so many different elements, and one of them is the track. I love the Ballarat track, because it's home. You tend to like the tracks where you do well, but not always. Tracks have such character. Warrnambool takes the jumpers across the road and up the hill into Brierley's Paddock. Eagle Farm in the winter sunshine is classically Queensland. Moonee Valley on Cox Plate Day, with the crowd right on top of you, makes for a great atmosphere. Flemington has its sweeping lawns and gardens.

Courses all over the world have such history. They have produced so many stories that sit in the memories of those who made them and shared them. The tracks in England and Ireland go here, there and everywhere, up and over undulating fields and through thickets of ancient trees, like someone marked out the course in 1839 and the horses have carved the path since. And then there's the long, straight tracks of Ascot or The Rowley Mile at Newmarket.

Racing is a big part of Australian culture. The carnivals here have their own distinctive characters. Warrnambool has scudding sideways rain during its three-day May carnival—so Irish. The four-day Flemington Spring Carnival is a riotous celebration. The Sydney Carnival, which for a long time was timed for the month around Easter, is not as big as the Melbourne Spring season, but the racing is excellent. I love the Randwick track during this time—its layout and the rise in the straight, a gentle-enough gradient that is not cruel to the horses but sufficient to test them. The track is all part of the experience, even for a jockey focused on their horse.

Yosei liked Randwick and had won the Sires Produce there. Stuey Webb mapped out a new campaign for her. She was now a four-year-old with three Group 1s to her name, so she would run in the very best races, and in the famous Doncaster Handicap, which Patrick had won twenty years before. She ran fourth in the Coolmore Classic at Rosehill behind Ofcourseican, ridden by Kathy O'Hara, and then didn't run a place in the Queen of the Turf, won by outstanding Sydney mare More Joyous, who was going to be hard to beat in the Doncaster a fortnight later.

The Doncaster Handicap is a textbook Australian race that dates back to 1866. Because it's a handicap, every horse is weighted to give all of them an even chance, and there are often blanket finishes involving many horses—so basically any horse can win. Long shot winners, like Soho Square for Patrick in 1992, are not uncommon. Yosei was well suited to the 1600-metre handicaps as she would get back and then fly home. Yet she was always sent out at a good price.

I walked the Randwick track and was surprised to find the best going on the inside, right up against the fence. But, with horses fanning out, I thought I'd be able to cut the corner. In the race I got back and, as expected, she travelled well. Just as I thought the field was drifting to the centre of the track I stayed hard on the rail and saved a lot of ground. When it all opened up in front of me I thought I might win.

Little Yosei hit the front just like she had in the Sires Produce. I got such a rush of blood as we dashed up the rise at Randwick but then More Joyous and Shoot Out just ran her down. She ran third by a length. More Joyous was a popular winner, but Yosei certainly won the admiration of the crowd. She was applauded all the way in, as if she'd won the race. The owners, John Pittard and Rob and Barbara McClure, were so proud of her.

They decided to give Yosei a break and I would wait for her to come back in the Spring, when she would be set for the Epsom in Sydney and the Toorak in Melbourne. Yosei had been taking me all over the country but back at home I was getting some nice rides for Darren Weir. His star was continuing to rise. Good judges respected him as a horseman. Initially I had been a little apprehensive about asking Darren if I could ride trackwork for him as I assumed he was a blokey bloke. My sisters had always got on well with him, though. He was very fair. Jockeys know that if you do the work for Darren and his big team, he will put you on, which is the way I think it should be.

Not long after returning from Sydney I was riding El Divine, which was having its second start, in a 1000-metre race at Donald, a little town in the Wimmera in western Victoria. Darren thought he had a really good chance in the race and, when El Divine was standing so beautifully in the stalls, I thought he could be a winner. But as he came out of the outside barrier he didn't move his front legs, so when he jumped so powerfully with his hind legs he face-planted into the ground. He just went smack.

Because I was ready to jump with him, I was speared into the ground as well. On the footage of the incident it looks like I had broken my neck. It was a sickening fall. I was immediately stunned but was soon fully conscious. The barrier attendants were there first.

'I can't feel my legs,' I said. Soon there were a lot of people around me.

'Don't panic. Just lie down.'

As they were gathering around me I was getting even more worried.

'I really can't feel my legs.'

'Just relax.'

Back at the rooms Darren was shaking his head—he didn't give me a chance. He thought I was seriously injured.

After a while the feeling started to come back into my legs, which was such a relief. I was less concerned about the injuries I might have suffered. I was placed on a stretcher and the ambulance took me to the Ballarat Base Hospital, where a CT scan showed I had five vertebrae fractured down the left-hand side, from T6 to T10, the fifth to the ninth cervical (neck) vertebra, and three broken ribs. I also had a terrible concussion again and was very sick.

To my surprise, I was allowed to leave hospital. At home in Melbourne, I had the same vomiting reaction as I'd had with my other falls. My brain felt really swollen, as if it was too big for my skull again. I started icing my head to alleviate some of the pain and pressure that were making me feel hideously nauseous. I couldn't keep the painkillers down once again. Everyone was really worried. Therese, who lives just around the corner, came over on the second day and insisted I come to stay at her place. The car trip of only a few minutes took thirty because we had to keep stopping for me to be sick.

Therese wanted to take me to hospital but I knew I couldn't travel and I was getting worse. The pain was excruciating, so bad I just felt like I wanted to die.

'We've got to get you to hospital,' she kept saying.

'I can't. I just can't.' I was not good.

Therese called Dr Mulkearns and he called around. He gave me an injection to stop the vomiting, which worked for a few hours and settled me, but I continued vomiting for two more days.

It was awful. When it stopped I felt a tremendous relief. Although my ribs were painful, the spinal injury wasn't too bad.

In the next few weeks I coped reasonably well. The same conversations took place, with family members suggesting I stop riding. But I knew that I had just been involved in some freakish incidents, things that horses never normally did. El Divine planted his feet. Vladivostok fell over. I thought it was just really, really bad luck and, if I was going to retire, I wanted it to be on my own terms. I had more to do, more to give. I also knew that Yosei was spelling in the paddock after the Doncaster, and that she'd be coming back around the same time I was. That was a tremendous motivation for me. She had something to give, too.

I also had a chance to get away again. My sister Maree and her husband Brett Prebble were living in Hong Kong, so I decided to go over and visit them. Later that year Brett would be back to ride in the Melbourne Cup and he would win on Green Moon. After spending time with them I went sailing off the coast of Croatia with friends Rosie and Kelly Myers. I trained every day while I was on the yacht and whenever we docked.

All the time I was travelling I was telling myself to stay positive, not to let my run of falls get me down. The thought of Yosei was a great help. Yosei, in Japanese, means 'the fairy', and she was my invincible spirit.

Around mid August we both returned to racing, to ride in the Cockram Stakes at Caulfield. She dropped back to last, then worked her way into the race, but made no real impression. She wasn't quite ready. Stuey freshened her and she came back three weeks later in the Let's Elope Stakes at Flemington in early September. She finished midfield. She was getting fitter. Next start would be the million dollar Epsom Handicap in Sydney. I was excited for this!

A few weeks later, on 21 August 2012, I was riding Julinsky, a first starter, for Darren Weir at Ararat, which is the next major town west of Ballarat, about two hours out of Melbourne. Another runner came out on the home turn and I nicked its heel. I went down again, face-first. I was flipped onto my back and Julinsky and I slid down the track together. I was lucky and grateful that she didn't roll over me. I woke up in the ambulance.

'Please tell me this is a bad dream,' I asked. I genuinely had no idea.

'No, it isn't. I'm sorry,' the ambulance guy said.

Oh, no, I thought to myself. No! Do I have to go through it all again? I was going to miss out on the Epsom, the Toorak, the Spring Carnival. I was devastated.

It was the same pain as the Donald fall only four months before. The same pain, except on the other side, so I knew I had a major back injury.

After being assessed at Ararat, I was taken to Ballarat Hospital. I'd had five breaks on the left at Donald; this time it was three on the right side of the same vertebrae. I knew it was going to be awful. Could I go through it again? The pain? The nausea? Mark Zahra was at the hospital waiting for me. By this stage we had broken up but we'd been through so much together; he was always there to pick me up and take me to be with Dad at Home.

Dad comforted me.

'Ahh, Little Girl,' he said in a gentle voice. It was the voice of pure love.

'I think that's enough, Dad,' I said. 'I think that's it. I think someone's trying to tell me something and I'm not listening. How can somebody be so unlucky?' Then Dad said something I wasn't expecting.

'You don't have to make a decision tonight; you've got plenty of time to decide. Sleep on it.' At that moment I not only realised my father loved me, I also knew he knew me.

Later that night, lying in bed at Home—there was actually a bed for me this time—with a broken back and aching head, as I was waiting for the same four days of nausea to kick in, I was thinking about everything. I had thought Dad would be happy; that he would be thinking, hooray, the penny has dropped and she will retire. But it didn't take me long, probably not even the time before I went to sleep, before I knew that I wasn't going to let this latest setback stop me. I still wanted to retire at some stage on my own terms.

The nausea arrived, on cue. True to form, it was four days of torture.

◆ ◆ ◆

I'd had too many concussions. I think everyone was worried about my head, including the racing authorities. A few months went by and I had to undergo a neuropsych assessment to be passed fit to ride. A woman came around to my house and put me through a series of tests, which included puzzles and memory exercises and other thinking challenges. I'd never done one of these before. It went on for well over four hours, and was easily the hardest series of tests I've ever done. I passed it sufficiently well that I was given the all-clear to ride. Thankfully, touch wood, I haven't had a fall since.

◆ ◆ ◆

That summer Patrick wanted to campaign a number of his horses in Tasmania. The Cup carnivals in Hobart and Launceston run through January and February. Our family has enjoyed success in Tassie but I wasn't ready to ride. It was a great opportunity for me to get away, though, and start on my comeback. Just after our big family gathering in Christmas 2013, I caught the ferry with my car to spend a few weeks in Hobart looking after the horses.

It was like a retreat, with time alone to contemplate. I stayed in a cabin at a caravan park. It was pretty basic, but it had all I needed. With a lot of time on my hands I explored, and found the beauty of Hobart, with its clear water and inlets and the hills and Mount Wellington, quite calming. I worked Patrick's horses along the beaches. I sat under trees, taking it easy, trying to work out what I would do. Wondering.

In passing the neuropsych test my short-term future was assured. I would return to race riding as soon as I was ready. But what about the long term? I could hear different voices in my head: Margie and her husband Nick wanted me to retire; the Loreto girls made the life of twenty-somethings, their work and play, sound like a lot of fun; I had my own ideas about buying a farm, somewhere near Home, and starting a life as a jockey–trainer, and hopefully having a family. Some people were suggesting a career in media. Not Dad, though. When I did a stint as a panellist on racing station TVN, he laughed at me and said, 'Little Girl, you were so boring I had to change the channels.' And then gave me a lecture on modulating my voice.

I decided I wasn't ready for these changes yet. Despite all of my falls and setbacks, I still loved horses, I was still a jockey and I still wanted to be the best jockey I could be. I hadn't come close yet. And I could still hear the voice of my little self: 'I just wanna win the Melbourne Cup.'

Patrick's horses were stabled at a property just near Seven Mile Beach and I worked them on the sand every day. It was idyllic. I was half-expecting a film crew with gorgeous models in white robes to arrive to shoot a perfume ad. I was also riding the horses on a proper racecourse. Patrick was ringing me often to check that all was well with the horses. He would occasionally come down to

Hobart. When he did, he trained me hard, getting me to do sprints on the beach, especially if we'd been out to dinner the night before.

With no racing commitments I was free to eat and drink as I pleased. I lived on oysters, straight from the water. I had six with a bit of lemon every morning and six more, lightly floured and fried, later in the day. I knew they were good ones because whenever Patrick came to stay he'd pinch them from the fridge. I'd also buy the freshest fish from a fisho who parked his van near the airport.

Fieldmaster had won the Devonport Cup for Patrick's great mate Steven Arnold and was being prepared for the Hobart and Launceston cups. My first ride back was on him, in a 2100-metre race. He ran fifth in that Hobart Cup, behind Darren Weir's Hurdy Gurdy Man. He was not quite right going into the Launceston Cup and finished fifth there as well.

Once that campaign was over I returned to Melbourne and dropped into the Weir complex next to Home. Stevie was still thriving there. He was helping with the horses and strapping. Darren was showing himself to be a very astute judge of horses and he was becoming more and more successful. I went to see him to tell him I was riding again.

'You can come and ride a few here,' he offered.

'Thank you,' I said, and immediately set about preparing.

I really liked working with him. I had been blessed to spend time with true horsemen over the years and Darren was one of them, with his deep affection for horses, and his passion for training and racing. I started riding for him and everything felt right about it.

After a couple of weeks of work for him, Darren and his racing manager Jeremy said there would be quite a few horses going to trial at Colac, if I was interested.

'Any good ones?' I asked.

'There's a few there,' he said.

It was February 2013. Colac is grey and wet, dairy country for much of the year. It's where the long-distance runner Cliffy Young and his gumboots came from. But in mid February there's dust and flies around, and the galahs are screeching in the gum trees.

It was a pretty routine sort of day, just another trial. With the Autumn Carnival underway in Melbourne and Sydney, lots of horses needed a run, so it was busy enough. Darren had a few making their trial debuts. I was on a three-year-old bay called Prince of Penzance. When I first saw him I noticed his walk—an athletic, confident stride. He looks like a bold one, I thought. Let's see if he can run.

At the course following this horse were some pretty excited first-time owners, every new experience was a thrill. There were also some old campaigners who'd seen it all before. My horse jumped out okay and travelled along fine, but the track was starting to chop up by this stage of the day, though, and when we got to the corner he slipped and nearly fell over. He picked himself up, though, and got going, charging powerfully.

Geez, I thought to myself. Horses don't really do that. We might have one here.

As I came back in I met Darren Lonsdale and his daughter Emily. They had a small share in a syndicate that had a 10 per cent share in the horse. Darren owned just a small portion of this horse's tail, but that didn't dampen his enthusiasm.

'What'd you think?' Lonsdale asked, as he patted Prince of Penzance on the neck.

'You're going to have some fun with this one,' I said. 'Don't you worry about that.'

14

Dancing with the princes

DARREN WEIR IS one of the great characters of Australian racing. You couldn't make him up, in the same way you couldn't make my dad up. You just have to meet him. Given the connectedness of Australian racing, and especially the fraternity of racing in country Victoria, there's a good chance you will if you have the slightest involvement in horse racing.

Under 'Owner' in a race book you will often see, especially with horses trained by D.K. Weir, the name A. McGregor. Alexander McGregor, known to all as 'Sandy', loves horses and has been involved in horse racing all his life. He and Darren go back a long way and he knows Darren's story as well as anyone. Stories of their past bob up from time to time. They've done a fair bit together and, although Sandy might try to tell you that having dinner with Darren Weir is a form of torture, they are good mates.

Sandy grew up on a wheat property at Callawadda just north of Stawell, near the Grampians National Park. It's good farming country that his great-great-grandfather selected in 1865. When it rains the paddocks are green with thick crops. By Melbourne

Cup time the growing is finished and the crops just mature in the summer heat until they're ready for harvest.

Sandy's father, Stuart McGregor, who is still trying to back a winner, was the president of the Stawell Racing Club for twenty years. He kept the club active and strong while running his farm and chain-smoking cigars. The club was formed in 1857 when Stawell was a gold town and prospectors were trying their luck, and Melbourne was a day's travel away. Stawell is a beaut track that conducts regular meetings. The time-honoured Stawell Cup is held on Easter Sunday during the world-famous professional foot-running race, the Stawell Gift.

The life of a country town revolves around its sporting clubs and other community organisations, pubs and churches. People know each other and they know the people in the next towns as well. Footy and netball are a big part of the life. Sandy played junior footy for Marnoo, 30 kilometres north of Stawell, until he gave it away for racing. But he still follows Richmond in the AFL. He says Richmond and racing horses have a lot in common: they provide a never-ending series of disasters punctuated by the odd miracle.

Darren Weir is from further up the bush at Berriwillock, on the railway line between Wycheproof and Sea Lake in the Mallee. It's tough country. Dry. The Mallee scrub only grows about 5 metres high. If you need a bit of luck to farm in the Wimmera, you need a lot more in the Mallee. The average yearly rainfall is about 300 millimetres. Farming on the dry plains is a punt. Some years more so than others. Farmers try to plant after rain and spend a lot of time and money to get a crop in. If it hasn't rained, you can plant in the dry ground—and hope. There's a lot of hoping in the Mallee.

Berriwillock was a thriving town in the first half of the twentieth century, when farms were smaller and it took a handful of blokes to work them. Photos of Berri from the late 1960s bear little resemblance to the quiet town it is today. In 2014 they even shut the pub, a sure sign a community is shrinking. The farms in the area are become bigger and more mechanised, needing fewer people to work them, and so everyone is drifting to the larger provincial centres, or even Melbourne and Adelaide.

Darren grew up on the family's grain farm, where they also had a piggery. They still have the farm, which is the key measure of success in the Mallee. He and his brother Chris were good footballers for the Berri team, which eventually merged with other clubs in the area. They played their last game at the Berri oval in 2015—it had become too expensive to maintain. When your pub and footy team are gone, you're battling.

Darren grew up with horses. They became his first love and as a teenager he wanted to work with them. His parents pushed him to finish school but he wasn't having that. Jack Coffey was happy to take Darren on and helped him develop his skills as a horseman. Jack was a bush trainer based at Birchip, a dusty Mallee town that had produced Ray Neville, who won the 1948 Melbourne Cup on Rimfire, when Ray was a sixteen-year-old apprentice. It was his ninth ride ever! Darren was an absolute natural, but also a very hard worker, desperate to learn. He became great mates with Jack's son Austy.

After a couple of years with Jack, and people talking about his potential, Darren got a job with respected Stawell trainer Terry O'Sullivan. Driving to work on his first day, pulling a float carrying two horses, Darren had an accident. A kangaroo had burst out of the stand of trees on the road north of Stawell and Darren couldn't avoid it. The horses were safe but the car was buggered. Unperturbed, Darren rode one horse bareback while leading the other the 8 kilometres to the Stawell Racecourse. When he arrived Terry was amazed. He knew then that he had a genuine young horseman on his hands.

Darren was keen to learn from a very capable country trainer who had a good strike rate, when he took one of his better horses to race in Melbourne. Apart from learning the training game, Darren played footy at Stawell, where he was a hard nut with a textbook case of white-line fever. Before long he bumped into Sandy McGregor. They both had dreams, and they were both starting out. Sandy wanted to own racehorses; Darren wanted to train them. It was a perfect match; only Darren had no money.

◆ ◆ ◆

The race book doesn't tell the story of the friendships and collaborations and projects and all the theorising that goes with it. At the O'Sullivans' there's a photo of two fresh-faced young blokes on the back of a couple of horses in the water at Lake Lonsdale. One is Darren Weir, the other is Brett Prebble. While I was now riding for Darren I also did so occasionally for the O'Sullivans. I am good friends with Terry and his daughter Karina, who train together these days. Family, friendships and partners.

The Stawell Racing Club helped Darren establish his own facility at the racecourse. Jim Holmes made chicken coops but could turn his hand to anything, so he built the Weir stables out of discarded railway tracks, creating what Sandy describes as the most over-engineered structure in racing—'It will still be standing in two thousand years,' he says.

Learning quickly as he went, Darren's obvious skill as a horseman won him respect and clients. People in racing could also see how genuine he was. When he first started training in the mid 1990s he would shoe horses, work and feed them, attend to their every need and still find eight hours in the day to work as a farrier and a barrier attendant. He had incredible drive. He also got results.

Like all the top trainers, he was on a mission to understand horses, to be kind and friendly to them, to train them to be the best they could be. He trained a lot of winners in the country and then started to have success in the bigger centres. And he wanted to win the Melbourne Cup, just like anyone else. Early in his career he very nearly did.

Worrall 'Woggsy' Dunn owned the boat and fishing shop in Horsham, and later the White Hart Hotel. Woggsy was one of those old characters you see on country racetracks. People would point to him and say, 'That's Woggsy Dunn. His horse ran second in the Melbourne Cup.' He had the racing bug and had his horses with D.K. Weir. He got hold of a good one called She's Archie, which won the South Australian Derby in 2002, Darren's first Group 1. She was an ideal cups horse and Darren got her cherry ripe for the 2003 Melbourne Cup. She flew home brilliantly but missed out by a length. Had she not been baulked at the top of the straight she might have run down Makybe Diva and got her first Cup victory.

Darren's skill as a trainer brought him more and more winners. Good judges thought he was gifted, a special talent. With those winnings came more owners, more horses and more resources, and the need for a bigger training complex. Rather than go to Melbourne he wanted his horses to have the country life, so he set up the complex at Miners Rest, just a stone's throw from Home. He also set up stables at Warrnambool, where horses seemed to thrive on the beach. He could move his team to and fro according to their need.

As I got to know Darren I could see that, like Bart Cummings, he was a thinker, someone who was consistently developing his understanding of horses. He knows his horses—like they're his own children. That's the sort of relationship I value, and that I wanted. Horses just don't get the better of him, no matter how naughty the horse might be. He wants his horses in peak physical and mental condition and to do that he has created an environment where they can thrive. He believes that horses will perform for you when they are happy and content, so he tries to get them in the best order with the least stress.

He also trains his horses his own way, on the 1400-metre straight track up the hill at the Ballarat Racecourse. Turning corners at pace puts stress on the legs of thoroughbreds, and the theory is that running up an incline is easier on their legs. Everything for Darren is about being as gentle as possible, about treating horses as best you can. At the same time his theory is they have to be fit to win races, so it's a very fine line, a balance. It's also a pleasant environment to work in, with trees on either side, that always reminds me of Chantilly in France and Newmarket in England.

While Darren loves horses, it's the owners, he says, he finds difficult. But I think that's his shtick, because he's always rapt for them when they have a win. If his post-race interviews are any indication, he likes it when larger syndicates have a bit of luck because he knows that will make for a good shindig. Darren is quiet and driven but he will come to life after a few drinks. Owners like him. I think they are fascinated by the understanding he has of horses and like that he is so successful.

These days he has to be very well organised because he has to manage so many horses and so many staff. The staff love how loyal he is. They give their all because he looks after them. He also has an incredible memory, which stores so much information about his horses—their starts and performances, their work and what's coming up for them.

About ten years ago Sandy and Darren were having lunch together. Sandy had had a number of good horses over the years. He was a huge fan of jumps racing and loved the Warrnambool carnival. He and Darren then decided they'd go one better.

'Let's win the Melbourne Cup,' Sandy said.

'We're all trying to win the Melbourne Cup.'

'No, have a real go. Target it. Plan it.'

So they did.

Darren, the master trainer, would prepare the horse; they just had to find the right horse. Some give you a better chance than others. They bought six.

◆ ◆ ◆

Prince of Penzance was foaled in November 2009 at Rich Hill Stud in Matamata in the Waikato region of New Zealand's North Island. He was offered at the Karaka Yearling Sales that summer. Highly respected Australian bloodstock agent John Foote, son of the legendary Queensland racing figure Loftus Foote, liked his breeding, and the look of him. Prince's sire is Pentire and his dam Royal Successor, so he was bred to stay. He was purchased for $50,000 for D.K. Weir. Darren then set about syndicating him.

Over the last decades racing syndicates have become more and more popular, which has altered the face of racing in Australia. For many years it was considered the domain of the wealthy and rather inaccessible. But that didn't stop small-time owners (like my dad, really) from trying. However, in spreading the cost, syndication has brought so many people inside of racing and that means the culture of racing is all the richer for it. You meet good people in racing. The friendships are long lasting, whether they are the result of success or struggle. Being one of the connections of a winner is such a thrill. I see it all the time.

As one of the initiators Sandy McGregor took a share, even if the shares in six horses was going to stretch the family budget. He took 25 per cent. John Richards, another long-time client of Darren's and friend of Sandy's—everyone seems to know each other—took another 25 per cent for his Galadi Holdings. The remaining 50 per cent of Prince was divided into five shares.

Winning Five is headed up by Arthur Rickard and includes his daughters Susan Cahill and Jenny Monks, Darren Lonsdale and his family, and Mark Hall. Arthur bought a share because one day at the races he saw Darren in the distance.

'Hey, Weiry,' he yelled. 'Have you got a decent bloody horse for me before I cark it?'

'Yeah, mate,' Darren yelled back. 'I'll send you some info.' And he did!

Men in Hats, a group of thirty-something blokes, some of who went to school together at Luther College in Croydon, an outer eastern suburb of Melbourne, also bought a share. The Men, Sam Brown, Tim Ashford, Greg Williams, Scott Jenke, Mike Botting and Adrian Brown, put some cash together to race horses. Prince was their last roll of the dice.

Andrew Broadfoot, a Melbourne barrister, has a share, as do Wilawl Go Racing, including Pam, David, Andrew, Michael and Stephen Wilson, and Neil and Ken Laws. Stephen is corporate affairs manager at the Gold Coast Football Club, so the Suns would have had a very big Cup Day if they'd copped the tip. Dalton Racing is brothers Joe Dalton (of Dalton Concrete Constructions), Jonathon Dalton and Bruce Dalton, a solicitor in Bundaberg, and they own another share.

The diversity of locations and occupations of the owners connected Prince to people all over the country. I have met most of the owners. I know John Richards very well. He has been a wonderful supporter of mine. Like many of Darren's early owners, John is from the bush, a lovely little town called St Arnaud, northeast of Stawell. He has a very successful farm machinery business, Goldacres, which manufactures sprayers for all different types of agricultural uses. They are used by farmers all over Australia. His father had sold farm equipment from a St Arnaud depot, and died when John was twenty-three. John developed the sprayers and they have been highly regarded for decades. He bought his first horse at twenty-eight and fell in love with racing. He will tell you that he's learned as he's gone along—not unlike Darren Weir.

Not long after the Pentire colt arrived from New Zealand, Sandy and John were at lunch discussing the progress of their younger horses. Usually they are given appropriate nicknames. Really, a horse is a pet and you become very familiar with them, and close to them. There's no need for formality. The colt was being called 'Success' because his dam is Royal Successor, and that became his stable name. They decided the colt's racing name was going to be Prince of Penzance. And they also had to decide what colours the syndicate should use, so they tossed for it. Sandy won. The McGregor family colours were chosen.

That meant John Richards, theoretically, got to choose the jockey. Because I was riding for Darren quite a bit, I was in the mix. But at that stage Prince was just another horse, checked out by the vets like any other horse, pre-trained like any other horse, just going through the preparations so he was ready to race. Who would know where he'd end up?

After impressing everyone in his trial at Colac, Prince was ready for his debut. His first start was at Stawell, which was nice, given how much Stawell means to Sandy and his family, and Darren, who started out there. It still has a feeling of home for them. Because I had ridden him at the trial, and had been riding him in trackwork, Darren gave me the ride.

Horses have to learn about racing and this can take some time. They need to get comfortable with being floated to a new track, with being in unfamiliar surrounds and with other horses, some of which are highly strung and tense on the day. They need to learn the routine of being boxed, saddled and taken to the mounting yard. Being walked around in front of people. The bigger the crowd, the more agitated they might be, until they get used to it.

Prince was a fiery character. We decided we needed to ease him in gently, to give him a good first-day experience so that he didn't resent what was happening to him, in the hope he might grow to like it. He was being difficult, playing up in the mounting yard, and generally not happy. I was in the maroon and white colours of the stable, rather than Sandy's colours. As he legged me up Darren asked me not to be too hard on him, and his final words were, 'I think he's going to go really well.'

I got Prince around to the barrier and he went in without a problem. He was slowly away, settled last, tracked through on the inside and then I got him to the outside and he finished strongly to win. For the first-time owners it was suddenly one of the great days of their lives—for the veterans it was a maiden win at Stawell. He'd done enough. Yes, I thought, there was no doubt he was handy.

Back in his box Prince was grumpy. He was kicking, pawing at the ground, biting the tie-up and generally being a bastard. For a long time no one could settle him down. Podge, who works with Darren, had a go, but no luck. Finally Darren came to have a look. You could tell Prince had spotted him. With a slightly cupped hand, Darren gave him a smack on the neck. It made a big noise and Prince went quiet. That was Darren's knack. No horse ever beat Darren Weir.

Prince wasn't finished, though. He waited for Darren to disappear and, once he was out of sight, he started again. He was so agitated he had to be led to an enclosed box so he didn't damage himself. We could hear him kicking away and I thought at least he has some fight in him.

His second start was at Donald. I was returning to the track where I had been lucky enough not to break my neck. This time I was in the McGregor colours. I settled last again and he raced comfortably. As I was bringing him into the race the favourite sustained an injury and dropped back through the field. I copped severe interference, which cost us a few lengths and our momentum. Prince picked up again and charged home for an unlucky third. On paper, that run made him no world-beater—third in a lowly rated race at Donald—but the signs were positive.

I led on him at his next start at Ballarat. It had been our intention to settle off the pace but as I brought him across to the fence he just landed in front, put his head down and settled nicely. Because Darren knew he was going to be a stayer he didn't want him to learn to get to the front but sometimes these things just happen. I took control of Prince and he responded and came back underneath me, and I really slowed the pace so when he kicked away, nothing was going to make ground on him. He won by three lengths but could have won by ten had I let him go flat out. He had a tendency to look around so I thought blinkers might suit him.

Darren thought he was ready for a metropolitan start so he was nominated for a 1800-metre three-year-old race at Caulfield. There were some good horses in the race—Backstedt for David Hayes, and Magnapal, who went on to run in a Caulfield Cup for the O'Sullivans. Prince had blinkers on for the first time and the idea was to ride him a bit more forward and hold a position that suits Caulfield. But he got back and was a little caught in traffic until I got him out at the 300. By the time he was revved up and asked to quicken, the leaders had dashed clear. Then, with 120 metres to go, he just took off and flew at them. He missed by a nose, which was a touch disappointing, but I was starting to think that, yes, we had a really good racehorse, and he seemed to be responding to me.

The new owners were already talking about the big races. The good three-year-old races weren't out of the question but he'd only had four starts and he was just starting to learn. Being a fiery type, it was going to take Prince a while to relax. Darren placed him in a 2000-metre race for three-year-olds at Flemington in early May. If he impressed again, Darren would take him to the Queensland Derby.

While Prince was finding his feet, I was also riding my little mate Yosei. She was set to return in Adelaide in a lead-up race to the Goodwood Handicap. While I was out with the Julinsky injury, Michael Rodd had ridden her to a fourth placing in the Emirates Stakes at Flemington, and then in Perth in the Railway Stakes, before she was sent for a spell.

On the plane going over to Adelaide to ride Yosei in the Robert Sangster—funny to be riding in a race named after the man who bought Our Paddy Boy—I got chatting with John Richards, who was going there with the Weir camp to watch his mare Lake Sententia. He had watched on in admiration as Darren blossomed as a trainer. It was the first time we'd had a chance to have a decent chat. He seemed like a really lovely guy. He was in his sixties and had been successful in pretty much everything he'd done.

Brad Rawiller had ridden Lake Sententia for luck in her previous start, trying to find a clear path through the middle of the field at Flemington, and finished second, and John did not ask Brad to ride the horse again.

'You can't ride 'em for luck,' he said. 'That wasn't Brad's best ride.'

'I thought it was a good ride,' I said, defending Brad. 'She doesn't finish second unless he rides for luck.' John and I didn't know each other very well then, but I wasn't concerned, even though I knew he had a share of Prince. Surely people can state their case in a rational discussion.

'I'd much rather my horse comes to the outside. I'd rather it finished fifth down the outside than be ridden for luck.' John was adamant. But I think he worked out that I would always hold my ground, too.

Ben Melham rode Lake Sententia that day in Adelaide, and came third. Funnily enough Brad won the race. After that, John gave me a go on Lake Sententia and we won. That's always good for a relationship. And then she won again. That was even better. Since then we have combined many times, for some nice results.

John runs the Galadi syndicate, which is sometimes part of other syndicates, as it was with Prince. But he always has a few on the go. He hadn't paid much attention to Prince at that time—he was just another young horse learning the caper—but he hoped he'd turn into a good stayer.

Yosei ran third in the Sangster at twenty-five to one. She was such a gutsy thing. Stuey was going to take her back to the Goodwood Handicap, one of Adelaide's biggest races, a fortnight later. These were good times for me. Spirits were high.

In the interim, we ran Prince in the 2000-metre race at Flemington. I tried to hold a slightly closer position on Prince this time without hopefully firing him up. Approaching the 1400-metre mark, when the pace slackened I was in a bit of trouble. Prince became really fired up with the blinkers on and over-raced badly. He was pulling and throwing his head around all over the place. I did my best to settle him but he had wasted so much energy I thought we'd blown our chances.

As we approached the straight I'd got on to the back of Saint or Sinner. His run had been beautifully timed by jockey James Winks but, remarkably, Prince had plenty left. Although Saint or Sinner shot four lengths clear, Prince put in a huge run. He just pinned his ears back and charged out after him and won by a head. It was phenomenal, made all the more so by the fact that Saint or Sinner shifted out and we were checked. Sam Hyland came over shaking his head.

'What about that!' he said. He'd been watching Prince because he is a good mate of Sandy's and because Prince's antics were the principal feature in the middle of the race. You couldn't help but notice it.

'Horses just don't do that,' he said.

'I know. That's what I've been saying,' I said.

Back in the rooms, watching the replay, we all stood there shaking our heads and almost laughing. Even Darren was surprised.

'That's ridiculous,' he said.

Prince was good enough to go to Brisbane and on that performance we knew he'd give the Queensland Derby a real shake. It was the first indication that he had inner strength. Then and there I thought, he's a Melbourne Cup horse.

◆ ◆ ◆

I was genuinely excited about Prince. Not I-hope-he-turns-into-a-good-one excited. Fair dinkum excited. From what I had seen and the way he felt, and given how much improvement he had made, I *really* believed he was the sort of horse that could win a Melbourne Cup. Then the bad news came.

In the days after the race Prince had gone lame. Waiting on any diagnosis is tense. You just never know. When the tests came back, they showed he had a bone chip in his right front fetlock, a common injury for thoroughbreds. The chip needed to be surgically removed.

Brian Anderson did the arthroscopy on the joint—the procedure is the same for horses as it is for humans—and took out a 2 by 2-millimetre piece of bone. Because it was sorted out quickly, the chip had not had an opportunity to cause damage to the fetlock and Prince was given a good chance—about 80 per cent—of recovering fully. That was pretty good odds, but we had to wait and see.

I really took that setback hard. Prince had given me such a lift and things were going well, and now he was out of action. At least

Ian Fulton and his colleagues at the Ballarat Veterinary Practice were happy with the surgery. I got the impression it was routine and that he'd be fine. Or was that just me being hopeful? They thought he'd be back at work in three months.

Margie and her husband Nick live in Geelong, so whenever I'm riding down there I try to pop in and say hello. Often they talk me into having dinner and that means I can relax and stay the night. Relax means have a couple of glasses of red, maybe a game of Pictionary and then another glass of shiraz. Not long at all after Prince's Flemington win, we'd settled in and the conversation turned to my plans for the future.

'It's just so dangerous, Michelle,' Margie said. 'You just cannot risk having another fall.'

'I still want to ride,' I explained to them.

'There's life outside of racing,' she said. 'More falls, and more fractures, and more injuries: what are you going to be like when you're older?'

I wasn't dwelling on that side of things. I was on a high. All I wanted to talk about was Prince. Prince this. Prince that. And then he did this. And then he did that. And he's so athletic. And he's so powerful.

'He just does things which horses don't usually do,' I explained. 'I really think this horse is good enough to win the Melbourne Cup.'

'Wow!' Margie said. 'And then what?'

'I'll retire,' I replied.

Well, Margie nearly jumped out of her chair with relief.

'Really!' She went and got her phone. 'I'm going to film this,' she said. 'Say it again.'

I didn't say anything.

'Okay, I'll say it,' she said. 'If you win the Cup on Prince of Penzance, you have to retire. All right?'

'All right,' I agreed.

She's still got that video on her old phone.

◆ ◆ ◆

We were all waiting for Prince to return to the track. I was getting lots of rides. Yosei did enough in the Goodwood, without threatening, for Stuey to push on to Brisbane to the big winter races. She was competitive in the Doomben 10000 and the Stradbroke Handicap at long odds, but didn't run into the prize money. Patrick also took some horses up there for the winter. I rode Turner Bayou in the Queensland Cup over the Melbourne Cup distance, and he won well. You don't get too many chances to ride the 3200-metre, so it was a good opportunity and I seemed to time things well.

Prince was recovering but he wasn't going to be back for the Spring. True to form, Darren was being patient, and was putting Prince's welfare first. This was one of the many reasons I liked riding for Darren, as well as the fact that it made Stevie and I work colleagues! He was doing very well with Darren and after six years was a real fixture around the stables. One night when I was at Home he was sitting at the table with pens and pencils and sheets of paper. He was looking very serious.

'What ya doing, Stevie?' I asked.

'Map.'

'Oh.'

'Yeah, I'm making a map. Of Darren's.'

'Oh, yeah,' I said.

'I've been putting the horses in the wrong yards, so this'll fix it.'

'Oh, good.'

'For tomorrow.' He wanted to get it right. Stevie always gave his best.

On Turnbull Stakes Day that Spring of 2013, I rode Platelet

in the Gilgai Stakes, a Group 2 down the straight at Flemington. Stevie was Platelet's strapper and being in the mounting yard with him before such a big race was very special. When they jumped she settled in behind the leader and travelled nicely. Coming to the 400 she was really motoring; she found the front and then sprinted powerfully to hold off the challengers.

Bringing her in was just fantastic. Stevie was really celebrating. He was absolutely stoked, and so was I. Everyone around the mounting yard was happy for Stevie. And it was one of those moments where you have to be grateful for people like Darren who have such a sense of perspective about things. Stevie felt like he was part of the stable, because he was.

Yosei also had a Spring campaign but she was coming to the end of her career. When she finished last in the Toorak I think we all knew her time had come. After an outstanding career, where she won three Group 1 races and was placed in three, she retired. She was always under-rated. She was incredibly brave, and she got the best out of herself. And that's all you could ask. We went well together. Coming back in that day and unsaddling her for the last time, I was so proud of her. She was off to stud.

Prince had taken a while to get back to the track but he finally had a run in December. It put me in a quandary as he was nominated for the same race as Sistine Demon, which I had ridden for two wins in his previous two starts. I didn't think Prince could win first up but he was my preference. In the end, Brad Rawiller rode Sistine Demon and won. Prince finished five lengths off the winner and his action was fine. I knew he would improve. I wasn't invited back onto Sistine Demon after that and he went on to win three of his next four. But I already believed in Prince and I wasn't giving him up for any other horse.

The family gathered for Christmas as always. The punch was excellent, if I do say so myself, and the soccer game full of magnificent highlights. A few days later I was riding Prince, who started favourite at Moonee Valley over 1600. He settled at the tail in the race and the pace was hot up front. They weren't the strongest horses in the world, so I was riding confidently—I knew he was better than this lot. I started to let him stride forward from the 800. Despite being seven-wide on the turn he sustained his long run and picked them up, streaking away comfortably.

It was an impressive win but I was keeping a lid on things. The lid was well and truly off for the Men In Hats and a few of the other owners. I was reminded numerous times by text message that the Cox Plate was also run at The Valley.

Prince won the Mornington Cup Prelude at Caulfield and that made him favourite for the Mornington Cup itself. He drew near the inside and we pushed forward out of the barrier getting the run of the race one back on the inside. I got him out at the 300 and we hit the front, but he couldn't sustain the run. He got swamped on the line, which was unusual. It was a big ask to have an inexperienced horse racing so forward in a high-pressured race, so it wasn't the worst run. I wouldn't hear a bad word about him.

He went to Flemington in early March, and raced forward again. He ran second but it was clear he wasn't quite right. The vets checked him out and, sure enough, after they did some scans, they found he had bone chips again. This was pretty concerning, and the odds were increasingly against us. How would he cope a second time?

Ian Fulton operated at the Ballarat Veterinary Practice and removed the chips without complications. Again, a full recovery was more likely than not. But there were still questions. Again, we just had to wait.

Prince recovered pretty well and Darren prepared him to return that Spring. His work felt okay and we were keen again. I drove to St Arnaud for a jump out. I was getting excited and so were some of the owners. Some even made the trip to watch. Darren Lonsdale, on the days when he wasn't working as a hospital theatre technician, was there. After Prince's run they were all standing around in a circle as I reported in. It was a sunny winter's morning and Prince had gone really well. I told them he was ready for his return to Caulfield. Everyone was feeling up. Darren asked me the question.

'He's gunna win the Melbourne Cup,' I responded.

They laughed, thinking I was just mucking around.

'That's two races you want to win,' Darren said. 'The Cox Plate and the Melbourne Cup.'

'Bit greedy,' I said. 'But, you know …'

They laughed again.

I was half-joking (at the most). I had such faith in him.

The whole stable was pretty excited. Two horses were being set for the Melbourne Cup—Prince and Signoff—and there was a healthy rivalry between the two camps. Sandy had a share in both horses but I reckon Signoff was his favourite, and not just because that's where he had the bigger share. Signoff is an absolute Rolls-Royce of a horse—and he is a joy to ride—so the general feeling was that Signoff was the better Cup chance.

Not for me, though. I wouldn't have it. My Prince was the one and I kept telling anyone who would listen. The comparison was a real talking point and it was fantastic for the stable to have two quality horses starting their Spring campaigns. If things went to plan, both were a chance to line up on the first Tuesday of November.

One day Jeremy Rogers, Darren's racing manager and a very old friend of his, and I were discussing the relative merits of the two horses.

'You blokes have got it wrong. I'm telling you, *Prince of Penzance will win the Melbourne Cup before Signoff does*,' I said.

'No way.'

'He will,' I insisted.

'No he won't.'

'I bet you $20 I have the Melbourne Cup in my hands before Signoff wins it,' I said.

'You're on.'

Prince and Signoff came back through the same races early in the Spring and while they were not expected to be competitive they still needed to run well. Prince especially, having returned from injury.

He didn't show much for his first three runs, so there was some doubt about whether he was as good as he'd been before the second operation. The conditions weren't helping. He was running on really firm ground and I didn't think he was trying. As soon as he felt the hard ground he would back off. I was getting really angry with the track managers. I wrote an article with Matt Stewart for the *Herald Sun* about hard tracks and the damage they do to horses, especially horses back from injury. I was very protective of Prince.

When VRC handicapper Greg Carpenter released the weights for the horses nominated for the Melbourne Cup, Prince had 50.5 kilograms. Signoff had been given 50 kilograms. I liked that. Greg obviously thought Prince was the better horse but when I mentioned that round the stables I didn't get much of a bite. At those weights both would have to perform well to make the field.

Prince's fourth start back was in the Moe Cup. He was a good chance, despite his mediocre form, and was expected to run really well. Unfortunately, on the day he had an abscess that, because of the bit, burst in his mouth. I could tell there was something wrong because he threw his head around like that day at Flemington. He still tried and when he got clear he finished strongly, but Count of Limonade was a neck in front.

If he couldn't win the Moe Cup, what chance was he against the rest of the world? But there were excuses. We continued to aim for the Melbourne Cup but we were a very long way off qualifying. We needed to win the Moonee Valley Cup to improve our position on the order of entry.

We drew the outside barrier and, with no obvious leader in the race, I convinced Darren we should lead. I just didn't want Prince to over-race behind a slow pace. Darren heard my argument and agreed. But when we jumped, the jockeys on my inside went forward and quickly I realised I was going to have to work very hard to get to the front. So I elected to go back. Going around the first corner he was throwing his head around everywhere and I was thinking, this is a disaster.

Soon after, he put his head down and switched off, and was perfectly relaxed. Instead of being first, I was running last! But you have to deal with circumstances as they unfold. The good thing about it was he'd never been so relaxed and I thought, If you finish as well as you do when you race ungenerously, Prince, what will you be able to do now? Going down the back straight, I had to decide whether to thread my way through or go to the outside. When I was at about the 800, I could tell the field was going to bunch and I thought they were all going to fan to get a run. So I took my chance and rode for luck. I knew Prince would take any gap that opened. Past the 600, I was following Precedence and jockey Glen Boss. Coming to the turn there were only three lengths first to last and I had Prince ready. The gap opened and I was in there. It was my run to take. I burst through, got around the leaders and shot away. Well done, Prince. We were a step closer to the Cup.

Unfortunately Chad Schofield had come down on the corner on Albonetti. There was an enquiry. I thought the second horse, Le Roi, had shifted from the inside to a horse and a half off the fence. But in the stewards' room I tried to explain what happened in a way that wouldn't get anyone in strife, and somehow took the blame. In blaming myself, I copped the charge.

When I came out, Brad Rawiller and Dwayne Dunn weren't happy.

'You go back in there and you tell the stewards that on the overhead shot there was a clear run for you to take, because they're going to get you for this.' When I was called back in to be charged for careless riding I pointed this out to Terry Bailey and his panel of stewards.

'I'd just like to point out to you that on the overhead shot there really was a run for me to take and I don't believe that I should be blamed for the interference.' The stewards weren't having any of it.

'You said there was no run,' they said.

'Well, I was pretty rattled, because there had been a fall, and as we were pulling up, Glen Boss had given me a spray for taking the run through a gap which he'd opened up. But on the overhead shot, you can see there actually was a full run for me to take.'

The stewards just kept going back to my original words. I made no impression. Thankfully, Chad was all right, that was the most important thing. Me, I was suspended for twenty-two meetings.

My heart sank completely. The horse I loved, and had complete faith in, was possibly going to make the final twenty-four of the Cup field and I was going to miss the ride through suspension. I had to do whatever I could. I had to appeal. I took it to the Racing Appeals and Disciplinary Board. When we lost there, I took it further, to the Victorian Civil and Administrative Tribunal. We had lawyers and documents and diagrams and footage and explanations, but it was all to no avail.

The idea of *watching* Prince in the Melbourne Cup was devastating. But I was still hoping he would get there.

◆ ◆ ◆

I was out for the whole Flemington carnival. It was very frustrating to be sitting on the sidelines watching. Signoff, ridden by Brazilian jockey João Moreira won the Lexus on Derby Day like a favourite should. He looked like a classic stayer who was right in the mix for the Cup. He was lightly weighted at 51.5 kilograms and was going into the Cup in peak condition and in hot form. Punters loved him. VRC handicapper Greg Carpenter thought Signoff had snuck under his guard, such was his improvement since the weights had been released.

The Melbourne Cup in 2014 was won by Protectionist, ridden by Ryan Moore. He exploded to the front over the final 200 and was by far the superior horse on the day. It was a very impressive win. João Moreira gave Signoff every chance and he ran bravely to finish fourth. Darren and Sandy were getting closer. I was still convinced Prince would win the Cup before Signoff.

Darren needed to find a replacement for me on Prince for the Queen Elizabeth Stakes. Hugh Bowman, a country boy from central New South Wales, now based in Sydney, took the ride. Prince ran second. It's the only time another jockey has ridden Prince in a race.

I came back for the Zipping Classic at Sandown a week after Cup week and again we thought about leading. Instead I sat third on the fence and he pulled terribly, really throwing his head around again. He didn't feel comfortable the whole way and in the straight when he wanted to fly we were held up. Once he was in the clear he still fought all the way to the line and actually came back to finish third.

Prince was due for a spell, but that was forced on him anyway. After the Zipping run he was very tender again, and it seemed he had yet another joint problem. He had to go back to the vets. The news wasn't good. He had bone chips again, in both fetlocks. When Ian Fulton operated he found they were very small and again the surgery went well. But the odds of a third perfect recovery surely weren't good, although Ian was really positive.

'He's made of good stock, this bloke,' he said. 'He's certainly more robust and resilient than fragile. If he was a footballer you could patch him up and get him out there. He'd have three hundred games in him.'

While we had the family Christmas at Home, Prince was put just up the road at Laura Dixon's agistment centre to recover. Ian thought he'd probably need about eight weeks. One morning, towards the end of January, Laura noticed Prince was unwell. He was showing signs of colic, which is simply a term for abdominal pain. Within hours he was in a bad way. Painkillers were having no impact and Laura was getting really worried. She called the Ballarat clinic and Nicola Lynch went out to see him. She thought Prince needed urgent surgery, as he probably had a twist somewhere in his intestine. The extent of the damage was difficult to know. If the blood supply to parts of the intestine was shut off a lesion could have formed and this would need to be removed. The surgeon would have had to cut the section where that lesion was out and the intestine be reconnected.

Prince went under general anaesthetic. Lying on his back, four legs in the air, he was opened up. All 22 metres of soft, sloppy small intestine were lifted from his abdomen and thoroughly checked. The twist was found and sorted. It had happened quickly enough that there was no lesion. The small intestine was put back into his abdomen. It really was major surgery. The success rate on small intestine operations is around 60 per cent. When you consider Prince was also coming back from a bone chip arthroscopy, the chance of him getting back to his best was probably less than toss-of-the-coin odds.

We had to wait again.

15

Gathering the troops

THE SUMMER PASSED slowly as I waited for Prince to recover. I wasn't hearing anything from his strapper, Maddie Raymond, or from Laura Dixon who was overseeing his recovery. That was good news. But I was enjoying being part of the Weir camp. Darren was going from strength to strength and with so many horses in his stable there were a lot of rides available.

Earlier in the year my friend Chris Symons, a jockey, introduced me to world champion surfer Layne Beachley and we got on very well. I found her inspirational. She seemed so genuine and I really liked how she was trying to help young women get started through Aim for the Stars, the foundation she had set up. When she asked if I would like to be involved, I was keen. Layne has an amazing story and the more I got to know her the more I wanted to do something with her. She knows struggle.

Born to Maggie Nickerson, who was seventeen at the time, Layne was adopted out. Then, when she was six, her adoptive mother, Val Beachley, died of a brain haemorrhage and Layne was brought up by another relative, Joan Tate. She grew up near Manly in Sydney. A brilliant teenage surfer, she worked three or four jobs to make ends meet, and to raise the money to have a crack at the surfing pro-tour. One of the restaurateurs she worked for admired her determination and helped fund her initial attempt to break into the professional ranks. She went on to win the world championship six times in a row and then, later, a seventh title. She is so generous of heart; I could only aspire to be like her. I was more than happy to do my bit to help. Besides, it was fun.

The deal was I was going to learn to surf, and Layne was going to learn to ride a horse. The idea of the swap was to generate some media interest, and that would help promote the Aim for the Stars Foundation race meeting, which was to be held in March at Moonee Valley. Even though I am somewhat anxious when it comes to the ocean, one day in February 2015 we went to Thirteenth Beach near Geelong, where the waves really crash in. I'd never surfed before but with some brilliant coaching from Layne I somehow managed to stand up. Then we got her on to one of Sandy McGregor's horses, King Krug, a fourteen-year-old thoroughbred who'd had half a dozen starts many years before. Layne did pretty well on the old boy.

With Darren's stables being at Ballarat I was seeing quite a bit of Dad during this time, often staying overnight before trackwork at dawn. Using Dad's place as a base also took an hour or so off the drive to country meetings in the Western District, the Wimmera and the Mallee. It was good to spend time with Stevie too.

Early that year Dad just wasn't himself. He didn't look well and there were a few signs he was suffering silently. He didn't have that characteristic optimism, his good humour, the banter with Stevie. I thought he was crook. We all did.

'You've got to see a doctor Dad,' I said.

'I'm all right,' he'd say, dismissing it every time. But he was getting worse. We were begging him to go to the hospital.

He must have felt shocking on the night of Saturday, 7 March, because he finally drove himself to emergency at Ballarat Hospital. He parked out the front, leaving the key in the ignition and money on the seat. He must have been in a hurry.

The doctors completed a series of tests that showed he'd had a heart attack. By the time Therese and Margie got to the hospital he'd been placed in intensive care. Further tests revealed three arteries were blocked. A few days later he was transferred to the Alfred Hospital in Melbourne but his urgent surgery had to be delayed because of the blood-thinning drugs he'd been on.

I was no stranger to hospitals and was very worried. We all were. It was the first time I'd felt Dad was vulnerable. The heart surgeon operated on 16 March, his seventy-ninth birthday. The next days in intensive care were awful for him, and for the whole family. He deteriorated so much that Maree came from Hong Kong and Cathy from Sydney.

Dad couldn't hold down any painkillers and the doctors couldn't get a needle into his veins to give him any relief. He was so, so ill. On the Thursday he just wanted something that would make him feel better. Of all things he could have asked for, it was stout and lemonade. We were worried this would not be good for him. We knew we couldn't ask the nurses and I started Googling to see if drinking a glass of stout would be dangerous. I think I was Googling 'stout and heart attacks'.

In the end, Dad couldn't keep the stout down and we had to try to hide the mess before the nurses came in and asked what was going on. Unfortunately, it was no joking matter. He was getting worse. I had to leave to get to Layne's Aim for the Stars night at Moonee Valley. Although the Weir stable was well represented, I didn't have a ride on the night. The race promoting Aim for the Stars was won by Nicoscene, ridden by Jordan Childs for Lee Freedman. It was a successful night, although my mind was elsewhere.

While I was away my sisters stayed with Dad. When I went to see him next, on the way home from trackwork on Saturday morning, he seemed even worse.

'Little Girl,' he said. 'I've told the Lord to take me. I can't handle this.'

I couldn't speak. I started crying.

'I've asked them to get the priest,' he said.

'Don't say that, Dad. You'll be right. This pain will only be for a short time.'

'They can't do anything,' he said.

'Dad. It's okay, you will be okay.' I'd learned a lot about inner strength from my father, and now I had to find mine to give to him.

'Dad, stop talking like that. You're going to get through this.'

'Little Girl, please,' he said. 'Will you get me the priest.'

Dad was so consumed by pain, he thought he was dying. I sat there. Feeling so close to him. Yet he seemed so alone. I needed to let the others know what was going on.

'I'm going to pop out for a minute,' I said. 'Can I get you something?'

He wanted stout again. It was breakfast time and no bottlos were open. I quickly texted everyone: 'You need to get in here as soon as you can. Dad's calling for the priest.' I took him back a banana smoothie. He couldn't drink it.

Nobody was ready for what was happening. No one could handle it. There were a lot of tears. We were concerned for Dad but we were also thinking of Stevie. How would he cope if Dad died? They were inseparable. Stevie sensed what was happening.

'What am I going to do when you go away?' he asked Dad.

'What do you mean, Little Boy?'

'You know, you know, when you go away.' Stevie was so sad, but he didn't want to say the words. Dad helped him.

'What, when I die?'

'Yeah, that's it,' Stevie nodded.

When I left, Dad was still in agony and the situation seemed grim. I had to prepare for the Bendigo races that afternoon. It was the Golden Mile meeting. I was in the spa when Dad rang. He sounded no better.

'How are you going with that priest, Little Girl,' he asked. 'Have you got on to him yet? Can you get him to come and see me?' He was serious. I felt I had to do what he asked. So I rang Des O'Keeffe.

'Dad's calling for a priest.'

Des contacted Father Brendan Dillon, the racing chaplain, and asked him to go to the hospital. Dad had known Father Brendan for years. They had met through Bob Skelton, a very successful jockey who'd also come from New Zealand and was a mutual friend. They would see each other at the races. Father Brendan was often at Caulfield and would come over to say hello. We all knew him.

Father Brendan gave Dad The Sacrament of the Sick. He heard Dad's confession, and he comforted him. He could see how low Dad was, but he also had every faith in the doctors' prognosis that Dad would pull through. I don't know what Father Brendan said—no doubt he prayed with him—but Dad really got a lift from spending time with him.

At the same time, the doctors had worked through Dad's gastro-intestinal issues and he started to feel more comfortable. He was over the worst and improving. We were all so relieved.

Later that night Dad rang me and I couldn't believe the change. He just kept saying what a lovely man Father Brendan was.

'I want you to thank Father Brendan,' he said to me. 'I mean, really thank him.'

I visited Dad every day and it was so hard to leave him. But he continued to recover and soon became desperate to go home. Eventually he did. I spent two weeks at Home with him.

Everyone else was busy with work, with kids and with just getting things done. And I wanted to be with him.

That time had a huge impact on me. Riding was not so important right then. It was part of me, but I realised my father and my family were even more important. I will never forget those days. Things felt so clear. I understood what mattered the most. I knew we were a racing family, and so much of who we are is expressed in our love of horses and of racing, but we are a family first. And I saw, even more so, that Dad had been our great example.

As Dad improved I returned to the track and, being more relaxed about my riding, I started to find form. I notched up quite a few winners. I still did the work, still did the preparation, still thought through the tactics, but I was willing to let things unfold. I was more accepting.

I felt, yet again, that things happen for a reason.

◆ ◆ ◆

I had a really good run through the first half of 2015. The Warrnambool carnival—three days of terrific racing, and a lot of partying in early May—proved to be very successful for the Weir camp. We all loved it. The Warrnambool region is perfect for horses. It has the beach as well as the lush countryside.

As well as the stables at Ballarat, Darren has a complex at a little spot called Wangoom, just outside of Warrnambool. It's dairy country, as it rains a lot there and it's green. A lot of Irish people settled in the area—probably because it seems like home to them. Some of the names of the people and the places there are so Irish. There's a town called Killarney, the river is the Moyne. There are country homes that make you feel like you're in Ireland. There are stone fences and Catholic spires. The region produces big families. Many of these people have been involved in racing.

Understandably then, the racing carnival is one of the most significant annual events in the life of the town and it includes some of the biggest jumps races in Australia, as well as the Warrnambool Cup and the Wangoom Sprint. People come from all over to punt and party and catch up with old friends, and are not disappointed. Darren has always loved it, and has had a lot of success there. He also loves the craic and can usually be found in the Whalers Hotel in the wee hours, rum and Coke in hand, chatting to someone. Everyone knows him. It's a bit harder for us jockeys. We have to behave ourselves.

That week Darren won the Warrnambool Cup with Tall Ship, and our resident Irishman jockey, Johnny Allen, saluted on Regina Coeli for Ciaron Maher, a Warrnambool trainer, in the Great Eastern Steeplechase. Jarrod McLean had a good time of it. I rode a double on the first day. The one disappointment was that John Richards' Lake Sententia didn't go so well for me in the Wangoom.

One of the attractions of Warrnambool was that it was a good chance to spend some time with the crew from Darren's two stables and, of course, to see Prince. Maddie was based at the Warrnambool stables; she's a Warrnambool girl. She'd filled me in on Prince's progress while he was spelling.

I did a lot of riding through the winter but I was getting increasingly tired. I knew I needed a break. It had taken me some years to realise that we jockeys need balance in our lives. As a young jockey I'd tried to push through the exhaustion. But the physical and psychological demands are relentless, and draining, and I'd worked out my suspensions and falls have often come when I was low, not as lively and alert as I needed to be. But I'd learned to read the signs and knew when it was time to get right away. Perhaps my falls happened for a reason, so I could learn to take a break. So I organised with some friends to travel to North America.

I travelled with Kelly and Rosie Myers, two Kiwi jockeys I'd got to know because their uncle is a good friend of Dad's and the two families have remained close, and their partners. It was my first trip to the States. We started in Vegas! Then San Diego, Mexico, then north to Canada. The couples then went home and I went to the Calgary Stampede. I hired a car and drove to Vancouver, staying in B&Bs along the way. I like travelling on my own as I always meet a lot of people, and love chatting to them, hearing their stories, like Dad does. I spent a fair bit of time wondering how Dad was going. He was getting better, but he'd had a tough time.

I was looking forward to the Spring. I had a strong feeling that good things were going to happen, and I was going to give myself every chance of being ready. I had to stay fit and not pack on the kilos. I made a deal with myself: party as hard as you like but you must train properly for an hour every day.

I was doing beautifully until I got to Canada, where I soon became addicted to chai lattes and these great raspberry and white choclate cookies they have there. I came home through Bali, where I caught up with a couple of jockey mates, Nikita Beriman and Holly McKechnie. We spent a week together and then I couldn't face going home just yet, so I extended my stay for another three days, catching up with Maree and Brett and their two kids, Georgia and Thomas, who were there at the same time.

Therese does my brother Patrick's race bookings. She texted me while I was in Bali: 'Do you want to ride Percy On Parade on Monday at Swan Hill?'

'Are you joking?' I replied. I warned them I wasn't fit even though I was keen and said yes. When I saw it was 2100 metres I freaked. I couldn't last that long. Six weeks away is a long time between races. Too long. Although I'd regularly done pilates and yoga and a lot of training while I was away, I was far from race condition.

Percy ran fifth but at least I'd had a ride and he'd had his chance, despite my lack of race fitness. Patrick was going to get stuck into me, I knew.

I was trying to get back into it but I wasn't getting any trackwork at Caulfield, so I went to Sydney to work for Gai Waterhouse for a few days. After initially coming home weighing 56.5 kilograms, I was 58 kilograms. I rode in a lot of trials, and worked with a personal trainer and we did a lot of traditional fitness stuff: medicine ball, boxing everything. I was eating more healthily by then and drinking lots of water. I always think positively so I felt it was only a matter of time.

Therese booked me in for five rides at Mildura, the lightest weight being 54 kilograms. No problem. I didn't check my weight for three days, I was working hard and eating healthily but when I got on the scales on the Saturday afternoon I was 59.5. I couldn't believe it. I had to lose 5 kilos in a couple of days to ride the horse half a kilogram over. Not a good start to my return.

As it turned out I was carrying a lot of fluid so I was able to make 54 kilograms without too much trouble.

I won my first ride but I'd had it by the end. I let him run well past the line because I couldn't breathe and I had to get back for the interview with the broadcaster. I felt I was back into it, but I was struggling physically.

Prince was still in Warrnambool. With not much happening at Caulfield I was happy to ride for Darren wherever he needed me to gallop his horses, all around the countryside. I did many kilometres in the car, to Camperdown, Casterton, Coleraine, Terang, Hamilton, Donald, all about three hours or more away. I especially travelled so as to ride Prince whenever I could. It's often a long way to go for a five-minute ride, one minute of which really matters. But it was all about building the relationship between me and him.

I was next booked to gallop him at Warrnambool in early August, and hadn't seen Prince since the carnival in May. He had turned six on 1 August, when all horses have their birthday. When I first saw him he looked absolutely magnificent.

'Wow, Prince,' I said. 'You've grown up.'

His head was mature, his body was mature, and he walked like a mature horse. I was smiling and laughing to myself. It was like seeing a puppy that's suddenly become a dog. In that moment I felt such affection and respect for Prince. Then when I was patting him he put his head into my chest, like an old friend.

Given he was coming back from yet another major injury, I was concerned about how he'd go on the track. But that day at Warrnambool he worked just as he looked, like a strong thoroughbred racehorse.

I was so excited for him. Darren wasn't there. He had warned me that he doubted Prince would be the horse I'd seen the previous Spring, but he looked better, he was behaving better, and he galloped fluently and powerfully. I couldn't get out my phone quickly enough.

'I reckon he's come back better than he was,' I said. Darren would not believe me.

'I've got to see him myself,' he said.

At that point I knew Prince's campaign would be planned with one trophy in mind: the 2015 Melbourne Cup.

◆ ◆ ◆

It was coming towards the end of footy season, and the better horses had started to return to racing in preparation for the Spring. They'd enjoyed their time in the paddock, eating as they pleased, getting chubby and hairy, before hitting the training track. It's a well-planned process. Trainers start campaigns by giving horses light work and then they're put on a program of trackwork, which gets the horse finer and fitter. Horses competing in the distance events later in the Spring, like the Melbourne Cup, resume in shorter races, and these are part of a horse's path to fitness. The trick is to get them absolutely peaking on the day of the race being targetted—the Caulfield Cup, the Moonee Valley Cup, the Cox Plate and the Melbourne Cup.

Bart Cummings was a genius at this; you can't ask more of a trainer than that. Darren Weir had built a reputation as a brilliant trainer, too. He knows his horses so well. He knows exactly where they are in their preparation and what they need to do next. He has the combination of science and art, the point at which rational thinking and gut feeling intersect to get a horse right.

Prince of Penzance was definitely a Melbourne Cup horse. He had the breeding, and he had the ability. His record was pretty good. He had the character. He was tough. Maddie always told me how tough he was, and how he just needed to stay sound. She rode him every day and she knew what a competitor he was, what a fighter he was. But he was coming back from major surgery, and the three other bone chip operations. Could D.K. Weir get him racing at his best? And would his best qualify him for the Melbourne Cup anyway?

For over 150 years people around Australia have dreamed of owning or training or riding a horse that wins the Melbourne Cup. The chances are ridiculously small, so you have to do everything in your power to give yourself the very best chance, to do whatever you can to make it happen.

That's how I was thinking. That's why I was determined to drive thousands of kilometres to the bush tracks to make sure I rode him at every gallop. Not too many people had noticed him and I don't think anyone had the belief in him that I did. When I told some of the owners that I thought we were in with a real chance they shared my sense of hope, but I don't think they shared my belief. We were one of many doing the same thing. But we had Prince.

He resumed in the Group 1 Memsie Stakes at Caulfield, a 1400-metre race at weight-for-age, meaning the horses carry a set weight depending on the age and gender of the horse. The Memsie attracts a strong field of very classy horses, many of which are targeting the main staying races towards the end of the Spring Carnival. Phar Lap won it in 1931. The champion mares Makybe Diva and Sunline won it. And Manikato took it out in 1982.

Prince drew an outside barrier and he was a bit slow out of the barrier, but I settled him at the tail of the field a couple of lengths off the second-last horse. Coming to the corner I was able to get onto the back of a horse with an unusual name, Weary, and he gave me a good trail into the race. At the top of the straight I thought I was going well enough to win, even in such a classy field, and as I pulled to the outside I felt like he was ready to fly. He worked to the line beautifully, but couldn't quite match it with Chris Waller's horse, the very talented Boban. That horse had an explosive finish and was much more suited to the race. Prince hit the line really hard, having come down the centre of the track, just two lengths behind the winner.

'Prince of Penzance has run out of his skin on the outside,' caller Greg Miles said.

It was a fantastic return for a horse that was coming off such a severe injury, a classic stayers' first-up run, storming home late against quality opposition. He really took me to the line.

A couple of weeks later, the Melbourne Cup weights were announced. Prince had 53 kilograms, which was pretty fair, really. Signoff was not nominated as he'd had some setbacks. Darren had nominated Prince for the Makybe Diva Stakes, another Group 1, at Flemington. On his Caulfield form Prince was well placed, even if it was so early in his campaign. He is a fighter, but Prince does not like hard tracks. I thought it was unwise for him to run if the going was too firm so I walked the track the night before. It was already rated a Good 3, so pretty firm on the ten-point scale, one being the hardest. The turf would dry out further before the end of the program of races.

I rang Flemington track manager Mick Goodie and asked him if he had any intentions of watering to take the jar out of the ground. I knew he wouldn't.

'No,' he said, 'and you're not going to change my mind.'

The conversation got pretty heated and I may have resorted to making my point with some colourful language. As a result, Mick had a word to the stewards. But, with the track so hard we didn't have any choice but to scratch Prince. It was too risky to run a horse with delicate legs that had endured three bone-chip operations. It's very frustrating to have to scratch a horse from one of the best racetracks in Australia because it's too firm.

Darren had nominated him for the Gold Nugget the next day in Ballarat. We ran, despite having to lug 62 kilograms, as he was the best-credentialled horse in the race by far. He ran fifth. It was a pass, just, but the weight had anchored him, as those very high weights will do.

As I was about to turn thirty my sister and I decided to organise a party at the Riverview Golf Club. Being a child of 1985—What a Nuisance's year, as they used to say up the bush, in reference to the Melbourne Cup winner that year—we thought we'd go with a 1980s theme, when the sisters were at their finest with their big hair, and large jackets with padded shoulders. We all love a party, especially one with a theme. I didn't invite a lot of people—family and family friends, the Loreto girls, a few people from racing. Darren was there, as well as a few other trainers, such as Andrew Noblet and Ciaron Maher. Everyone was in top form. Cathy and I had put together a dance to Mel and Kim's 'Respectable', which was more like a Kath and Kim in Moonee Ponds version. We hadn't told anyone about this, but when the DJ put it on, we took over the dance floor.

So, so eighties.

It was a fantastic night, but even though it was my birthday I took it easy as I had to be at the Monday meeting at Stawell to gallop Prince between races. Prince was always my priority, always at the front of my mind.

I drove to Ballarat and Darren drove me to Stawell. He didn't say much. Prince looked as good as he always does. Maddie had been riding him every day at Warrnambool and she was always impressed. Again Maddie wanted to tell me how strong and tough he was. She really shared my belief.

'He'd run through a brick wall, this one,' she'd say.

The other horse in the gallop, Our Voodoo Prince, was very handy. He'd won in Melbourne and had been considered good enough to be sent to Sydney to run in the Metropolitan. He was being prepared for the bigger country cups and went on to win the Pakenham Cup later in the year. Darren had his stable apprentice, Harry Coffey, riding him. Harry is the son of Austy Coffey, one of Darren's best mates, and the nephew of trainer Jack Coffey, who helped Darren get a start in racing. Harry is a fantastic young rider who has to deal with the challenges of having cystic fibrosis. He knows about chance. And he was nervous because he had to lead and was worried about setting the right pace.

'If you're going too slow or too fast, I'll come alongside you, and you just stay with me,' I said to him. I'd walked the track to find the best ground. The girls in the jockeys' room were laughing at me.

'You what! You didn't party last night, so you could gallop one. And you're walking the track!'

'Prince of Penzance might win the Melbourne Cup. You won't be laughing then.'

Harry and I took our horses out and just quietly I was a little nervous, too. Every gallop can make such a difference to a horse's preparation, for where they are, fitness-wise. If the gallop was too soft or too hard it could put everything out. We worked off from the 1000 and when we got to the 800 I let Prince go. He ran the last 800 in 45.5 seconds, a very quick time. He was extremely impressive. The signs were good.

His next start was in the JRA Cup at a night meeting at Moonee Valley. The United States was the favourite. Prince settled back and we had a nice run, fifth on the outside. The roughie Escado set a slow pace up front. When the leaders quickened, Prince laboured, and it took a while to accelerate, which was out of character. Then he ducked in. When I straightened him he hit the line about two lengths from Escado, which had kicked on to be the surprise winner. When Prince got into the clear he finished well enough, and he did cross the line with The United States and was holding him. I had the feeling he didn't like the firm ground and he was going through the motions. I knew he had more fight in him than that.

On Caulfield Guineas Day, two weeks later, he went to the Herbert Power Stakes, an important staying race for horses looking towards the Melbourne Cup. He was fractious in the barriers and then he came out awkwardly. He was four lengths last. Something just wasn't right with him. I let him get into stride before I tacked on to the back of the field. He made a run down the side of the course and then was really getting to the line, but all too late. The track was pretty firm that day too, and he had 59 kilograms. Later he was found to have irritated a ligament in his back. I'd say it happened when he came out of the barriers.

In the Caulfield Cup, Mongolian Khan took the honours. Trip to Paris flashed home along the inside to run second, and there were a number of impressive runs from international horses.

As punters were trying to make sense of it all, Amralah's name was now being mentioned. Prince had dropped right out of the conversations, but there were explanations. Or, as they say in racing, excuses. I still thought he had a chance in the Melbourne Cup.

16

Keeping the faith

I LOVE COX PLATE Day at Moonee Valley. All racing people do. It's the middle of Spring, the week before Derby Day and the Flemington carnival. Footy is long forgotten and racing is the talk of the town. Trackwork is exciting—not like work at all. Trainers are trying to get their horses right. Jockeys are vying for the best rides. Punters have been trying to stab a winner.

The W.S. Cox Plate is the premier weight-for-age race in Australia. It's regarded as the championship, contested by the very best horses in the land, and these days from overseas as well. It's filled with action and drama. It's my favourite day on the racing calendar.

It's an important day for the Paynes. When my family first came to Australia from New Zealand with Our Paddy Boy, he was good enough to be nominated for the Cox Plate. Our champ ran a brave third in 1980, the first of Kingston Town's three wins. But by then Dad had sold him to Robert Sangster and Colin Hayes was training him. But he always felt like one of ours. The race also means a lot to my brother Patrick. He rode Northerly to victory in 2002. And, of course, Prince and I had won last year's Moonee Valley Cup.

I also love the track. The Valley, as we call it, is different from classic Flemington, which is quite formal and so traditional. The Valley's a crazy shape, made to fit into the local surrounds, and you have to ride it accordingly. It's in Melbourne's older northern suburbs and it sits on a flat surrounded by 1920s homes filled with people who live everyday lives. It's Dame Edna territory. The back section runs alongside Moonee Ponds Primary School (where Edna Everage probably went), which for years has been a reference point for jockeys, punters and race-callers: 'To the school now, and Sunline is doing it magnificently, four lengths clear. Where are the challengers?' Just round the corner is St Monica's Church and convent.

I was pretty excited. Prince was in the Moonee Valley Cup again—defending his title. That 2014 win qualified him and continued to keep him high on the order of entry for the 2015 Melbourne Cup—high enough to be a good chance to get in. A win now would take the chance out of it. He would get a run in the Cup. I was pretty confident he'd run a big race. He was just slightly down on form.

The Sunday before the Cox Plate Darren had taken him to a meeting at Warrnambool for a hit-out between races. I was happy to drive the two hours or so from Dad's place at Ballarat. I wanted to see what sort of nick he was in. On this Sunday in October, the Warrnambool racetrack was very quiet. No one took much notice of Prince. He was coming off the eight-length failure in the Herbert Power but I still thought Prince had it in him to be competitive. He produced some nice progressive work and I felt that he was getting back to his best.

Darren didn't say much—again. I didn't say much. But we both thought he'd run well at The Valley.

On Cox Plate morning, when I walked the track, I felt the best ground, by far, was close to the fence. With the rail out 3 metres from its usual true position, I felt that bias was going to be even greater. The camber in the track, a slight angle, can propel you around the corner; you just kick off and it can save two or three lengths sometimes.

Walking off the track I ran into Peter Ellis, Darren's stable tactician. His job is to anticipate how the race will be run, to predict where jockeys will position horses, and what will happen as the race unfolds. He is very experienced, and a fine judge. I also got Deane Lester's speed maps, which are always very good. And I do my own.

Soon after, I saw Darren. We had ten minutes before I came out of the jockeys' room.

'Can I lead on him?' I asked.

Darren was unsure, so I suggested he have a think about it and that we should talk about it when we came out. When I emerged from the jockeys' room just before the race I spoke to the owners and said that I wanted to lead, but without firing him up. It wouldn't take much to get him going and if we could lead comfortably that would be perfect. Then we could take advantage of the track bias.

About twenty of the owners had gathered around and they were happy with him going forward. Owners generally prefer to see their horse up on the pace, close to the lead, and this would be a change from Prince's pattern of settling back. Leading still seemed the right option but in the mounting yard Darren said, 'No, don't change it, unless he gets there easy and without you doing anything.' He wanted me fourth or fifth.

When we jumped from barrier three I gave Prince a good squeeze after 100 metres, without stirring him up too much. I looked across to the outside and around and the other horses weren't going very hard. They looked like getting to the best part of the track without being made to do much work and, if he sat in behind them, Prince was likely to start pulling because I already had him out and going. So I elected to take up the running and lead.

He found a good rhythm. Darren probably thought that that's what I intended to do from the outset, but it was a genuine response to the situation. For the first half of the race I was rapt because he was going at a really nice tempo, quick enough to make it hard to take him on, but relaxed enough where he could give a good kick when I asked him. I was hoping to stoke him up and get him to pick up from the 1000-metre mark.

But, around the 1400, Kerrin McEvoy moved up around me on Gai Waterhouse's horse Bohemian Lily. He was looking for the lead, trying to find a way to win, doing the best he could for his connections.

You are kidding, Kerrin! I thought. What are you doing?

I wasn't giving up the lead at that stage of the race. I said something to Kerrin and he came back off me, so I was leading again. He just kept looking straight ahead. Unfortunately, though, that challenge set Prince alight a fraction early and then in hindsight I think I let him stride 100 metres too early. Hugh Bowman was stalking us on The United States. He picked his way through the field, cutting the corner. He had the sit, came off heels and went past in the final 100 metres. Prince had something left after the line and ran on well, so I had to pull him up. As I rode up to where Hugh Bowman was, The United States looked like he had had it from the run.

I was extremely happy. We'd had a really strong hit-out, which is what you need for the Melbourne Cup, and we still had something to offer. I was confident we had more left to give than The United States. Coming back in, the owners were delighted. It was obvious he'd bounced back to form. And Darren was happy enough. I wasn't sure about my ride, though. I try to ride intuitively and instinctively, and sometimes things work out for the best, sometimes they don't. But I always reflect on things. I always wonder: did I do the right thing? What could I have done better?

Later that day I saw Hugh Bowman in the jockeys' room.

'What do you reckon?' I asked. 'If I'd waited that bit longer, would I have won the race?' He didn't say too much.

'Maybe it could have brought his horse undone but The United States was tough.' Peter Ellis was somewhat critical. He thought Prince needed to be fourth on the outside. But second-prize money moved us higher up in the order of Cup entry, and because we didn't win we avoided a penalty. Handicapper Greg Carpenter gave The United States an additional 2.5 kilograms for the Cup. That's a lot.

I rang Patrick. He thought the run was good enough.

'It was fine,' he said. 'But if you're looking for perfection, you could have got your wrists down a bit when you were trying to settle him again.' Later, having watched the video a few times, Patrick got back on the phone.

'Hey, Stinky,' he said. 'That was actually a great run. I hope they decide to carry on to the Cup. I reckon he'll race well.'

I did too.

◆ ◆ ◆

That evening Prince was floated back to Warrnambool, a four-hour drive. When I woke the next morning I was concerned about how he'd pulled up after his Moonee Valley run. I sent a text to Jarrod McLean, one of Darren's assistants and in charge of Prince: 'How's Prince?'

I was getting ready to head down that way to ride some other horses for Darren at the Hamilton meeting. The phone beeped. 'Couldn't be better.' I was so relieved. Horses are such delicate creatures that you never know how they'll pull up, especially a horse like Prince. He'd been so susceptible to injury.

The phone then beeped again. It was a photo of Prince on the beach at Warrnambool, looking bright and well. He'd had a solid run at The Valley but not a tough run—perfect preparation for the two miles of the Cup. Jarrod was on top of things down there. He's a fantastic horseman, very gentle. He certainly doesn't overwork them.

I was still thinking about my ride the day before, still kicking myself that I'd reacted to Kerrin's pressure. But Patrick's phone call had been encouraging. The owners were also ecstatic. They were almost certain to have a starter in the Cup. But not everyone was satisfied I should retain the ride. When a couple of them raised the issue, Darren was quite practical about it.

'Look,' he said to them, 'if you take Michelle off, who would you put on?'

Prince had been given 53 kilograms in the Cup and not many jockeys can ride at that weight. More importantly, no one else knew Prince the way I did. Not only had I been on him in all bar one of his races, I had ridden him for nearly all of his track gallops. Darren and I had trekked around western Victoria to gallop him, around our home country, really.

That Sunday after the Cox Plate it took over three hours for us to drive to Hamilton, knowing we'd have to come back again that evening. So it was nice to win on Ha Long Bay for Simon Morrish. But I hardly rode the rest of the week after as I'd managed to score a dose of tonsillitis. I did do a couple of events. One was a launch for the TAB.com.au, hosted by James Brayshaw, Glen Boss and a couple of footy players, Hawthorn's Luke Hodge and Geelong's Steve Johnson. We were racing on mechanical horses. I beat Glen, then Steve beat Luke, and then Steve beat me in the final. He's a competitive bugger. The Melbourne Cup itself was also there. The photographers wanted shots of us with it.

'Glen, can we get a pic with the Cup?'

'No way. It's bad luck.' Glen wasn't having any of it.

'Michelle?'

'No worries.'

I wanted to see how it felt in my hands.

◆ ◆ ◆

On the Thursday I rode at Cranbourne but I was looking forward to Prince's last track gallop on the Friday morning, although it was going to be a massive day. I had to gallop eight horses for Darren at Terang in the morning and then come back up the highway for eight trials at Camperdown. Kyle Maskiell, an apprentice from Tasmania who was trying to find a master in Victoria, was coming with us.

Terang is near Warrnambool, so only about half an hour for Prince to travel, but a couple hours for us from Ballarat, so it was an early start to be there by seven. It's dairy country with plenty of rain, and the Terang track is usually in good condition and great to ride on. I'd won the Cup there in 2010, a day when the first four horses across the line were ridden by women. I was on Picalero, Holly McKechnie finished second on Lady Avacan, Lisa Cropp, a Kiwi, third on Crocodile Canyon, and Nikita Beriman fourth on Nicastral.

Darren had organised the session and track manager Michael Beauhayden had given the track a light water. The surface was perfect. It's a big track too, with a really long straight—quite like Flemington. With the Cup just days away, Prince needed a solid gallop. Darren paired us up with Dandino, a quality stayer who'd been set for the Melbourne Cup but had not qualified. He'd started favourite in the Geelong Cup the week before, running second to Almoonqith, which was given some hope in the Cup. Dandino was nominated for the Queen's Cup on Emirates Day, which he went on to win impressively.

Johnny Allen was riding Dandino. Johnny's an Irishman, from County Cork. He's a real horseman and since deciding to stay in Australia he's won some big jumps races, including that 2015 Grand Annual during the carnival at Warrnambool, aboard Regina Coeli. We headed out onto the track and Prince felt fantastic.

It was a sunny morning, but pretty breezy. That meant there were no flies, for once. Terang's right next to a chicken farm and there's always flies. And the chook shed has the loudest phone in the history of telephones. You can hear it all around the track, which always makes me laugh—it's so Australian.

'You lead,' Darren instructed Johnny. 'Michelle, you sit back a couple of lengths.'

We rolled off a nice strong canter from the 2000-metre and we went a mile at evens, which is 15 seconds for each 200 metres, and then worked into it over the last 1000. We just let them increase their tempo. I set Prince off at the 400 to join Johnny and Dandino head and head and he had plenty to give. We both built our pace to the line, together.

I couldn't get the smile off my face initially. But as I was coming back I spotted racing journalist Bruce Clark and his camera-man—they were doing a story on me and a story on Darren for G1X Racing.

'Oh, that was good,' I said.

Darren didn't say anything.

'Are you happy?' I asked Darren.

'Yeah.'

Nothing more was said.

A few minutes went by. Bruce Clark drifted off, and Darren was legging me up on the next horse.

'That's the best he's ever worked,' Darren said.

'I was thinking exactly the same thing,' I replied. At that moment I felt Darren had managed to bring it all together perfectly—just like Bart—that coming off his final track gallop Prince was going to peak on Cup Day.

After the trials at Camperdown—eight or so more rides—Darren dropped us back to Dad's. On the way back to Melbourne Kyle was knackered.

'Big day,' he said.

'It's not over yet,' I said.

'You going out?'

'Nah, I've gotta train.'

'What!'

He couldn't believe it. But I knew that if I was going to win the Melbourne Cup I had to do everything I could. And everything I always did.

As Kyle was flying back to Tasmania, I made my way down to the Aberfeldie footy ground, where I often punched out some interval sprints the best I could. Music in my ears: Pat Benatar's 'All Fired Up', 'The Fighter' by Gym Class Heroes, Rachel Platten's 'Fight Song'. More thinking time. Prince. Tuesday. Would we get a start? Just keep pushing the laps out. Breathe. Derby Day tomorrow. Prince was fit. I had to be fit, too.

After my run, I rang Andrew and told him about the Terang gallop.

'It's the best he's ever worked.' I was not able to contain my excitement.

'Well, I'd be surprised,' he said, 'you never know.' I could tell he was just as hopeful for me as I was.

After a gruelling day I climbed into the spa, which was a relief to every joint and muscle in my body. While relaxing I started to play the replays of the races of the European horses who were in the Cup field on my phone. I really liked the run of Max Dynamite.

◆ ◆ ◆

The whole Spring Carnival builds towards the four meetings at Flemington: Derby Day on the Saturday, Melbourne Cup Day on the Tuesday, Oaks Day on the Thursday, and Stakes Day on the second Saturday. The racing is fantastic—there's always drama. And it captures the focus of people everywhere. Melbourne is alive with revellers who have travelled from all over to be part of it. Spirits are high. The pubs and restaurants are filled. Newspapers and TV are full of racing stories. Punters are trying to find a winner. Everyone is making their Melbourne Cup Day plan.

The first day of the Flemington Spring Carnival, Derby Day, is regarded by many as the best day of racing in Australia. Big fields. The best horses. It's a festival day, like Christmas or Easter. I had one ride, on Darren's mare La Passe in the Group 1 Myer Classic. She had improved over her previous two starts and had surprised a few people by winning two Group 2 mare races—the Blazer at Flemington at forty to one, and the Tristarc at Caulfield. I thought she had a chance.

Making my way to Flemington, I was still wondering whether Prince would make the final field. Even though he was almost certain to, I just wanted to see his name in that list of twenty-four. The 53 kilograms he'd been given was a handy weight for him to carry. It was well below the weight of the European and Japanese horses that were highly rated on the international scale, and the classy Australasian horses who had come through the traditional derbies. The Caulfield Cup winner, the Kiwi horse Mongolian Khan, would have carried 56.5 kilograms had he started in the Cup. So, chance had played its part again. Prince's injury as a three-year-old meant he missed those classics and hence they did not impact on his record. Yet had he been fit at the time he would almost certainly have been competitive.

With various scratchings during the week, including Mongolian Khan to injury, Prince was number twenty-two on Derby Day morning. But that still wasn't good enough for me. Just after I walked the track I saw Simon Marshall, who was getting ready for his afternoon at the Channel 7 desk with Bruce McAvaney and Francesca Cumani. Simon was a fine rider and has always been very supportive. He'll take time to offer some quiet advice, or to comment on something that's happened. He just wants jockeys to be the best they can be.

'Will we get in?' I asked him.

'For sure.'

'How do you reckon we'll go?'

'He's hard fit,' he said. 'And, on the basis of your daring ride at Moonee Valley, you'd have to be hoping for a big run.' I suppose he thought leading was daring.

'Just ride him for a top-ten finish,' he said.

'I think we'll go better than that.'

'Well, I hope you do,' Simon said.

There was good racing happening all day. Darren took out the first with Mahuta, with Brad Rawiller on board, and Terry O'Sullivan's Patch Adams finished second for Steven Arnold. A Stawell quinella. Mentor and protégé! Darren was unlucky in the Lexus when Zanteca finished second for Damian Lane, after seemingly copping interference from Dwayne Dunn on Excess Knowledge. He protested but the stewards didn't overturn the result. Gailo Chop won the L.K.S. Mackinnon Stakes, giving Francesca Cumani her first Group 1 win as a connection, and the Derby went to the hotpot Tarzino for Mick Price and jockey Froggy Newitt. The jockeys' room was on Froggy's side as he'd had a run of outs. In the Myer Classic, La Passe, who'd had an easy run, got tucked away on the inside. She needed one crack at them and the run didn't come at the right time. She finished well back but her run was better than that suggested. She was a bit unlucky not to finish closer.

The barrier draw is one of the rituals of Derby Day. After the last race, and the final Melbourne Cup field is officially declared, the connections of the runners are invited to a room to draw the barrier for their horse. Barriers can make a big difference. Drawing an outside barrier makes it much harder for a horse to win. From a wide barrier jockeys have to use all their skills to get their horse into a position close to the fence. An inside draw can be enormously advantageous. So this is yet another aspect of the Cup where luck plays its part.

The chief steward, Terry Bailey, draws a number between one and twenty-four. That number signifies the horse. A connection of that horse—an owner or the trainer or racing manager, and occasionally the jockey—then comes out to the table where twenty-four mini-Melbourne Cups sit. Each has a number on its base, face down to the table. The connection lifts the little Cup and you can tell immediately from their response whether it's a good barrier or not. Expectations can be shattered in an instant. In recent years the draw has been televised and makes for terrific theatre.

Right from the time Prince had a chance, however small, of running in the Melbourne Cup, Sandy McGregor was adamant Stevie should be given the task of picking the barrier at the draw.

'Stevie can draw the barrier. That would be brilliant,' he always said. 'Stevie's our man.' Stevie wasn't usually Prince's strapper. Maddie Raymond did that job perfectly. But it seemed a good idea that they should share the duties on Cup Day. Maddie was so gracious about it all. She is a total team player.

Emily Lonsdale, the daughter of Darren, one of the owners, had had the same idea about Stevie doing the draw and had been chatting with me about it from the time we thought Prince was a Melbourne Cup horse. Stevie had been strapping all day for Darren. He freshened up, put on a maroon shirt, the colours of the Weir stable, and we all set off for the Phar Lap Marquee. It's a fantastic room to be in. It's full of hope and expectation and excitement. Everyone there has a runner in the Melbourne Cup. There are connections from all over the world. I was praying for barrier one or two. I was actually thinking two, as I didn't want to be too greedy. But one would have been the ultimate.

As we were walking in, Darren was joking with Stevie.

'Stevie, if you get number twenty-two just put it back!' Stevie laughed and gave Darren the same look he gives Dad when he's teasing him.

'One or two, Stevie.' I put my arm around him.

'I'll just get barrier one,' he said.

Racing.com broadcaster Jason Richardson was the compere. Richo is a very warm and friendly guy. (And he's no stranger to the world of racing and punting. As an athlete, he won the Stawell Gift in 1993.) Terry Bailey started the draw. After a while he drew horse ten and held up the marble: 'Trip to Paris.' One of the owners of Trip to Paris, Englishman Andy Gemmell, a sports fanatic, music buff, pub intellectual and all round ripping bloke who has been blind since birth, was helped forward. Andy chose barrier five. A great barrier for one of the highly fancied runners. He was rather pleased with himself.

Stevie was so nervous, really feeling the responsibility. And our number was yet to be drawn.

'Which area?' he muttered. 'Which part of the table?'

'Stevie, you choose,' I said. 'You'll be right.' I was loving the moment. My brother was about to pick the barrier for the horse I was going to ride in the Melbourne Cup.

'Number nineteen: Prince of Penzance.'

I thought I'd go up with him just for support. But Stevie shot out of the gates and strode towards the table before I could get moving. Richo spotted him and said, 'The best strapper in the business, Stevie Payne, is going to come forward and pick the barrier.'

I was no match for Stevie. As he was getting to the table Richo continued: 'Stevie told me he was after barrier one or two and he's picked ...'

Stevie leaned forward, picked a Cup, looked at it, and thrust it high.

'Barrier one,' Richo yelled, nodding, as if the universe was always going to deliver this moment.

The room erupted. People were cheering, clapping, laughing, even crying. Stevie was triumphant. I had seen the number at the same instant Richo had and had immediately given the thumbs up and then placed my hand on Stevie's shoulder. Our family was watching and recording it on TVs all around the countryside. Margie and Nick watched it over and over again. Patrick also just kept replaying it. Stevie!

There was media everywhere. Darren couldn't hide his delight, but he was cautious when asked about Prince's prospects.

'It's a great draw. Yeah, just happy to have a runner in the Cup. We're a good chance to finish top ten,' he told the press. Later, he said the same thing to me.

'We might win it,' I said.

'Oh, well,' he said.

◆ ◆ ◆

I woke up the next morning feeling terrible; the tonsillitis wasn't improving. I had a couple of nice rides for Darren at Kilmore, but I didn't want to take any risks. I never think like that, but I was worried something might happen and I couldn't stand the thought of not riding Prince in the Melbourne Cup. So I rang Darren.

'How ya goin'?' he asked in that classic Mallee drawl.

'I'm a bit crook, actually,' I said. 'If I'm going to be right for Tuesday I reckon I need the day off.'

'You do whatever you think's best,' he said. 'Just give the owner a call and explain to him, and it'll be right.'

◆ ◆ ◆

On the Sunday before the Cup the racing fraternity gather for a special racing Mass. It's been conducted every year since 1959. I have been a few times and my racing manager, Phillip Roost, always goes. This year Father Brendan Dillon, the racing chaplain who'd visited Dad in hospital earlier in the year, had invited me to come along. Walking into St Francis's Catholic Church in Lonsdale Street, I made my way towards the front and found a pew—beside the part-owners of Winx, Mr and Mrs Tighe.

'Congratulations,' I whispered, when I saw they had the Cox Plate with them.

'I'm going to have it blessed,' Mrs Tighe said. 'You should get your saddle blessed.' I thought that was a great idea, and quickly snuck out to get the saddle from the boot of my car.

It was the first racing Mass since Bart Cummings had died. Bart and Valmae Cummings had never missed it in previous years. They had always gone to Mass regularly. Their grandson James Cummings did the first reading, from Revelation chapter 7. Edward Cummings did the second reading, from the First Letter of St John chapter 3. The Gospel was the Beatitudes. It was great to hear Anthony speak about his father, Bart. After Mass, I went to see Father Brendan in the church courtyard and asked him if he would bless my saddle. That afternoon I took it easy. Margie rang me.

'I've got a really good feeling about this.' I could feel her smiling down the phone. 'I really do.'

'So do I.'

◆ ◆ ◆

Monday morning and everyone was talking about the Melbourne Cup. Trip to Paris was shortening in the market; people were debating the merit of the run of Japanese horse Fame Game in the Caulfield Cup. Some were criticising Zac Purton for his ride on Fame Game. Others thought it was the perfect preparation for the Cup. But so many names were bobbing up and, as always, it was hard to line them up. Horses from all over the world had form. There were so many in with a chance. I was waiting to hear from Peter Ellis and Deane Lester about what their speed maps looked like. Prince of Penzance was hardly being mentioned in all the talk.

I had to see Dr Mulkearns to get clearance to ride.

'You've still got a fever,' he said. Thankfully he thought I was fine and that I'd get through the day without a problem—I'd just wind up really tired. A relief.

Then I was off to the Melbourne Cup parade. Melbourne loves a parade, whether it's Anzac Day or the Grand Final or Moomba. When I got into the city I'd misjudged the weather, which is a very Melbourne thing to do. It was suddenly overcast and cold. I ducked into Target on Bourke Street and bought myself a long-sleeved cardi—a grey one for $20. Then I found the start of the parade. Darren Weir, Emily Lonsdale and I sat in the back seat of a Triumph convertible being driven slowly up Collins Street. People everywhere were waving. Cheering.

'Go, Michelle!'

'Go, Prince!'

'Go, Weiry!'

I doubt anyone was giving us a chance. We were just a colourful part of the story: the trainer from the bush, the horse back from injury, the only woman to be riding in the Cup. Photographers snapped away. Interviewers jumped out of the crowd with their mics and headphones. Thank God I bought that cardigan.

◆ ◆ ◆

There's always a stack of things happening on the Monday—all day. After the parade we went to the Palladium at Crown for the Call of the Card, a three-course lunch where the betting frenzy on the Cup begins. The booze is always flowing on the tables of friends and connections and people from the racing industry and punters and media, although many of them are working. The idea of the lunch is for the big bookmakers to open the betting on the Cup, by putting up their odds and adjusting them as the punters in the room place their bets. Bookies and punters have been in battle forever. Bookies try to take bets on horses that they don't think can win the Cup. Punters want to back the horse they most fancy and are looking for the best price.

Hamish McLachlan from Channel 7 was the host and when it came time to assess the chances of Prince of Penzance he called me to the mic to have a chat. He was trying to get a funny yarn out of all the jockeys but, just like Dwayne Dunn and Michael Walker, we had nothing for him. I wanted the crowd to know that I thought Prince was way over the odds at $101. If The United States was one of the fancied runners then Prince had to be in the mix as well.

Some of Prince's owners were there, and not overly cashed up. The minimum bet at the Call of the Card is $400 and they were falling a little short. There were no casino owners or American billionaires among them. Adrian Brown found himself sitting at a table with comedians Mick Molloy and Lehmo. They were per-suaded by his analysis of the form and his love of Prince—and I suppose I sounded confident enough—so the table pooled their resources and had $200 each way on him.

Across the Yarra at The Footy Almanac Cup Eve racing lunch at the Royal Melbourne Hotel in Bourke Street, VRC handicapper Greg Carpenter and Andy Gemmell were guests. Andy had a dozen arguments for why Trip to Paris would win. But as Greg worked his way through the field he didn't dismiss Prince. Again, he knew he was well-weighted and he was drawing the same comparison with The United States.

Other Prince syndicate members were at work, some were flying in from interstate. Quite a few had backed him already.

◆ ◆ ◆

I went home and had a short workout. To ride at 53 kilograms in the Cup I needed to get down to 52.5 kilograms. So I did a light workout in the shed then jumped in the spa. I was watching the Music Channel on the TV and playing Conundrum on my phone. I felt so ready, but I had to find a way to pass the hours, to stay relaxed.

There's a real danger at this point. I think people involved in sport at any level have the same problem; that is, of playing the game in your mind, of over-thinking it. That's what had happened to me with Azkadellia on Caulfield Cup Day. She's an outstanding mare and expectations were high. I was concerned with how our race would pan out, and I just kept running the race over and over in my head, imagining what might happen.

What I needed was sleep. I got into bed determined not to think too much about it. But how do you do that? How do you stop yourself? How do you accept that you can only prepare as best you can and then trust that it'll all come naturally when the race is being run? You need a plan but you also need to respond to the circumstances of the moment. You need to understand that some things go your way, and some things don't. Is that luck?

There I was, lying in bed, by myself, in a simple little house in the suburbs, thinking about it all. Again and again. About Dad. About my brothers and sisters, and what racing means to our family.

The passion we have for it. And the hard work we've all put in. And about how Dad helped us learn to believe that all we can do is give our best, and accept what life offers, by showing us his great capacity to accept.

'Racing people are good people,' he always says, 'because they know how to take a beating.'

Don't over-think it. Don't over-think it.

But then I let myself go a little and think about what I will say if I do win. I think of all the people I want to thank. Everyone who has helped me. I don't want to forget anybody. And then I run the race in my mind again.

I have to hold my position on the inside. I just have to get him to settle. If he fires up I have to get my hands low on his neck so he can get his head down and relax. Then I think, if we are coming up to the 600 and we're travelling, I am going to be so excited. So composure will be key. I know the race can be completely lost in just a few seconds by going too early or by pushing somebody out. Unbalancing a horse can be critical at that stage of a two-mile race. So I am thinking, if I'm in that position and he's travelling, just keep your composure. And be patient. I have to keep him balanced and the rest will come naturally, just as it does in every other race.

I feel so prepared. So ready.

Thankfully I fall asleep.

17

The day of all days

CUP DAY. I wake up feeling really rested, and really fresh. The best I've felt for ages. Which is something of a surprise. That makes me feel even better. I definitely made the right decision to have two days off riding.

I start with a workout in my gym, ten minutes on the cross trainer, followed by a hit-out on my equiciser, my mechanical horse that helps warm up the right muscles and really opens up your lungs for the day. Then a hot spa. I get in drenched from the workout and try to stay in for around an hour to sweat out the last of the weight I have to shed for the day ahead. I sip on soda water with a Berocca in it, or a mini Coke Zero, to help keep me in there, keep me sweating. To pass the time I watch race replays on the TV or play brain-training games on the phone. It can be a real mental battle at times but today I feel great—I'm so ready!

As I am getting ready to leave, Bernadette rings. It's out of the blue, because she never rings me on race morning. As a jockey, she knows it can be stressful when you're in the zone. But she tells me she felt she had to ring.

'I just wanted to tell you that I've got this incredible feeling about today,' she says.

'So do I.' I'm pleased she's rung.

Bernie gave me a little medallion years ago. Our Aunty Bertha, my mum's only sister, had given it to her when she was a teenager, before she left to go to Italy as an exchange student. It's St Agnes.

'You should take it,' she suggests.

'I will,' I assure her.

I go looking for it, but I've put it somewhere really safe—a little too safe, because I can't remember where. But I am thinking about the medallion. And about the way all my sisters are feeling about me today. I love the sense of expectation and possibility on the morning before the races—but especially on the big days. It's exciting. And it's even bigger on Cup Day.

All over Melbourne, and Australia, people are preparing for the day. Packing. Getting dressed. Having theories about who'll win: some have studied the form, some have listened to the experts, some have a favourite jockey or trainer, others like the names or the colours or the numbers, or maybe they use their kid's birthday to decide. Such diversity. I imagine the international connections in Melbourne's best hotels, waiting for their drivers to turn up. And I also imagine the Men in Hats crew looking for their myki travel cards and a bit of change under the couch cushions for the train to Flemington.

I back out the driveway. The white roses are in need of some care, but at least they are blooming.

I should do something with those four bags of potting mix down the side of the house, I think.

I *am* relaxed.

◆ ◆ ◆

I get to Flemington midmorning. The weather is perfect. At the jockeys' car park the men in green on the gates, always so friendly, are up for a chat. One has backed the Prince. They find me a park and I wait for the buggy to pick me up so I don't have to drag my kitbag all that way to the jockeys' room in my nice heels.

Quite a few of Prince's owners are already on the course. They've put a Prince of Penzance scarf on the Bart Cummings statue and sent me a photograph, along with another photo of Bart and me together when I was riding Allez Wonder for him in 2009.

One of my friends from Loreto, Rebecca Ludbrook, works for TAB.com.au. I do an interview for their marquee and then as I am making my way back to the jockeys' room, Neil Kearney from Channel 7 grabs me. We sit on a garden seat not far from the stabling area. Channel 7 also wants some short grabs for their pre-race coverage, so we do those too.

I am keen to walk the track. I change into my silks and racing boots and a Melbourne Cup jacket. I head back up the straight and wait around the 600-metre mark. Just after the horses of Race 1 gallop past, I walk after them. It's much easier to tell after a horse has galloped on the surface how far into the ground they go. The marks from the fence to 8 metres out looks the best ground.

I am riding Falamonte for Henry Dwyer in the third, a race named the Bart Cummings Tribute, over 2800 metres, almost the Cup distance. Falamonte is an outsider. Cantering her towards the gates I pretend it is actually the Cup. The crowd is already coming to life—all the food and drinks start to turn the lawn into a huge party. Sitting in the barriers, I get nervous. A few nerves are not the worst thing; I think it shows something matters to you. Every ride is a test of you. And I always want to do my best for the owners and the trainers. But I am *really* nervous.

It is silly. But it makes me realise I *am* being silly and that I need to stay composed. And that helps settle me down. Once we jump I am fine. Falamonte tries hard but finishes well back.

I need to make sure my weight is right. I have left myself with half a kilo to lose once I am at the races. It is better for me to lose it closer to the race so I am thirsty for less time. So while I'm still sweaty from my ride, I jump straight in the sauna in the jockeys' room. It doesn't take long till I am 52.4 kilograms, just under what I need to be for the Cup.

Then I catch up with Peter Ellis to talk about the Cup. He is confident Max Dynamite and Criterion will get the run of the race. From their good barriers they'll come across easily to take a position on the fence and he says we should follow them. We agree they are two of the better chances and they will bring us into the race. We want to be somewhere between eighth and fourteenth on the fence, smothered away with the nice trail, and then find a way into the race between the 800 and the 600. That's how Makybe Diva did it. If we can angle off we'll try to get as wide as is necessary to get a clear run. Once in the clear I'll wait for as long as I can before letting Prince rip. It seems simple. But so much can happen in an instant.

Peter wishes me all the best.

On the way back to the jockeys' room Des O'Keeffe wants to have a word. The men's jockey room is overflowing and he asks if he can put a few of the guys in our change room.

'As long as I like them,' I say, half-joking.

There's always tension among jockeys. You don't always see eye to eye with everyone over incidents in races, and when you appear before the stewards during protests and enquiries you have to state your case. The fraternity of jockeys is ultimately strong, but that doesn't mean you want to spend the last hour before the Melbourne Cup with them all. Des says he'll send the internationals in, which seems fine to me. No history there!

One is Gérald Mossé, who's ridden with Patrick in Hong Kong. He wants to know how Patrick is going. The others are William Buick, who is on Sky Hunter for Godolphin, and Ryan Moore, on

Snow Sky for Sir Michael Stoute. Ryan won the Cup last year on Protectionist. Both are quiet. Everything is going along smoothly.

I don't have much more preparing to do. I just have to wait, and stay away from the fridge in the jockeys' lounge. I can't drink or eat anything until after we weigh in after the Cup. Your mouth gets pretty dry after sweating and with the heat and underlying nerves you become really thirsty, but you get used to not having anything.

The jockeys' lounge overlooks the mounting yard. It has a couple of TVs, two bunk beds and a masseuse called Jose in the far corner. There's a big fridge full of drinks (not many get drunk) and a few platters of fruit, ham, salad and sandwiches.

All that is left for me to do is some final stretching and have another look at the form, even though it is all done by now. I know every horse in the race and where they are likely to race and what their pattern of racing is.

Layne Beachley has asked me to go in to her Aim for the Stars event. Generally, I never agree to visit a marquee between races as I worry about losing focus. But I know that what Layne is doing is really worthwhile and I want to help by doing an interview. Having competed in so many world championships, Layne really understands the position I am in two hours before the race. I am totally relaxed about the interview, and it seems to go well. There are a small group of about a hundred people and the room has a real intimacy and warmth about it. I feel I can talk freely about my family and being a jockey, and about Prince's prospects. I explain how I think the race will be run and why Prince has a good chance.

I must sound confident because, as I am leaving, they are all lining up at the betting terminal to back Prince. They wish me all the best, and send me on my way.

It's just over an hour until the Cup but next I have to find Dr Turf, who is broadcasting for SEN, a sports radio station in Melbourne, with Kevin Bartlett, the champion Richmond footballer and racing enthusiast, and anchor Kevin Hillier. Dr Turf is a mad punter and always looking for a laugh. He wants to talk about Bart Cummings.

'Bart gave me awesome support,' I explain.

'You rode a Group 1 winner for him,' Dr Turf notes.

'Yes, Allez Wonder,' I say.

'She was your first ride in the Melbourne Cup. Tell us about the nerves that day, or today; or is it just a matter of going through your usual routine?'

I explain how different I am feeling, as I only have to ride at 53 kilograms, and carrying just 50.5 kilograms with Allez Wonder my main focus then had been on getting down to the weight.

'This time I've been able to enjoy it a lot more,' I say. 'I'm feeling really good.'

Kevin Bartlett asks me if I will lead from barrier one, like I had in the Moonee Valley Cup. I laugh. I am happy to tell them precisely what I think I need to do to give Prince his best chance.

'Unless they go ridiculously slow and I land in front, I'll be three, four or five pairs back, along the rail. I just have to get him to relax. And then bring him into the race at the right time so he has one last crack at them.'

Back in the jockeys' room I find all three internationals are calm, too. Even though I am already calm, they seem to make me more so. Not long to go. We chat. I am with three of the very best in the world and they are asking me questions.

'Is this your first ride in the Cup?' They are so friendly. There is no frosty gamesmanship. They are just going to go out and jump on and give it their best.

In big races, when jockeys feel the pressure of the moment, the room goes quiet. In those last minutes before you go out to the mounting yard, to face your challenge, you are suddenly alone. I feel alone, not that I am alone. So many people have done so much to get Prince to this moment. I am the one who now has the responsibility of giving Prince the best possible chance. The funny thing is, this responsibility does not feel like a burden. I don't feel nervous.

Coming out of the rooms I spot Stevie and Maddie walking Prince around the mounting yard. It is the first time I've seen Stevie today and he looks so proud of Prince, and so thrilled to be strapping a horse in the Melbourne Cup. He certainly has his game-face on; he looks serious and mature, but at the same time he is Little Boy to me.

The owners are in the mounting yard enclosure, too many of them to greet individually, but I say, 'Hey, how're you all going?' We stand around together.

Peter Ellis is there and he runs through his thoughts for the owners' benefit, and I add mine, but basically it has all been discussed earlier and we are letting everyone know how we hope things will work out. I also have a look at Deane Lester's speed map and his view of how the field will settle in the running. It is almost the same as Peter's. I feel great confidence in those around me.

All of Prince's owners are completely rapt to be in the owners' enclosure at the Melbourne Cup, with *their* horse racing against the best in the world in our greatest race. Who wouldn't be proud! I think they are all pinching themselves that they have a horse in the Cup, especially the first timers. Even Sandy, who finished fourth in last year's Cup, seems excited.

'If we're in a position where we're a chance of winning, I'm just going to make sure I wait long enough so I don't go too early, and let's just hope for some luck and basically go out there confident we can give our very best,' I tell them.

They tell me to enjoy myself and ask me to try to run in the top ten! I am more hopeful than that.

I see Darren just before getting on Prince. He tends to stand back a bit, and leaves the owners to Peter and me—but he is funny.

When he thinks he has a good chance in a race, he can get a bit on edge but he is way more nervous today than I've ever seen him before. I have a little smile to myself and think, thank God I'm feeling calm, he'd have tipped me over the edge!

'Should work out perfect, what do you think?' I say to him.

Looking down at Peter's speed map, he says, 'Just stay on the back of Max Dynamite and Criterion for as long as you can, and try and run in the top ten.'

There is a pause.

'What do you think? Should work out perfect,' he says.

'Yeah, I think the same,' I reply.

I smile and agree.

We were both itching to say it.

'What do you think are our chances?' I ask.

'What do you think?' he throws back at me.

I have to say what I am really thinking.

'I think he'll run top five.'

'So do I,' he says.

And I reckon Darren Weir believes it.

◆ ◆ ◆

The mounting yard is crowded. I weave my way through owners and horse trainers and officials. Some jockeys are already up. Stevie and Maddie are leading Prince around on the grass. Prince, you look magnificent. How can you be one hundred to one?

Stevie is with Prince, concentrating hard.

'Hey, buddy, how ya going?' I ask him. It's the first time I've talked to him.

'Good, thanks.'

'Whaddya reckon?'

'Yeah, bloody good,' Stevie says earnestly. 'Nice and relaxed.'

'He *is* nice and relaxed,' I say to him and Maddie.

'He's been good,' Maddie says. 'Couldn't be happier with him. Darren's nervous, though.'

Darren comes over.

'Gee, he's relaxed,' he says.

'Sure is.'

'Looks great.'

He usually doesn't give much away but I can tell how much this means to him.

'It should work out perfect,' he says, as he legs me up. 'Good luck!'

We leave Darren at the mounting yard, and Stevie and Maddie lead me and Prince down the path, along the famous Flemington roses walk, out to the track. People are already going crazy, yelling, screaming, whistling. Some revellers are aware, some not so. It's noisy-party mode. I frown at them.

'Shhh! Shhh!' I am worried about Prince reacting.

'Shhh!' I don't want Prince throwing his head around. Once he's fired up it's very hard to settle him down. The yahoos keep yahooing. But thankfully he handles it pretty well.

'Good luck,' Maddie says. Stevie usually wishes me good luck as well, but he breaks from his routine.

'Don't get beat,' he says, 'I've got my money on you.' That makes me smile. He had $10 each way.

Once Prince steps out onto the track he is perfect. I get him moving. He is such a naturally athletic horse he doesn't take much warming up. He's loose from the start, so a bit of a canter and he's right. He rolls back up the straight, head down, as quiet and as relaxed as he could be. He is in absolutely perfect condition heading down to the start for his grand final. A true testament to Darren and his team to have him peaking but relaxed for our greatest race! I can't believe it is falling into place so perfectly. It all feels right.

Margie already has her position in the stand. She claimed it early, as she does. Cathy and Maree are in the mounting yard in the first place stall, funnily enough. Patrick is at home on his farm in Plumpton. Therese is at home in Essendon North with her kids and the next-door neighbour. Dad is at Home on his own. Andrew is watching with Jacq and Karl at their place but I think they are going straight to Dad's after, living as they do just five minutes away. Bernadette is in the members' stand with some friends. The Loreto girls are dotted all over the place: Stephanie in the car park; Stacey in a marquee; Liz and Jackie somewhere.

Glen Darrington, a former jockey and now one of the barrier attendants, will be loading us into barrier one. He leads us around a bit and gives me a bottle of water. I have a few sips, wetting my mouth, which is pretty dry, spitting most of it out so I don't put on any weight but allowing a little bit to trickle down my throat. Snowy, another barrier guy who always looks after me so well, wishes me good luck as we walk around waiting to be called up. Prince is still really relaxed. I ask Corey Mallyon, one of the starters, if I can get a man back up with me before we jump. Just to make sure I have Prince right as we have to wait till all the other horses are loaded.

'No worries,' he says.

'Michelle Payne: barrier one.' We are led in.

'Frankie Dettori in two.'

Frankie comes in next to me on Max Dynamite. It's funny to be next to Frankie after meeting him in Dubai all those years ago and then on the platform at the Newmarket railway station a few years later. And here we are, side by side, in the barriers before the Melbourne Cup.

Racing can be so cut-throat, but in this moment, it is rather friendly. We are having a bit of a joke. Usually I'm so in the zone I won't say anything unnecessary to anyone, worried I am not concentrating enough.

João Moreira comes in on The United States in three, Michael Walker is then loaded on Criterion in barrier four, and Frankie and I are chatting away as if it is just another race.

'Make sure you give yours a good ride,' I say, 'coz I'm following you all the way.'

He smiles and gives a bit of a laugh.

'What are you doing after the race?' he asks.

'I told you before—I'm going to be celebrating. You coming?'

We have quite a wait for the twenty other horses to be loaded. It can be an issue if you have a fractious one but Prince is calm—and I am calm. Everything is silent for a moment. I think of Bart for a second. Then I think of my mother. I always feel like Mum's with me, looking after me.

Prince hasn't moved. He is standing straight. Nothing like Caulfield and Moonee Valley, when he was all over the place. I'm thinking maybe I don't want to upset him by getting a man up. If he gets a bit irritable before they jump and I miss it, I'll blame the man. Patrick is the same. He never wants to create an excuse.

As the horses are coming into the outside barriers I call out to the starter, Paul Didham, 'Don't worry about a man, I'm all right.'

'You sure?' he yells back.

'Yep, he's right on his own.'

The last couple of horses go in and we are ready.

'Are you right, Michelle?' Paul Didham calls. 'Do you want a man?'

'No, I think he's right.'

Prince feels like he is going to jump even though he is being really quiet.

'All clear.'

Crash!

The gates open, and … he walks out like an old steeplechaser: just what I didn't want to happen.

I am cursing myself, which is not the best thing to be doing for the first few strides of a Melbourne Cup, especially when so many have done so much to get us to where we are. Unfortunately, where we are is three lengths behind the field. And in danger of losing the spot that was ours for the taking. Frankie has brought Max Dynamite straight across to the rail, no trouble at all, and now I have to make a decision: do I still hunt Prince up to get on the back of Max Dynamite?

Righto, I say to myself, I'll get him there, but I won't fire him up. Yeah, sure.

I gotta give you a squeeze, Prince.

I click him up, and he goes forward. I haven't even heard the roar of the crowd. I am so focused on Max Dynamite and Frankie.

Michael Walker has Criterion across too. He's on the fence in front of Max Dynamite. From barrier five Tommy Berry has Trip to Paris one off the fence, outside Criterion.

I get Prince in behind Max and I'm concerned he's going to race fiercely. Coming onto the course proper Prince wants to throw his head around a bit, but he's not too bad. I'm telling myself to get my hands on his neck so he'll tuck his head down and relax. Easy, boy. He's not quite settled but now he's not throwing his head up in the air either.

There isn't a lot of speed going down the straight for the first time. If anything, the speed is slackening. I keep bringing him back under me.

The speed is still slackening. What are they doing up the front? But no one's copping any backwash; everyone has time to steady.

Round the corner and I have to bring him back again. He's getting strong. He wants to show us he's an athlete, a powerful athlete. But he needs to relax.

'Hey, Prince,' I think, 'hey, your time will come.'

I'm sitting on him, wishing the best for him and us and every-one. But I still can't get him to relax. He can sense the horses around him. He can hear them, feel them, even if he can't see them with his blinkers on. He's a competitor and he wants to race now, and I want him to wait. Up the back and he's wanting to race. But I've still got hold of him and he's in a rhythm and his breathing is fine.

I'm calm. And things are going to plan. Sort of.

Kerrin McEvoy is second, up outside the leader, and Brett Prebble is three wide outside me, on Bondi Beach. I look across. Damn it. Brett's got Bondi Beach switched off, totally relaxed. And I'm pulling.

Forget about them. Forget about them all. Run your own race. Prince and me.

I'm doing my very best to stop Prince from racing too keenly. As I sit there, all muscles straining, I am grateful for all the training I have done for this day. It's all come to the fore. I can do this! He's still in a rhythm. He's not reefing and tearing. It's okay. It's okay. It's okay.

It's quiet. There's no voices. There's no interference. No jostling. Jockeys aren't calling out. Everybody is in their position. Just the thunder of the horses.

At the 1400 the leaders steady again. What's happening? It's already been a slowly run race. No pressure. How much longer? Who's going to move?

Frankie's got Max going well. Criterion's going well for Michael. I can hear Darren's voice in my head: 'Stay on their backs.' I can hear Peter Ellis's: 'Stay on their backs.'

We've picked the right horses. We're in the right place. We're in that sweet spot. Makybe's spot. We're about eighth. And Prince is travelling.

Composed, stay composed.

Follow Max.

Composure.

Just ahead, Trip to Paris looks really strong. Tommy Berry pops Trip to Paris off his one-out trail and urges him forward, three-wide, to the outside of Snow Sky. At the 1000 there's a nice gap in behind Trip to Paris. Three-out Sky Hunter is starting to feel the pinch. If I get off the fence, I'll be on the back of Trip to Paris and he will drag me into the race. I've gotta take that one. I just have to take that gap.

Trust your instinct. Just get on Trip to Paris's back and see what happens.

I'm worried about Jimmy Cassidy on Grand Marshal behind me but Jimmy isn't saying anything. No one's calling me. I get on the back of Trip to Paris very easily. We're in this, Prince. We're right in this.

Sky Hunter's on my outside, battling away. Trip to Paris is second favourite and he's about to extend. I am trying to be patient again. I'm really travelling. Prince has so much to give but I don't want to come off the back of Trip to Paris too soon. I don't want to go too late either. The horses running on from the back might box us in. I don't want to bump Sky Hunter getting out. I can't afford to take any energy out of Prince.

I keep a straight line on the corner, like a tangent to the curve of the bend. Sky Hunter drops off and drifts out under pressure. Suddenly I've got heaps of room and I'm bolting.

I pull out. I've got a lap full of horse and a clear run and I'm looking up the Flemington straight. As I get Prince into the clear the wind hits me. Oh no. I should've stayed on Trip to Paris's back for longer. Oh well, too late now.

I've got him in the right position but I don't want to go. Yet. He's building but I haven't let him go. Hold him together. Count to ten. Count to ten.

There's a lot of shouting inside and behind me. It's nothing to do with us. We're going too well.

Approaching the 300 I let him go.

'Yah! Yah! Prince! Yah!'

Prince sprints. I go past Trip to Paris easily.

I've hit the front in the Cup. I've hit the front in the Melbourne Cup. Then everything goes silent.

'Keep going, Prince. Keep this run going. Brilliant, Prince. Brilliant.'

There's action on the inside. Criterion makes his run. Something's coming from behind. It's Max Dynamite. As he makes a dash at us, I swap the whip into my left hand. It's totally instinctive. It straightens Prince up. He's going as well as anything else and he fights off Max. We hit the line. I raise the whip.

'Oh my God!' I feel an overwhelming sense of …

I think I feel …

◆ ◆ ◆

'Well done!' Frankie calls. But Prince is still running, as he always does. And only one horse comes near us. It's Damien Oliver on The Offer. He congratulates me.

For a moment Prince and I are on our own. I pat Prince. This magnificent athlete who, despite patched-up legs and no one noticing him, comes out and wins the Melbourne Cup.

I pull Prince up. Channel 7's Sam Hyland comes over, perched up on his horse, Brian, mic in hand. He's absolutely beaming. We're looking at each other.

'Can you believe that?' he asks.

I feel … this overwhelming sense of fullness, of completeness. And gratitude. I catch my breath and say to Sam:

I was lying in bed last night and I gave myself a chance. I thought what if I'm talking to you after the race? What he's been through! Darren Weir: unbelievable trainer. To get him here today. All of the staff. Jarrod McLean. Maddie. Tyson. Everyone down at Warrnambool. They got this horse here in the best shape he could be in. The owners: I'm so thankful, and grateful to them. When I was on the horse as a three-year-old, he won and I thought, 'This is a Melbourne Cup horse.' He just felt he'd run the two miles out *that strong* but, far out, I didn't think he'd be this strong. John Richards: he stuck up for me. Jeremy: Darren's racing manager. And Stevie: Stevie drawing barrier one is the key to this.

Back in the mounting yard Stevie is being interviewed by Neil Kearney for Channel 7. Stevie sums it up beautifully: 'Great moment. Great win. Great ride. Ten out of ten.'

Neil says, 'You've won the Melbourne Cup.'

'Yesss! We've finally got one in our hands,' Stevie replies.

◆ ◆ ◆

I start the walk back along the path, along the roses, waving to the crowd.

People are cheering, some are just standing and clapping and calling to me.

People are taking photos.

I throw my goggles into the crowd.

People are yelling from the inside of the track, calling for a wave. I'd forgotten about them—some from Layne's marquee perhaps. As I looked across I noticed Red Cadeaux for the first time. He's been injured and has been pulled up before the line. My heart sinks. The screen is already out and he seems to be in a lot of trouble.

Stevie and Maddie appear to lead Prince back. I feel so close to Stevie. He just says, 'Well done.' He is so excited. He holds the sash above his head like a soccer fan. People are so happy for us. I am giving the thumbs up. Maddie walks behind. She is trying to hold it together.

'Can you believe that?' she says, with her huge smile.

John Richards meets me at the gate. He's not an overly emotional man, but he can't speak. When I jump off I fall into Stevie's arms and we give each other a massive hug and a kiss. My brother! He has tears in his eyes, the first tears of joy I have ever seen Stevie cry. It is beautiful.

'This is because you drew barrier one,' I say to him.

'Well done,' he says again. We both have things to do, so that is all we have time to say.

My sisters appear! I am not expecting that. They are all kissing me and we are all crying. Chief steward Terry Bailey is letting me enjoy a few seconds but he has to step in.

'Right, Michelle, let's get you on the scales and get everything out of the way, and then you can get back to the congratulations!'

After I get off the scales I see Nick, because he's so tall. He is jumping over the top of everyone.

'Michelle, I can't believe it.' He is thrilled.

Kerrin McEvoy is there, happy for me and so animated. Then Brett appears. They are as excited as my sisters.

People are photographing the Payne girls, arms in the air. It is pure joy. And a fair bit of pandemonium.

Darren is being interviewed but we embrace.

'Thank you,' I say.

'Well done,' Darren says. And I don't see him again until we are all on the podium.

The Channel 7 guys grab me. Suddenly I am in a huge crush of media, with Channel 7 mounting yard commentator Peter Donegan trying to hold his ground, and sort of shepherd me. We face the camera, and digital recorders and mics come out from everywhere. I am not really thinking about where my words are being heard. I am just telling the story—to Peter.

'The most funny thing,' I start, with the finest grammar I can muster in the moment, 'is that my sister Margie and I had a feeling I was going to win. Then we said, "Don't be stupid, it's the Melbourne Cup!"'

The Channel 7 guys get the scrum to back off so we have some space and I relax:

> I can't believe we've done it. To think that Darren Weir's given me a go. It's such a chauvinistic sport. I know some of the owners were keen to kick me off Prince and John Richards and Darren stuck really solid with me. I put in all the effort I could. I galloped him every gallop he had and did everything I could to stay on him because I thought he had what it takes to run a race in the Melbourne Cup. I just can't say how grateful I am to them and I just want to say to everyone else to 'get stuffed' if they think women aren't strong enough because we just beat the world.

There are more photos and people to greet. Hugs. Kisses. Handshakes and high fives! As I am walking back to the jockeys' room, I wish I'd mentioned Johnny Allen—damn!—and a few other things.

By then Des O'Keeffe, Sarah Peatling from Racing Victoria and jockey Chris Symons are looking after me. They have at least seen the mayhem before, and know I'll be mobbed and my mind will be all over the place—they are like theatre nurses in post-operative care. I race into the jockeys' room to freshen up a little. Just to catch my breath. And make sure the hair is presentable. I can hear the presentation has started so I get out there as quickly as I can, making my way to the podium. I spot Jarrod. We embrace the moment and I thank him for all his input in getting us to this moment. I find my place between Stevie and Darren. It's the first time I've had a real chance to speak to Stevie, so nothing can stop us from chatting away. We can't help it. He is so stoked. Then it's my turn to approach the mic:

I'd like to say that, you know, it's a very male-dominated sport and people think we're not strong enough and all the rest of it. But, you know what? It's not all about strength; there's so much more involved with that—it's getting the horse into a rhythm, it's getting the horse to try for you, it's being patient. And I'm so glad to win the Melbourne Cup. And hopefully it'll help female jockeys from now on to get more of a go because I believe that we sort of don't get enough of a go and hopefully this will help. I wanted to thank also my manager Phillip Roost. He's an enormous support for me because it's always so nice to have somebody to talk to when you finish your day that actually cares about everything that's happened and he's always there whenever I need him. As well as my first-ever manager, Joan Sadler. She'll be so proud today and I can't thank her enough for what she's done for me. Lastly, but not least, I'd like to thank my family—my dad and all of my brothers and sisters. Especially Stevie. It was a dream come true to pick barrier one and how it all worked out, and it was so funny when he let me go, he said, 'Don't get beat, I've got my money on you!' So … so proud that I could get the job done for him today. So, thank you very much and, yeah, it's just unbelievable. Thank you.

Stevie is a star. He is presented with the Tommy Woodcock Trophy for the best strapper. He steals the show.

'Thanks to everyone at the stables,' he says, 'and all the crowd we had at the races here today. I hope you have a good night.'

Well, it is going to be a good night.

◆ ◆ ◆

Soon after, the press conference is underway and I walk in late. I sit down. Darren and Sandy give the win a very Australian flavour. If the world has never heard of Berriwillock and the dusty Mallee, it is about to. The pub's been shut a few months but the best bet of the day is that it's about to open again. It's time to celebrate.

The three of us, off farms in country Victoria, each with a love of horses and racing, and an understanding that if you are keen enough and determined enough and capable enough you can win the Cup. There is admiration and affection for Prince, and for Darren's ability to have him perfect on the day. He has been 'through the wars', as Darren explains. When I am asked what impact a woman riding the winner will have I am circumspect: 'I don't know whether it will help but I certainly hope it does.'

I haven't seen the replay of the race so I go off to the Stewards' Room and watch it. How deeply satisfying it is.

Layne and Kirk Pengilly, her husband and INXS band member, find me. They are so happy, so happy for *me*. Kirk is keen to show me the photo he took before the race as I was off to the barriers.

'Look at this!' I am riding Prince in front of the big screen on the inside of the track and the caption reads 'Who will be king!'

'That's funny,' I say.

We have to do so much media. Stevie and I tape an interview for *7.30* with Leigh Sales. I have a shower and I do more media in the mounting yard, and then I get rushed off to do yet another interview, for *The Project*. They are waiting for us.

At home we watch the replay again and then we go to The Emerald pub, where there is another line-up of media—about five or six different TV and radio stations before I even get in there. Sarah Peatling looks after them.

The Emerald in South Melbourne is a classic old Melbourne pub—a racing pub—perfect for the Prince of Penzance crew. My sisters are there and all our friends, and Darren and the owners. We are asked for so many photos. It's really hectic.

Margie and I get the chance to spend a moment together, thinking about Mum. We thank her. I finally got a chance to ring Dad, too.

'How'd you go?' he asks.

'Well, I got to pack my bags and come home,' I say.

He laughs.

The party is in full swing. People are drinking from the Cup. My Loreto friends arrive and we sit out the front together. They bring me a nice bottle of champagne—which they get stuck into, of course. I am drinking water, because I think if I have a drink I will fall into a hole. I also have to ride in the next day's race at the Kyneton Cup and get up at 5 a.m. the next morning for interviews. And I haven't eaten. I'm also drinking water because I want to remember every second.

I want to remember the joy in the pub, among the people; the feeling of connectedness. I am happy to watch their faces and listen to their conversations, which get more and more animated. To hear yet another cheer go up for Prince and a toast raised to the Boy from Berriwillock.

We Loreto girls decide we should do something to mark the occasion. We agree that we'll all do our very best to spend a week in Bali together between now and Christmas. We can't even find a night to have dinner together, yet I have a feeling we will all make this happen.

With the owners showing no sign of moving, and the Weir contingent organising to get back to the stables in Ballarat for the second act of the celebrations, it's time for me to go as well. On the way home I order a pizza—a meat-lovers with pepperoni from my local in Essendon. I get home after midnight. I am on my own again. Eating pizza—the rarest of treats. Watching the replay—again. Prince and me. Darren. Stevie. Maddie. Everyone.

What a day. I drag myself to bed. I lie there, thinking, again. Feeling so blessed. Trying to make sense of it all. Believing there was something absolutely right about the day. Believing that this has happened for a reason.

18

What a chance

I T FELT PRETTY good to wake up on the Wednesday morning knowing there was a little Melbourne Cup next to the salt and pepper shakers on the kitchen table. Even if it was five in the morning and I'd only had a couple hours of sleep—and I had to get ready for what I was warned was going to be a crazy day.

I stood in the shower, shaking my head and smiling, still overwhelmed with a feeling of gratitude. If I hadn't been certain of it before, I am now convinced that many things that have happened in my short lifetime have happened for a purpose.

So many things came together in the moment of Prince's triumph that it feels like it was truly meant to be. It caused me to start asking, why me? I wondered how I could use the moment to help other people.

Little did I realise that the moment had *already* helped a lot of people. But I soon learned. I received dozens of messages of congratulations and support—and that was just from people who knew my phone number. They were about how inspirational they found the win. How when I reached down to Stevie they cried, because the family moment was as important as the victory, and those elements were all wrapped up together. How what I said about the place of women in racing touched them. But, mainly, they are all just so happy for me, and just happy. You can hear it in their voices. So many messages start with, 'Can you believe that?'

That's exactly what Margie said after the Cup, and I wondered whether she was going to start hassling me about retiring. Where did she put that phone recording? Did I really say I was going to retire? I am certainly not thinking about hanging up the saddle now. If anything, I think the Cup win might open up *more* riding opportunities. But this isn't the time to be thinking about that.

There are messages from Kelly and Rosie Myers, who tell me they were in the jockeys' room in New Zealand. They said the room went quiet at the 300-metre mark and when I crossed the line it exploded. Tears flow over the phone from Jade Darose, who had just ridden a winner at Echuca and was on the Bolte Bridge near the centre of Melbourne, on her way home, when I crossed the line. Tears also from Liz Francis, who was at Flemington with family and friends—the first time she has ever been to the Cup. Emily was in an Australian bar in New York with dozens of expats and backpackers, cheering me on. The Daltons in north Queensland were drinking champagne and having a few nibbles when Prince came home. While they were going crazy the dog ate the entire cheese platter. Aunty Bertha in New Zealand tells me she was in tears. The Men in Hats were dancing. Neil Laws, whose celebratory dance after the Moonee Valley Cup win posted on YouTube had won him the moniker 'Australia's happiest bogan', was even happier. Patrick sat at home shaking his head. Dad got more phone calls in an hour than he'd had in the previous six months.

With the sun barely up, Sarah and Des O'Keeffe take me down to Riverside Golf Club and we find a nice spot for the TV crosses.

I do interview after interview after interview. I lose count but I am told it's about thirty. They are all a blur but I reckon they have some common themes: have faith that life will serve you well, pursue your dreams with all your heart, fight through your setbacks, prepare as best you possibly can, and hope things go your way. And if they do, however you understand that, be thankful and do what you can to share that joy. Above all, be grateful for your blessings.

Roger Federer once said something that has stuck with me: 'It's nice to be important, but it's more important to be nice.'

I am a jockey, but it seems people are interested in what I have to say. Some interviewers want to talk about my 'get stuffed' comment. I want them to know that I am looking forward to a time when people don't think about male and female jockeys, but just jockeys, when prejudice won't exist. And that that should be the same across all fields of endeavour. If I am perceived as a strong woman standing up for what is fair, and other women take encouragement from that—especially young women—then I feel I have done something worthwhile. I believe you have to be outspoken and forthright when something is unfair. My sisters always say that if I thought something was unfair as a kid, that's when I got most fired up. In a family of ten people who speak their minds, we all suffered our share of injustice.

People want to know more about my family background. Some are already familiar with the story of us losing Mum but they may have been a little surprised when I explain that I still feel close to her, that I know Mum is always with me, that I pray to her often, and that she is my protector.

Other television crews are up at Home, just outside Darren's place. It is a bit of a circus. Dad is being the master of the understatement, telling Australia I had the will to win, pouring cold water on any gender issues in the racing game, while Patrick is ensuring I remain grounded.

'She's so un-co,' he says in one interview. 'She runs like a baby elephant.'

Nothing has changed in our family; it is just that now the world is seeing us. Dad is a great one for picking you up when you are down and bringing you back to earth when you are flying.

In another interview, in front of Darren's place, a streaker appears in the background, although I suspect he is an all-night partier from Weiry's place.

Ultimately, the media drive Dad mad and he is glad to close the door on them and get back to watching the replays of the races on the TV in The Next Room.

People want to know more about Stevie. Stevie had more to do with the win than people realised at the time, like drawing barrier one. How we greeted each other after the race was totally natural— a family moment first, and a racing moment a close second. Both are so meaningful to us. Stevie is hilarious and inspirational throughout the day talking to the media, and I am so happy for him. He means so much to us. For his thirtieth birthday we made a DVD of photos of him set to music. When I am feeling low, feeling I need a lift, I pull out that DVD, and all feels well with the world again.

Stevie has a big impact. I love it that by Emirates Stakes Day, Channel 7 is talking with Brad Thomas from Down Syndrome Victoria about how this Melbourne Cup was certain to change the public understanding of Down's Syndrome. That's an enormously positive effect.

After we finish doing the interviews at the golf club there is a press conference to attend and then I speak at a women's lunch at Crown. It is one thing after another. Off we rush to one side of the Yarra for a photo shoot, and then a helicopter picks me up from a helipad on the river near Crown. Everyone—the pilot, people in the crowd who see what's going on—say congratulations and well done. A photographer comes in the chopper, shooting away to

LIFE AS I KNOW IT

record every moment. I do my form for the Kyneton Cup in the chopper. I think I've got a good chance.

When we land at Kyneton Racecourse I have to make my way to the jockeys' room. Daniel Miles from Racing Victoria assists me. I am applauded all the way. I am laughing to myself—I am still just me. That means I want to walk the track as I always do. This time I am accompanied by a number of security guards! People are clapping and cheering as I walk all the way up the straight, and clapping and cheering me all the way back. I give a little wave here and there. I am pretty embarrassed.

In the Kyneton Cup I have a nice run, and as we get the split in the straight I think we are going to win, but Akzar runs out of puff and finishes fourth.

Cathy and her kids, Jake, Rhys and Charlie are at Kyneton and they give me a lift to Ballarat to see Dad at Home. That is a moment, getting out of the car and walking up the steps to be greeted by Dad. He's really had enough of the media! We chat as we normally would have. It's so nice to be Home.

I ride at Flemington the next day—Oaks Day—without luck. There is a massive thunderstorm and Ciaron Maher's filly, Jameka, wins the feature. Again, so many people are happy for me and want photos and want to tell me their stories. I can feel people have a strong connection with mine. I suppose it is a story common to all, although most struggle privately and silently. People want to tell me about their families and their personal battles.

I am still on a high but I am already starting to wonder when things are going to slow down, and when I will have a minute when someone isn't ushering me towards the next person or engagement or duty or function. After two days I am drained. Sarah and Des certainly knew what they were talking about when they warned me about how my life has changed and how frantic things will be for quite a while.

The next day, Friday, the City of Ballarat puts on a civic reception, which really is something. It means a lot to me to be welcomed by my home town, with people I know from Loreto and Our Lady Help of Christians in the crowd, people from local racing, people I know from living there. It is such an affectionate and giving crowd. They are so happy for me. Hundreds want a photograph.

The craziness continues back in Melbourne, with requests for media interviews and appearances at functions, and invitations and offers. I am approached by management companies and I soon realise I am going to need some sort of assistance. There is interest from all round the world.

On the last day of a remarkable Carnival week I ride the talented three-year-old Palentino for Darren and he wins impressively. I will always have Prince but will Palentino be another special horse?

Over the next couple of weeks I make two more trips to the centre of the universe—Ballarat. I am invited to speak to the girls at Loreto. Miss Baird does the interview. I feel I am doing something worthwhile talking to the girls. I hope they take something from Prince's win, from my story—something as simple as being passionate, having a dream, and giving life a real go. Being at Loreto was important to me, and I hope it is for them.

I also ride at the Ballarat Cup meeting. As I drive past Home and up to the boom gate to the racecourse, where I'd spent so much of my childhood, and where I rode Reigning all those years before, I feel so connected to the place. The welcome is phenomenal. I have rides for Darren, Gai Waterhouse and Terry O'Sullivan. I ride Akzar, again, in the Ballarat Cup but, despite being one of the chances, I have to ease him out of the race when he shows signs he isn't handling the run. That's racing.

With such incessant demands on my time, I have been counting down the days to the Bali trip that we have managed to arrange.

When we Loreto girls gather at the airport, I am more than ready to escape. It doesn't take long for us to return to our Year 9 selves.

'G'day, Dopey.'

'G'day, Stupid.'

Sitting round the pool at the hotel there is a lot of reminiscing.

'What about the time you made us do synchronised swimming?' Liz says to me. 'And then you were the judge.'

It's so good to be with them. Inevitably, as we are all just on thirty, we get to talking about plans and thoughts and, after a few drinks, why things happen the way they do. The discussions turn to what is important to us, how we understand the world, what matters. The girls are talking about some of the things I said after the Cup about being blessed. They are surprised but, as someone said, 'Surprised in the nicest possible way.' I think we have similar understandings, that life matters, that people matter, that we have a duty to make a difference.

Although I have had moments of great doubt, some of them long moments, I have tried to have my father's faith. I see grace every Christmas Day when I look around and everyone is at Home. I sit for the family photo and I look across to my father, who is never in the centre, never making a fuss, and I believe.

I still love going Home. Two years ago I bought the farm a stone's throw up Kennedys Road from Dad's. For Stevie and me. Dad turns eighty in March this year and we have had to think about what will happen to Stevie in the future. He will love living at our place. After we bought it, he and I tried to think of a name. We decide to call it *Nottingham Farm*. That's what happens when you watch *Robin Hood: Prince of Thieves* one hundred times.

I have planted trees there—liquidambars, elms and Cypress pines. Hundreds of them. It's a start. I want to make *Nottingham Farm* a special place of stables filled with horses, one hopefully as good as Prince, and a home filled with children, who I want to give the richest of lives—a life of love like we have had.

I have travelled the world to learn how to live with horses. And what I have learned is what my father, who grew up at the end of the earth, already knew. That people and horses respond to love and kindness and to those who, they come to understand, want the best for them.

How things change

DAD TURNED EIGHTY in March 2016. He didn't want us to make a fuss, and he certainly didn't want a party with invitations and speeches. We'd organised a big seventieth for him, and he hated it. So we just had tea together at Home, with family and a few friends, the way he likes it.

It was exactly what I needed, to sit with my family and pause for a moment. Everything had become so frantic in the months following the Cup win—dinners and lunches, speaking engagements, media interviews. One of the highlights was the Moomba Festival, which I was able to share with Stevie. It was a tremendous honour to be made King and Queen of Moomba, as the parade has always had such a big place in the life of Melbourne. Stevie had grown into his role as a monarch! I don't think there has ever been a happier King of Moomba, nor one so committed when it came to waving at the crowd. It was a delight to be his queen. So many people saw the telecast of the Labour Day parade; so many commented on the joy in Stevie's face.

Everyone wanted to know about the movie that was to be made about my Cup win. The writers were spending time with me and the whole Payne family. Who's going to play me? How are they going to shoot the racing scenes? Will it be as it happened? Because people have a fascination with the big screen, they wanted details! They wanted to know what the director, Rachel Griffiths, was up to, what she was like and which actors would be involved. People asked the same questions. So did the broader media. That's what happens when you land on the public stage. I have found that people are fascinated by very mundane things about my life.

I was incredibly busy getting ready for my winter overseas trip. I had a stack of engagements. I was to attend the Longines Ladies Award in London, and open a new racetrack in Sweden and ride in the first-ever all-women's race. I was also really looking forward to riding in the Shergar Cup, which is a teams event for jockeys at Ascot in England.

However, I was beginning to feel worried about the whole trip and its various demands. The Cup win had given me the opportunity to do a lot of amazing things, which I didn't want to miss out on, but how was I going to stay fit? As the time to leave was getting closer I became really anxious, and was constantly trying to keep fit to ride, and be in form, as well as meet my other engagements.

◆ ◆ ◆

My commitment to being a jockey never changes, and it has always been my main focus. But I also had an exciting new venture to add to the mix. Having secured my dual licence as a jockey/trainer, I was following in the Payne family jockey/trainer tradition and taking on my first horse. *Nottingham Farm* was coming along very well. It was going to be a huge job to establish it, but I had a strong sense of how I wanted it to look. The trees were enjoying the summer warmth, growing nicely with a bit of water, to add to the Ballarat showers that blow across. I was making plans to have the stables and yards built and I was talking to family and friends about purchasing horses. I was spending more time up at Miners Rest, staying at Home, just up the road, and that meant seeing more of Dad and Stevie, too.

Darren's horses were going well. From late March, once things had settled down a little, I started working pretty much every day for him, and was back on his team, getting lots of race rides. With an ever-expanding stable, he had competitive runners in so many races and was attracting more and more owners.

Prince of Penzance was returning from a spell. I was riding him in work, as Darren prepared him to have one run for the Autumn at Morphettville in Adelaide in May. The Melbourne Cup winner always creates interest and there was a lot of love for him. But Prince was also the subject of scrutiny and speculation. Was he a lucky country handicapper who'd pinched a Melbourne Cup? Did everything merely fall into place for us, getting the clear run in a rough race while his opponents belted each other up in the scrimmages around him? Or was he a better horse than that, a horse that could be competitive in classic weight-for-age races? Analysts had studied his pre-Cup form and some were willing to admit that they'd missed a few clues. Again, there were those who thought, given his ability, tenacity and fighting spirit, and from the way he always hits the line, that he could be competitive in those weight-for-age events. But, of all the people in racing, of all the people in the world, I knew how delicate he was and what it would take to get him there. As Dad always said, 'You and Prince. Some horses and jockeys go good together.'

His owners certainly thought he had the ability to be competitive in Australia's feature races. Prince was still down at Warrnambool and I had a chance to see him in the first week of May. As always the Warrnambool carnival was a lot of fun. Patrick's horse, No Song No Supper, won the Grand Annual—he really is having success with his jumpers—and Darren won the Warrnambool Cup with Master of Arts, ridden by Dean Yendall, one of Darren's stable riders.

I was working hard for Darren, to ensure that I got some decent rides, in good races. And that included Prince. I was so looking forward to riding him at Morphettville on 21 May. The week before that ride was even more hectic than usual. I was riding trackwork, which, on Friday morning, meant I had to be in Ararat. I rode a dozen or so horses for Darren there. Then I climbed into the little four-seater plane we'd chartered so I could get to Adelaide in time to speak at a lunch. The next day I rode Prince. He was the top-weight in the RA Lee Stakes, a 1600-metre Group 3 race, which he was not expected to win. Darren just wanted him to have a good run. His other runner, Tonopah, to be ridden by Dean Yendall, was the stable's better chance.

Prince was drawn wide and I didn't want him to pull at the back of the field, so I chose to stay wide and let him find his rhythm and balance. Unfortunately, we got caught three and four wide. But when we got to the straight, he picked up beautifully and just kept coming. He was entitled to die on his run but he just kept finding more and we hit the line strongly, wide out, and came second, a length off the winner, Tonopah.

Everyone was impressed. Prince was all the talk; he had come back better than ever. It was just one run, but if he could stay sound, he looked like being a real competitor in the Spring. My Prince! The owners were thrilled and feeling super-confident. Darren was all smiles. The whole camp was ecstatic. Prince would have another short spell and return for what would be a standard Melbourne Cup preparation with his first start in August. I was so looking forward to riding him again, especially in the Cup.

But there was no time to even think about this. The day after Prince's start in Adelaide there was a change of plans. Dean Yendall had injured his ribs and was unable to ride, so Darren asked me to take Dean's mounts that afternoon at Casterton in the Western District of Victoria. That meant another chartered flight from Adelaide. It's a cute little town to fly into, with its beautiful green farms and rolling hills. I had four rides, without success, with Try Four finishing fifth in the Casterton Cup.

I was starting to think I should get my pilot's licence. I was flown to Mildura, where Patrick had quite a few horses in races on the Monday. It was a lovely late Autumn day. His horses were beautifully prepared and had been well-placed. From five rides we'd had two wins and three seconds. I had one ride to go on Patrick's mare, Dutch Courage, which was the favourite and she was expected to go well.

We had drawn the very outside barrier at the tricky 1200-metre start, where there's a short run to the first corner. As we got going I was five wide. I needed to get at least a little closer to the rail. I know that corner so well. I know that some horses struggle to make the sharp turn and shift out. Sure enough, a couple of horses shifted out and I just nicked a heel. Dutch Courage stumbled forward and I went forward over her neck. I tried to hang on, thinking in that split second I could get back on. I held on too long and I ended up around her neck and fell underneath her.

Dutch Courage stood directly on my stomach. All 500 kilograms of her, at pace.

I was briefly knocked out when I hit the ground. When I came to I knew there was something seriously wrong. My legs had automatically tucked up to my chest and I was rocking back and forth in the foetal position. The ambulance attendants were with me on the track.

'I'm bleeding internally,' I said. 'Something's happening inside.'

They were trying to get me to lie flat so they could put me on the stretcher but the pain was excruciating. I was calm and just kept saying in a quiet voice, 'No, you can't. No. No. You can't. I'm bleeding inside and I can feel something ripping.'

They weren't sure what to do. They tried again. 'You can't touch me,' I said. 'You can't do that.'

I was on the track for a very long time, about 45 minutes, which always makes people incredibly worried that something drastic has happened. Patrick was there. Eventually they managed to put me on the stretcher with my legs tucked up. I was holding on to my legs.

A second ambulance had arrived and I was given some heavy painkillers. I'm not sure if I passed out; all I remember is being aware that my body was fully extended, in the ambulance. I don't know how they did that!

My mind was wandering. I had some vague recollections. 'Did I win a big race last year?', I thought to myself. 'Yeah, I think I did.' But for the life of me I couldn't remember which one.

I had to find out. I had been given my phone so I Googled myself while I was in the ambulance and found I'd won the Melbourne Cup. Not any race, *the* race! So that was a nice surprise—it was like winning it a second time.

But I knew I was in a bit of strife. 'Something's wrong inside,' I kept saying. 'I can feel it, I'm bleeding or something.'

The doctors at the Mildura Base Hospital were so attentive and professional. The scan was inconclusive, and as they waited they became more concerned. During that time one of the nurses took a photo of the bruise and marks on my stomach. The pattern of my riding vest was imprinted on my torso. Somehow I tweeted that photo with a message that I was okay but having further tests. That abrasion was deep enough to eventually scab over and peel off a couple of days later.

I was also assuring the doctors that I was not exaggerating the level of pain or the message my body was sending me. Patrick, who was with me throughout, was worried. 'Michelle doesn't bung it on,' he said to the nurses.

After about four hours the doctors decided I needed to be airlifted to the Alfred Hospital in Melbourne. The plane took off at about midnight.

Because I was pumped full of painkillers the flight was fine and the two or three members of the medical team were very comforting and supportive. The only problem was I had the driest mouth. They couldn't give me anything as I was heading straight to the operating theatre, but they were able to give me saline from a little tube.

Patrick had remained at the hospital in Mildura, so I was on my own at the Alfred, in the care of the emergency specialists and surgeon Marty Smith.

As soon as Marty started to operate he realised I had serious internal injuries. The weight of the horse had trapped my pancreas against my backbone and the organ had been almost severed. Two pieces held it together. The other internal organs were intact. Marty Smith and his team worked through the night. He stitched the smaller piece to the larger piece and then connected the larger piece to my stomach. What he did to save my pancreas seemed like a miracle. He later told me it was a procedure he'd performed many times in pancreatic cancer surgeries.

When I woke up on Tuesday I was on another planet. The incision had been enormous. I had a little button to give myself a dose of a painkiller, which I needed, but it got to the point where I started hallucinating, so they transferred me into the intensive care unit. Everything was orange and swirling around. I couldn't make out the nurses' faces. They looked like weird creatures.

I have endured a lot of pain over the years but this, unfortunately, was the worst. On the Wednesday, there was no relief. No regimen could control my agony at that stage. I felt I had no escape. By Thursday they inserted an epidural. That worked for a couple of days, so I was pretty comfortable, but then it started to wear off and the pain became excruciating again. Night times were the worst. They lasted forever. Poor Lauren West, the night nurse, who had to look after me through the small hours. All of the staff were fantastic and, yet again, I was left thinking about who the heroes are. During the day, Em Ryan was my nurse. She's from Woolsthorpe, near Warrnambool, and knows Ciaron Maher and has a horse with him. We had lots to chat about.

As a last resort I would walk laps of the ward and up and down the corridor. The nurses could see how much pain I was in, so they were happy for me to do whatever it took to alleviate it. They connected my tubes to a trolley and off I'd go! It was a matter of doing anything to get my mind off the pain.

The medical staff warned me the pain wasn't going to go away quickly; that, if anything, it would get worse around day seven. I found that so challenging. And I didn't know, despite the success of the operation, whether function had been restored to my pancreas. The tube down my throat was scratching my oesophagus. I was so thirsty and my lips were peeling. The drops of water trickling into my stomach from an ice cube would make me throw up.

However, I was surprisingly positive about it all. At the time it happened I was at first amazed that someone could survive the force of a horse standing on them. Then, after I endured the appalling week of severe pain and started to come good, I felt lucky. I was in a ward where people were seriously ill or injured but most were nowhere near able to get out of bed to walk, as I was. Eventually I found a walking buddy, a man from Eastern Europe, and I would get the paper for another guy who couldn't move. I talked with some of the patients, and became friendly with them.

My family and friends sat with me. Therese and Margaret took away my phone—a huge blessing! I didn't feel the weight of obligation to respond to the many, many calls and messages I was receiving from people in racing, from other friends, and from the media. People were obviously really worried about me.

I was in my own little world. I had no idea of the level of media interest in my story. Apparently they were probing here and there, and keeping an eye on my progress. They spoke to my family and the same questions came up. Should I retire? It wasn't time for me to be thinking about that stuff.

I was in hospital for two weeks and two days. When I left I spoke briefly to the journalists who had gathered at the hospital entrance. They asked me whether I'd made any decisions about my future. 'Initially, when I started feeling better, I definitely thought I would make a comeback, but at the moment I'm just weighing up my options and having a think about it,' I said. 'I still have the fire in the belly to come back. I have to weigh up everything and make sure I've got the energy to put in to make sure I can give 100 per cent.'

And I went Home—to Ballarat.

◆ ◆ ◆

I was told I was going to take months to recover. Thankfully the signs were positive. My pancreas was working and there was no damage to the other internal organs.

I needed rest. The pain was still severe, if unchecked, so I remained on strong medication. I wasn't allowed to do any fitness work that involved my abdomen, which had been pretty much sliced in half. But it wasn't long before I was walking further and back on the bike.

There was no shortage of thinking time. But it became pretty clear to me that I wasn't finished as a jockey. I was determined to recover in time to ride Prince in trackwork and help get him ready for when he resumed racing in August. That was going to be tight.

Some people thought I was crazy to put myself through the physical demands of another comeback but, as Patrick always says, and as I have been saying all along, some of us have to keep doing the things we love; the things that are a part of us.

This forced rest did me the world of good but, with Spring looming, I was keen to get back into training. The doctors kept a close eye on me and gave me permission to ride in the sixth week after the operation, which was pretty incredible. Once back in the saddle my mind and spirit were willing, but for once my body wasn't. I had responded differently to this fall. I had the drive but I physically couldn't do the amount of fitness work I needed to do. I had to listen to my body. The Rio Olympics were on at this time and I found many of the athletes' stories so inspirational. They were so determined. That helped me to train harder and push myself through the pain. I saw a documentary about Usain Bolt and what he does and that was so uplifting. That was reinforced when I later met him when we were both invited to speak at an Oaks Club lunch during the Spring Carnival. He looks as though he does everything without effort, but he has had to find the will to drive himself to that level.

For the first two weeks back I rode for my brothers Patrick and Andrew. I spoke to Darren Weir but he wouldn't let me ride trackwork. I think he wanted me to retire, but he also knew that wasn't an option for me.

When, eventually, he did let me ride track work, he started me off with eleven rides on the first morning. Eleven! I don't know if his plan was to make it so hard that he'd be able to say, 'You can't handle it. Maybe you shouldn't come back.'

For the next few weeks I was really sore and battling my way through it. The work knocked me around.

Then, a few weeks later, Darren gave me eighteen horses to work! 'He's got to be joking,' I thought to myself. I got to twelve and I was struggling. I reached the end of the morning, went home and threw up. But pushing myself helped me back to full fitness.

'I don't understand why you want to do it,' Darren said one day. 'You've got nothing to prove. Why would you want to risk yourself getting killed next time?'

But I knew I didn't have to explain why.

My family didn't pressure me. They were pretty quiet about it. Patrick felt somewhat responsible for the fall because I was on one of his horses. Of course he wasn't responsible. He thought I should stick with the main tracks, where the more experienced jockeys ride.

By early August I thought I was ready to ride in a race. I'd work a horse for Darren and ask, 'Can I ride that one?'

He wouldn't let me.

Time was getting away. If I was going to ride Prince when he resumed after his spell, I needed to get some race rides under my belt.

Prince was nominated for the Memsie Stakes at Caulfield in late August. Obviously I wanted the ride and I thought I would be fit enough to take it. Some didn't think I'd be ready. Darren and I had dinner with John Richards at the classic old North Britain Hotel in Ballarat. John told me the owners were worried about me getting injured again. And they didn't think I would be fit enough in time. It also seemed that some of the owners thought Prince could win first-up, which would mean a possible change in his riding pattern. If he was just having a run as the start of his campaign he could drop to the tail and come home strongly, which is how he races. That was an easy ride. No pressure on me or Prince. Just a first-up run. But to win the race, he'd need to be ridden closer to the speed, which meant being in the field. This placed a lot more pressure on the horse and the jockey.

I was adamant it was the wrong approach. 'John, he is going well,' I said. 'He's better than ever. But you have to remember how hard it is to win a Group 1 race, especially when it's not his distance.'

I wasn't going to change his mind.

At least John could see my passion. He was warm and friendly, as he always is, but he was also businesslike in how he presented the situation.

◆ ◆ ◆

A fortnight or so before the Memsie Stakes there were trials at Burrumbeet, a tiny town half an hour west of Ballarat. I drove out with Darren and we got talking about *the* issue. He was up-front. He told me nothing had changed—the owners didn't want me on. I wasn't impressed. It was a pretty awful morning, the track was wet and cut up, and I was coming off a dozen trials at Casterton the day before. After seven trials I went to talk to Darren. 'I've had enough,' I said. 'I'm not riding any more today.'

I was so disappointed. On the spur of the moment I tweeted: 'not anymore I'm done. Why work your arse off for people who don't appreciate what you do and write you off anyway. #moretolife'.

It certainly made a splash! It was retweeted so quickly. I felt bad about it, so I took it down. Of course the media got hold of it and put their own interpretation on it. But I was just really upset. I thought the owners were getting it wrong. It seemed to me they hadn't grasped what it had taken to get Prince to where he was.

Harry Coffey was given the ride. After missing the start Harry hunted him up, so he was closer to the speed. This is not Prince's style. It looked to me like Harry was following instructions. He finished back in the field.

I was getting close to full fitness and I was adamant I was going to be ready to ride Prince in the Makybe Diva Stakes two weeks later, in early September. I drove Darren mad asking if he'd put me on. But he stood his ground. 'You're not race fit. Tactics wise, you're nowhere near ready.'

'I don't need the match practice,' I said. 'He's going to get back and get home. It's a mile race, it's going to be too short for him.'

I wasn't giving up easily. I asked Darren for four days in a row and he just said, 'No'.

Johnny Allen rode him in the Makybe. He settled second last and sprinted home well. Darren had the quinella with Palentino, which was too brilliant for Black Heart Bart.

I had my first ride back the very next day, for Henry Dwyer on Lucky Liberty at Sale. Lucky Liberty was also coming back from injury. A very capable three year old (I rode him in his first three wins) he'd had eighteen months away from the track. He finished fourth that day. It was good to get the ride away for both of us. I later won on him at Caulfield on Boxing Day.

Prince's next start, a fortnight later, was in the Underwood Stakes at Caulfield on 24 September. Johnny Allen kept him mid-field, within striking distance of the leaders, and throughout the race he was just a couple of lengths behind the winner, Black Heart Bart. Prince finished at the tail.

About ten days later I went down to Warrnambool to ride Prince on Lady Bay Beach. Photographer David Caird took some photos for an article about banning horses on the beach. Darren's horses thrive on the beach. It was odd to be on Prince when I wouldn't be riding him three days later, in the Herbert Power Stakes.

I was riding against him in that race. Johnny Allen was on Prince again. I was on Dandy Gent. It was hard to take, but in racing you just have to move on. Cantering to the barriers I glanced over at my old mate and thought, 'How things can change ...' I put it all out of my mind. I had my own horse to think about.

I sat Dandy Gent outside the leader, Assign, who was travelling beautifully for Katelyn Mallyon. We weren't good enough, and drifted back. Prince was going well as he passed me and ran an honest fourth. But he'd been knocked around a bit on the corner and he pulled up lame.

The vets diagnosed a fracture in his off foreleg. He was operated on a few days later and retired. I was so sad. Sad for Prince. Sad for everyone. I was also frustrated because I had looked after Prince every step of the way. He is so precious. So fragile. I believe I knew what I had had to do to get him to the Melbourne Cup. I knew him. And, in his last race, I had ridden *against* him.

◆ ◆ ◆

My body was strong again. The only health issue I had was the tricky process, as my doctor had warned me, of weaning myself off the painkillers. One morning, three months after the operation, after cutting back to the minimum dose I woke up pain-free and I thought that was the time to stop. The withdrawal was shocking. I was rolling around on the floor. I suddenly knew what it was like to be battling an addiction. After a few days, I was fine. Thank God.

◆ ◆ ◆

Although riding was still number one for me, training horses was also starting to occupy my days, and I was talking to people about building my team as a trainer. Ultimately I would like to have about fifteen horses—not too many, as it's equally important to maintain solid relationships with each horse. I had finished building the stables at *Nottingham Farm*. The first horse I trained was He's Our Woody, who we nicknamed Woody. Cathy's kids named him after the horse in the film *Toy Story*. A beautiful chestnut with a white blaze, he was bought by some friends of mine. I tried to do too much training too quickly and he became fractious whenever he was put into the barrier stalls. My brother Andrew thought he could fix him up, so Woody was transferred to his stables. I had a lot to learn.

Then Dad and I found Duke of Nottingham at the Inglis sales. He had been with Sue Ellis, a trainer from Diggers Rest. She kept a share and also did three weeks of pre-training with him at her place with her daughter Emily. I fell in love with training Duke. I really started to get to know him and he made it very easy.

Duke had two starts, which he needed. By his third start he was pretty fit and I thought he'd race well at Swan Hill, and I decided to ride him. I loved that I was riding my own horse in a race. He settled about sixth or seventh and he had a nice enough position; he moved up on the outside, he balanced up and he just ran them down in the long Swan Hill straight for an excellent win. This was my first win as a jockey/trainer, and the first win for a Victorian jockey/trainer. He also won his next start, in a race for apprentice jockeys at Echuca, with Lucy Doodt riding him. She is apprenticed to Dan O'Sullivan, our neighbour at Miners Rest.

I have also set up the Women in Racing initiative with Darren Dance of Australian Thoroughbred Bloodstock. The idea is to put together syndicates where women who previously would not have thought of being involved in racing have a share in a horse—5 per cent—with some of those shares being syndicated. It's about bringing people together—which is what racing does—and sharing the cost. It's not expensive when it's done that way. We have three two year olds—which the syndicates will have fun naming.

In October, I bought and syndicated Queen of Zealand, from New Zealand. I thought she might be an Oaks filly. After a run at

Warrnambool she went to the Wakeful Stakes on Derby Day. That was a buzz too, even though she didn't show her best that day and then went out for a spell.

◆ ◆ ◆

And then it was the big day. Cup Day brought back so many memories. I had fun working with Channel 7 in the lead-up to the carnival as they were re-telling the story of our win, but I didn't get to see too much of the coverage, as I had riding commitments of my own. In the Cup, Kerrin was on Almandin for Lloyd Williams. Another one of Lloyd's horses, Assign, was to be ridden by Katelyn Mallyon.

I watched from the tower alongside the track just after the 300-metre mark, with Therese's son Harry and quite a few of the jockeys. I wasn't focusing on Almandin but when Kerrin got in the clear and settled down to fight it out with João Moreira, we were all jumping up and down and screaming for him. He was going to fight it out with the best jockey in the world! What a chance. It was a magnificent finish and Kerrin rode brilliantly to just get home; two perfectly balanced jockeys, fighting out our greatest race. Beautiful to watch. I ran straight down to the mounting yard. Cathy was at home in Sydney in the final week of her pregnancy, trying to hang on in all the excitement. Jockeys aren't allowed to have phones on the course but Des O'Keefe had rung Cathy and had given me the phone to pass on to Kerrin. It was fantastic. Then, on the Monday after, she had Eva May, a sister to their three boys.

It was a wonderful time for our family. We felt blessed—again.

It's been a remarkable twelve months of highs and lows, which struck me most during the Flemington Carnival. The memory of Prince's win—the day, the ride, those wonderful minutes just after the race—felt so good. The sadness of him not being there, not so good. But life moves on, because it has to.

Nottingham Farm is coming along so well. I'm now looking forward to building a house there and settling down; I've spent a fair bit of money setting the facility up properly. I am busy with riding and appearances and getting things organised. I can imagine life as just a trainer, giving each horse the individual attention it needs, coming to understand each one. I think it's such an advantage for them to have that.

I've worked hard my whole life; I just want to enjoy it now. The training. The people. My family and friends.

I will be at home. With Stevie. And Dad, just up the road.

Acknowledgements

I was not expecting *any* phone call from Louise Adler of Melbourne University Publishing in mid-December of 2015, especially not one about the possibility of writing a book with Michelle Payne. The suggestion she made, to work closely with Michelle to write a book about her life, was attractive even if it seemed ambitious to complete a book in the suggested timeframe.

However, the sense of purpose that developed around the project made it all achievable. The editorial team was led by publisher Sally Heath, who rode us with the whip from the barrier and never let up. Thanks, Sally. Also thanks to other team members, editors Louise Stirling and Joanne Holliman for their calm professionalism and commitment to the book, and to Yael Cohn for transcribing interviews.

Thanks to the wonderful Payne family. You were all a tremendous help. You have so many stories!

Thanks to all those people who returned phone calls and emails and set aside other matters to enable us to meet and talk sooner rather than later. They include: Father Joe Giacobbe, Tony Cavanagh, Greg Carpenter, Father Brendan Dillon, Layne Beachley, the Men in Hats (but especially the most organised man in the world, Sam Brown), Darren and Emily Lonsdale, Rebecca Ludbrook, Emily Hall, Liz Francis, Kellie Baird, Roger Morris, Maureen Fithall, John Richards, Andrew Rule, Ian Fulton, Chris Byrne, Aunty Bertha Hughes, Father John Keane, Joan Sadler, Phillip Roost, Jade Darose, Sandy McGregor, Adam McNicol, Wes Clarke and Maddie Raymond. In addition to these inter- viewees, thanks to all those who offered their insights in incidental conversations—Michelle's story has resonated far and wide.

Thanks to Neil 'Lofty' Longden for reading the manuscript with a racing aficionado's eye.

I also wish to acknowledge Tony Kneebone, whose fine book *The Paynes* provided a foundation on which to build. And Neil Kearney, whose documentary *The People's Cup* shows, yet again, his skill as a story-teller with a sense of what matters—that people are at the heart of sport.

I could mention many newspaper, magazine and radio reports. There was such interest in Michelle's story that it dominated press and radio for some time.

Finally, thanks to Michelle Payne, who is an uncommonly thoughtful and contemplative sportsperson. Michelle's uncompli- cated values are rock solid: love of family, love of people, love of horses, and the quest to be the best she can be in all her endeavours. Like her father, she has an inspirational faith in life.

John Harms